Body Wars

Making Peace with Women's Bodies

AN ACTIVIST'S GUIDE

Margo Maine, Ph.D.

gürze books

D1018660

Body Wars
Making Peace with Women's Bodies

© 2000 by Margo Maine, Ph.D.

Gürze Books
P.O. Box 2238
Carlsbad, CA 92018
(760)434-7533
www.gurze.com

Cover design by Abacus Graphics, Oceanside, CA
Cover Painting: Deux femmes courant sur la plage (la course)
by Pablo Picasso (1881-1973)
Used with permission from Musée Picasso, Paris

ISBN 0-963077-34-4
LC 99-075415

The authors and publishers of this book intend for this publication to provide accurate information. It is sold with the understanding that it is meant to complement, not substitute for, professional medical and/or psychological services.

1 3 5 7 9 0 8 6 4 2
First Edition

*To my Mother
whose grace, clarity, and courage taught me,
by example, to care for others, never to be afraid,
and to make the world a better place.*

*To my nieces, D'Arcy and Erin,
who are learning these same lessons and carrying the torch
for the next generation.*

Table of Contents

Acknowledgments

There is a safety in numbers and comfort in connection—we need each other in the fight against Body Wars. I thank my fellow crusaders for their support, their efforts, and their inspiration.

First, thank you to my husband, George Coppolo, for his love and understanding of the time devoted to my passion to end Body Wars. And deep appreciation to my "other husband," Rob Weinstein, for his support and partnership in our clinical work. Many thanks to Lindsey Hall and Leigh Cohn of Gürze Books for their dedication to this cause and their extraordinary efforts—they are far more than publishers, as anyone who knows them understands. I am also grateful to their staff, to Cate Baker and Susan Cakars for their editorial work, and to my associate, Michelle Gauvreau, for her secretarial support and endless enthusiasm for this project.

I have been blessed with wonderful friends who add much love, laughter, and light to my life. I am enormously grateful to all of you. I especially want to recognize my friends in Eating

Disorders Awareness and Prevention for the zeal, energy, and clarity of purpose in their efforts. Thanks to the staff, the board members, the benefactors, supporters, and the countless volunteers across the country who dedicate themselves to the cause of preventing eating disorders. And thanks to my staff and clinicians everywhere who help women rebuild their lives after eating disorders destroy them. And finally, thanks to the patients who so bravely trust me as they struggle with recovery from Body Wars—it is a great honor to be part of their lives.

These pages are full of numbers of the women affected by various Body Wars. Remember: statistics are people with the tears wiped away. Let us not be immune to the pain and suffering these numbers represent and let us commit to empower women, respect their bodies and their wishes, and enter the millennium dedicated to ending Body Wars.

Introduction

I have always been an activist—agitated, and ardent whenever I witness injustice, abuse, discrimination, or other wrongs. I owe this quality to my family and the other significant people in my life who encouraged me to be aware of the world, to question authority, to stand up for what is right, and not to fear others' opinions. Especially during my college years, I devoted much of my time volunteering for important causes: befriending the disenfranchised, advocating for social change, protesting the Vietnam War, and working for political candidates who cared about such issues.

After college, I continued my activism, but decided to go in a different direction in graduate school. The effort required to change systems and structures was endless and exhausting; clinical psychology sounded simpler, more effective, and more rewarding. So, I pursued clinical training, learned enough theory and technique to last a lifetime, and shifted my focus to individual rather than societal problems.

Before long, however, it became clear to me that I was still dealing with sociocultural forces, not just individual "pathology." More often than not, the patients I met were young women who hated their bodies, struggling each day with self-doubt, self-deprecation, and self-denial. Unable to eat without fear, they either starved themselves or did dangerous things to deal with their discomfort with feeling full. So, I learned as much as I could about eating disorders, body image, and the psychology of gender, and helped many to address and overcome these problems. But it seemed that I was not alone in my office with my patients: something bigger and more powerful was eroding the shaky self-esteem and identity we were busy constructing.

I began to realize that there was a new war being waged: an assault of women's bodies by an economic system and culture intent on keeping them in their place. And each day, more calls came in with the same constellation of symptoms, suffering, and pain, because more and more women were internalizing the enemy and destroying themselves. Soon, therapy seemed like an inadequate solution to a pervasive problem: a culture that dismisses, disrespects, and disempowers women by promoting a war against their bodies—what I call the "Body Wars."

Before I knew it, I had returned to my earlier activism. Now I am convinced that only major changes in the role of women in postmodern culture will stop the epidemic of self-hatred, disordered eating, and body dissatisfaction that has expanded exponentially in the twentieth century. As we enter a new millennium, we must transform our society into one where women and their bodies will be respected and nurtured instead of abused and neglected. We have been talking about the problem long enough: we must move into action. This book provides ideas, action plans, strategies, and tactics to do just that.

Each chapter addresses an issue that contributes to women's discontent with their bodies within a sociocultural perspective. The topics will help you to question the culturally-endorsed assumptions that support Body Wars, such as our misguided and misinformed beliefs about weight, dieting, and obesity. A number of chapters focus on aspects of the beauty industry, including the role of fashion, modeling, beauty pageants, plastic surgery, and media influences via magazines and advertising.

The book also addresses the impact of violence against women, ageism, and a healthcare system historically biased to meet men's needs and not women's. Special influences on children are also examined, such as the pressure to diet, the impact of the Barbie doll, and how schools, sports and activities such as dance can contribute to Body Wars. Finally, a chapter is dedicated to men, who are increasingly the target of industries promoting Body Wars and who are desperately needed as teammates in the fight.

Each chapter concludes with strategies and resources for both personal and political change. I hope you find these both useful and inspiring.

Every day, this issue becomes more urgent. Body Wars are now a global problem. No one is safe, as western media and information technology become integral influences in less developed countries. The damage to the human spirit and potential is growing exponentially. We must fight back.

1

The Challenge
RESPECTING WOMEN'S BODIES

"No one is free who is a slave to the body."
—Seneca, Roman Statesman,
ca. 4 B.C. - A.D. 65

In affluent, peaceful, western culture, hidden wars are being waged. I see the victims in my clinical treatment program every day. They are locked in the prison camps known in the health care system as cells 307.10, 307.51, and 307.50, the psychiatric diagnoses for Anorexia Nervosa, Bulimia Nervosa, and Eating Disorder Not Otherwise Specified. According to conservative estimates, four percent of high school and college-aged women are currently prisoners of these wars, many for lifetime sentences. Between five and 20 percent of them will die.[1] But these women are not the only victims. In fact, *most* women in westernized cultures are waging war against their natural bodies.

Ours is not the first culture to maintain ideals for beauty; every place and time has evolved its own prototype to emulate. But in our society, people are drastically altering themselves to reflect the recognized standard. For that, physical appearance must be valued as the ultimate achievement and representation of the self, considerable technology and resources must be devoted to changing the human body, and the economy must market these ideals. Such is the case in twentieth century western culture.

In fact, the past hundred years has been an epoch of unrelenting attacks on women's bodies and self confidence—what I call the "Body Wars." Their tactics render women insecure and dependent on the latest product, technique, or trend, by convincing them that their ultimate value is their appearance. The Body Wars are systematic, institutionally sanctioned, and economically driven. They are insidious and ubiquitous. They obliterate any respect our society has for women, or a woman has for herself. In essence, Body Wars keep women "in their place."

"More women have more money and power and scope and legal recognition than we have ever had before, but in terms of how we feel about ourselves physically, we may actually be worse off than our unliberated grandmothers."
—Naomi Wolf, author of
The Beauty Myth

American women feel worse about their bodies than any other group of their contemporaries.[2] Margaret Mead did not find this shame, self-doubt, and self-consciousness in any of the cultures she studied.[3] Rather, these appearance-altering preoccupations are most widely found in "the land of opportunity," as our advanced technology allows a constant proliferation of body-changing practices: pills, surgeries, body-shaping clothes, diets, etc. Seductive marketing conveys that these are normal activities, a part of daily life. Fashion magazines frequently feature articles about the latest plastic surgery techniques, immunizing us to the atrocious concept of unnecessary elective operations, with all their risks, just to achieve a different look. With each article, our perspective becomes more jaded and our objectivity regarding the absurdity of body alterations is compromised. These invasive practices have become socially acceptable, if not socially expected. The "land of opportunity" is a rich one for those whose fortunes are at the price of female disempowerment.

Confronted by lives ravaged by Body Wars each day, I must question: Why does the body represent so much to women and why do they torment themselves for a new one? Why do we limit girls' goals to their potential as consumers and dieters? How did the Body Wars overtake the self-esteem, logic, and judgment of women who are capable of so much?

Liberation or Consumerism?

By maintaining the status quo, Body Wars represent the clash between women's potential and their actual position in western culture. As a society we are ambivalent and afraid of the implications of female power; better to keep women worried about their looks than to deal with the real issues of equality! Although women have slowly gained rights, privileges, and public status, the marketing of body dissatisfaction has replaced the antiquated laws and customs which, in the past, had limited women's power.

The result of this invisible corset is, among other things, "do-it-yourself income discrimination."[4] While women may be earning more money than ever before (although still only approximately 75 cents for every dollar their male counterparts earn[5]), they are compelled to spend much of it on their appearance, investing in clothing, make-up, endless beauty rituals, dieting, and other obsessive activities in order to garner status, social acceptance, and feelings of worth.

In 1990, *Time* magazine announced that the fight for women's equality "has largely been won,"[6] and marketing strategies have been capitalizing on this concept ever since. By manipulating the quest for equal rights, advertising campaigns for the products of Body Wars subliminally suggest that strong, liberated women will benefit from their purchases. Madison Avenue constantly conveys that women are free and powerful, virtually unstoppable. But for the majority, the right to choose means the right to buy, as women seek their souls at the mall. Meanwhile, companies like the advertisers of Virginia Slims, using skinny cigarettes and skinnier models, seduce women to smoke as a weight control technique by announcing "You've come a long way baby." The association be-

"If the image makers and pharmaceutical companies and fashion designers have their way, we will always be made to feel that we don't fit. Either we don't fit the clothes, or we don't fit the ideal, or we don't fit the lifestyle. We just don't fit, period."
—Emme, model & author, *True Beauty*

4

tween freedom and a thin, attractive female body always sells. As a result, smoking is on the rise in young women, who soon will become the majority of smokers. Although they hope for the image of liberation with these purchases, women are actually buying enslavement to an unhealthy body image.[7] Ironically, in the current era of reproductive freedom and educational opportunities, women do not feel they own any part of their bodies. The obstacles to a woman's rights are simply packaged differently than in less progressive eras.

Necessary Evils: Weapons and Ammunition

It took our postmodern era of advanced technology and mega-business to foster full-fledged Body Wars. Advances in science, industry, and production have given us superior weapons to tame and defeat the natural body. Legitimate professions and industries have become emissaries, promoting the cause. New customs and institutions have developed, each a violation of our inner life.

Pharmaceutical companies produce new pills and concoctions to change weight, metabolism, fluid balance, appetite, energy, and bowel habits, so we can exert greater control over our bodily functions, contours, and appearance. The insurance industry publishes unrealistic weight guidelines to manage their decisions about applicants, and increase their profits. While the public scrutinizes and questions many other insurance company practices, their recommendations about weight have become sacred law.

Medicine has also fueled the fires for Body Wars. At an American Medical Association meeting in 1988, the president of the American Aging Association proposed that, "It would benefit physicians to look upon ugliness not as a cosmetic issue but a disease."[8] Once being fat or ugly became pathological conditions requiring treatment, the market for "remedies" or "cures" opened wide. Physicians began treating weight as a disease and prescribed diets and medications to take off pounds. Plastic surgeons made far more money after normal fat was labeled cellulite. Publishers did as well. *Thin Thighs in Thirty Days* sold over 425,000 copies in less than two months after publication. In 1995 alone, American women spent $100 million on cellulite creams that have no proven effectiveness.[9]

"Imagine us shaping that new woman, dream of the future, out of the transformed obsessions that presently rule our lives."
—**Kim Chernin, author,** *The Hungry Self*

Assisted by widespread marketing, the fashion, beauty, fitness, cosmetic, and dieting businesses are now the experts, offering easy answers to ever-increasing questions regarding our self-worth. Dependent on body hatred for jobs and profit margins, they are resourceful and creative, coming up with one idea after another, to keep women's self esteem and body image on edge. A secure person doesn't need all that "stuff." So, to make money, they have to instill us with insecurity. And they have.

Some of the weapons of Body Wars are external—girdles hold us in while clothes and cosmetics cover-up our natural selves and create a certain image. But there are internal weapons

6

as well. Pills and chemicals change our body chemistry. Even more importantly, our belief in self-discipline, mental toughness, and the importance of improving ourselves has been turned against us. The diverse industries creating the ammunition for Body Wars convince women that if they buy their products and follow their advice, they'll be morally superior, in control of their lives, and capable of anything. In reality, they have become prisoners of war.

New Recruits

Since women make about 85% of the purchases in countries like the United States,[10] they are critical to the success of a capitalist economy and to the Body Wars businesses. Women have more independent economic power than ever before, due to their hard work and the opportunities afforded them by the feminist movement. But the change from financial dependence on men to increased, and even total, financial independence brings with it a level of anxiety. Women are often confused about their roles in a male-dominated job market and

"When enough people change their consciousness to embrace a new set of values, the values of their culture change."
—Marcia Hutchinson, author, *Transforming Body Image*

power structure. Obsessing about appearance, hoping to be accepted in the work world, and shopping for a self, packaged just right, has become the lot of many women today. And they are being aggressively recruited!

Women are not the only targets of Body Wars, however. Armies need new recruits, and must attract younger and more diverse enlistees. After all, there is money to be made. In fact, kids under 18 years of age are responsible for $600 billion of our annual consumer spending.[11] This target market has both their own cash and significant influence over how the family's money is spent. Their hours in front of the television make them avid and knowledgeable consumers, brainwashed to incorporate Body Wars into their routines, values, and attitudes.

Listen to young children and you will hear words like, "diet," "fat-free," and "exercise" sprinkled throughout their conversations. You will hear them critique and describe their mother's bodies, competing to have the thinnest mom. Listen more carefully and you will hear them describe fears of becoming fat, the need to control what they eat, and hopes of losing weight. Meanwhile, fat kids are not even spared by their peers, who inflict ruthless ridicule and taunts directed at their body size.

"When will women not be compelled to view their bodies as science projects, gardens to be weeded, dogs to be trained?"
—M. Piercy, poet

Body Wars also recruit the male population. How did men become easy marks? Quite simply, people in the midst of change are vulnerable. The roles of men, as well as women, have been in transition for the last quarter century. As a result, men are less certain of their power and authority both at home and at work. The erosion of influence and the additional insecurity at work due to technological change and corporate downsizing has caused many to be more anxious and unsettled than ever. If men can be convinced that looking younger, thinner, and fitter will assure their success and end their confusion and existential angst, they will also readily spend on clothing, exercise equipment, skincare, pills, diets, and the rest of the arsenal of Body Wars.

We all know the strategy has worked. Men are increasingly concerned about their image and appearance. It is unlikely, however, that their numbers and their suffering will ever reach what we see in women today because, as a culture, we have traditionally respected men's bodies, power, and influence. They are not as vulnerable to the mass production of self-hatred and self-doubt.

The Right Climate: A Spiritual Ice Age

During the *Renaissance*, the essence of the self was thought to originate as a star in the heavens.[12] People believed that the core of a human being was connected to the energy and spirit of the eternal beyond—a peaceful image of harmony, tranquillity, and joy.

Today, the essence of the self is no longer considered a lifeforce or a process; it is a product. We believe that we must "work on" ourselves endlessly and mercilessly to achieve value. Spiritual awareness is *passé*. Exercise, once a source of pleasure and camaraderie, has become a science and an obligation. We treat our bodies like machines—not as the container for the self, but as the representation of the self. A spiritual ice age has allowed Body Wars to grip our culture.

Radical and rapid technological, medical, and economic

change has brought us to this point. Even though we have more comforts and advantages than our ancestors could have ever imagined, Body Wars have left many women feeling that their lives are lacking. Instead of embarking on a more meaningful quest, they have placed their faith in products and images. Rather than loving their bodies, and being peaceful, respectful, and gentle with them, women have attacked, manipulated, and controlled their physical selves, never feeling satisfied or content.

A Woman's Right for the Millennium

The new millennium introduces tremendous possibilities and opportunities for women. Girls in unprecedented numbers are playing competitive sports, studying math and science, going to college and graduate school, and functioning in impressive jobs. We can detect and prevent many of the health problems that used to limit or ruin their lives. Yet, the pressure to meet constantly changing, arbitrary, and unrealistic cultural standards for beauty has not changed. In fact, it has increased markedly over the past 20 years.

Years ago, Freud asked, "The great question that has never been answered and which I have not yet been able to answer, despite my 30 years of research into the feminine soul is 'What does a woman want?'"[13]

Well, Dr. Freud, the answer is simple. Women want what men want: life, liberty, and the pursuit of happiness. They want to be in charge of their lives and destinies, to share the earth and their responsibilities here with men, and to have the same opportunities in education, employment, and leisure. They want to express their creativity and beauty. They want to live as freely and as safely as men. But they cannot as long as Body Wars exist.

It is time to fight back. Until now, Body Wars have been a one-way battle. Attacked by powerful and destructive messages and industries, women have, in turn, assaulted their bodies with every technique available. Sadly, they have internalized the enemy, and become their own worst critics.

So, how can we fight back against the big business, endless weaponry, and constant propaganda? Only through radical personal and political transformation.

STRATEGIES FOR CHANGE

Fortify Your Own Defenses

Change begins with the self. The process of individual change challenges the systems and opens the door to other viewpoints and actions. Each of us needs to be painfully honest by doing a personal inventory of how we have absorbed Body Wars into our psyches and souls. Most of us, immersed in this culture, spend more time tending to our appearance than to our self-awareness and inner being. The more we comprehend how we have been personally affected, and the more we cultivate our internal resources, beauty, and values, the less Body Wars can infiltrate our world.

Next, we have to develop a value system that puts appearance in its place and honors our bodies as wonderful gifts regardless of the external packaging. In this age of distraction and external hype, inner wisdom can seem elusive. Think of the intrinsic functioning of our bodies. What could be more wise? What a woman's biology can do is awesome: menstruation, ovulation, pregnancy, lactation, childbirth—all miracles of life. So why do we instead reduce a woman's value to a number on a scale? We must begin to honor nature! Our bodies constantly change to keep us alive, recreating themselves in orderly, predictable cycles. One instant, hydrogen, oxygen, carbon, and nitrogen are locked in our organs. The next instant, we exhale and they're gone! Consider these amazing facts which reflect this inner wisdom:

• Skin replaces itself once a month.
• Stomach lining replaces itself every five days.
• Liver lining replaces itself every six weeks.
• Skeletal system replaces itself every three months.
• Within one year, 98% of our atoms are replaced![14]

Why let Body Wars attack such a wonderfully-working system?

Become an Activist!

Once you understand how you are affected by Body Wars and have fortified your defenses, you can take the next step toward social change, and that is action. In order to reclaim our bodies as our own property, each of us needs to make noise, be rabble-rousers and overcome the social conditioning to be silent. We need to help others fortify their defenses! Also, loving one's body is a revolutionary act with far-reaching effects. We must all become revolutionaries!

Never underestimate the power of one person's actions. In 1955, when Rosa Parks refused to give up her seat on a bus to a white person, her arrrest helped to launch the civil rights movement, radically changing racial awareness and relationships in America. Anger, correctly and consistently channelled, can lead to constructive cultural change. Share your outrage, your worries, your concerns with others. Challenge your friends or family members if they say or do things that promote Body Wars. Be "thy brother's keeper" by confronting others in a caring and instructive manner. Bring people together who share your views, or brainstorm how you could make your community a more positive and safe place for everyone.

> "We must restore a humanistic vision in which self-improvement means cultivating the mind and enlarging the soul: developing generosity, humor, dignity, and humility; living more graciously with biology, aging, and death, living with our limitations."
> —Roberta Seid, author, Never Too Thin

Decide to challenge everything and anything that promotes Body Wars. Write letters, make phone calls, keep records, enlist help. Make speeches, take out ads, speak up! This cannot be just "women's work;" both sexes need to work together. We *can* transform our culture and make peace with our bodies if we try. As Margaret Mead once said: "Never underestimate the ability of a small, dedicated group of people to change the world; indeed it's the only thing that ever has changed the world."[15]

25 Ways to Love Your Body

As with most worthwhile pursuits, most people have to work hard to make peace with their bodies. Review this list of 25 Ways to Love Your Body. Spend at least five minutes on these every day yourself, as a couple, or with your family or a small group of friends. Share your reactions and experiences as you learn to love your body. Remember, this is a revolutionary act!

1. We are born in love with our bodies. Watch an infant sucking their fingers and toes, not worrying about their "body fat." Imagine being so "in love" with your body.

2. Think of your body as a tool. Create an inventory of all the things you can do with it.

3. Be aware of what your body does each day. It is the instrument of your life, not an ornament for others' enjoyment.

4. Create a list of people you admire who have contributed to your life, your community, or the world. Was their appearance important to their success and accomplishments?

5. Consider your body as a source of pleasure. Think of all the ways it makes you feel good.

6. Enjoy your body: stretch, dance, walk, sing, take a bubble bath, get a massage, have a pedicure.

7. Put signs on your mirrors like, "I'm beautiful inside and out."

8. Affirm that your body is perfect just the way it is.

9. Walk with your head high, with pride and confidence in yourself as a person, not a size.

10. Don't let your size keep you from doing things you enjoy.

11. Remind yourself: your body is not a democracy—you're the only one who gets a vote.

12. Count your blessings, not your blemishes.

13. Replace the time you spend criticizing your appearance with more positive, satisfying pursuits.

14. Did you know that your skin replaces itself once a month, your stomach lining every five days, liver every six weeks, your skeleton every three months! Your body is extraordinary—respect and appreciate it.

15. Be the expert on your body—challenge fashion magazines, cosmetics industry, or Metropolitan Weight Tables.

16. Let your inner beauty and individuality shine.

17. Be your body's ally and advocate, not its enemy.

18. Every morning when you wake up, thank your body for resting and rejuvenating itself so you can enjoy the day.

19. Every evening when you go to bed, thank your body for what it has helped you do throughout the day.

20. Find a method of exercise that you enjoy and do it regularly, not to lose weight, but to feel good.

21. Think back to a time in your life when you liked and enjoyed your body. Get in touch with those feelings now.

22. Look at family photos. Find the beauty, love, and values in those bodies and faces. Hold those close to your heart.

23. If you had only one year to live, how important would your body image and appearance be?

24. Make a closet inventory. Do you wear clothes to hide your body or to follow fashion trends? Keep the clothes that give you feelings of pleasure, confidence, and comfort.

25. Beauty is not just skin-deep. It is a reflection of your whole self. Love and enjoy the person inside.

RESOURCES

Guidelines For Letter-Writing

Letter-writing is a particularly effective tool for change, especially when done as a campaign. It also provides a clear record of your communications. Here are some general guidelines for writing letters to companies, advertisers, magazines, newspapers and the like.

- An individually crafted letter is preferable to a form letter. You can take a form letter, change some of the language, personalize it, and put it on your own stationery. If you do not have the time or resources, however, a form letter, or adding your signature to a group letter, is better than nothing.

- The more personal you make the letter, the better. Call to get the name of the individual in charge of customer complaints, the manager, or the CEO. If you are writing to a local affiliate of a large corporation, get the names of both parties and send copies to each.

- Make it easy to read, preferably typed or, if necessary, clearly written or printed. Try to make it look user-friendly, with your address at the top. (Envelopes are usually tossed quickly.) Check it over for spelling, punctuation, and format. Take the time to redo it if you find mistakes rather than send something that is messy or straining to the eye.

- A short letter is better than a long letter. If possible, keep it to one page or two if necessary. Get to the point quickly. Be specific. If you are writing about a TV show or a newspaper ad, give the date it appeared and the name of the show, product, or article.

- Be specific. Are you complaining? Do you have a suggestion? Do you want them to take action to respond to you?

- If you are complaining, use your letter to educate, not to attack. Often, the receiving party has never thought about the issue you are raising. Be kind but clear in your attempt to make them more responsible and more aware of their potential impact on viewers or consumers.

- If they do not respond, send a second letter with a photocopy of the first, or call the customer relations department and ask when you will hear from them.

- Write letters to acknowledge the positive efforts of companies or concerns that are promoting respect for women, healthy body image, and other prosocial, anti-Body Wars messages.

Websites devoted to helping you make complaints

www.consumerworld.org
Consumer World Website, helps you with the process of filing complaints, identifying company consumer affairs offices, Better Business Bureaus, and relevant government agencies.

www.consumer.gov
The U.S. government website, for access to consumer resources and agencies.

2

Weightism
The "Politically Correct" Form of Prejudice

"Being overweight may seem like the worst possible fate . . . it isn't. A worse fate is feeling rejected and unloved because one is overweight."
—Joanne P. Ikeda,
Nutrition education specialist
University of California, Berkeley

You won't find "weightism" in your dictionary or in books about discrimination or civil rights. However, it is Big Business, responsible for billions of dollars spent on Body Wars each year.

Like other forms of prejudice, weightism encompasses a system of damaging beliefs that pre-judge people—in this case, those with large bodies. Discrimination intensifies as weight increases, but size bigotry also affects those who are only 20% above their ideal body weight.[1] Weightism affects people of all sizes who are plagued by fear of becoming fat and, hence, stigmatized. Considering its impact on millions of people, the term "weightism" clearly belongs in the dictionary.

Many affluent western nations exhibit excessive concern about size and appearance, and this is especially true in the United States. Not only do economic and sociocultural factors promote weightism in this country, but our culture steadfastly believes that shape and size are things we can and should want to change. Even though research shows that genetics account for at least 25%, and possibly as much as 70%, of the factors influencing weight,[2] obesity is still considered sinful, a rejection of the highly valued ethics of self-denial and self-control, particularly for women. For this reason, weightism has become a "politically correct" form of prejudice, potentially more powerful and pervasive than racism, sexism, or ageism.

"It really doesn't count if you're smart, kind, funny, sweet, generous, or caring, because if you also happen to be heavy, you may find yourself on the receiving end of more cruelty than you ever knew existed."
—W. Charisse Goodman, author, *The Invisible Woman*

In this day and age, a lean body is a symbol of health and power; being fat or even average size is considered inferior. According to a recent study, over half of the females between ages 18 and 25 would prefer to be run over by a truck than to be fat, and two-thirds would choose to be mean or stupid rather than fat.[3] Genetics researchers found that 11 percent of parents would abort a fetus that was genetically coded to be overweight.[4] Even very young children restrict eating, refuse favorite foods, and desire weight loss, having absorbed the negative stereotypes about large people. As they grow older, these behaviors and attitudes only multiply.

Research has repeatedly shown that weight affects teacher evaluations, admissions into higher education, personnel decisions, landlord decisions about tenants, and assessments by mental health and medical personnel who see fat people as emotionally weak and responsible for their own problems.[5] Most employers, who are reluctant to act in a prejudicial way toward minority groups, feel free to discriminate against large people, creating a unique type of "glass ceiling." In one study, 26% of respondents reported that they had been denied health benefits, and 17% said that they had been fired or pressured to resign from their jobs due to their weight.[6]

> *"Our culture really hates fat people. . . There are billion-dollar industries invested in me hating my body. . . If women of my size were to actually enjoy being their size, those industries would collapse."*
> —Camryn Manheim, actress, author, *Wake Up, I'm Fat!*

Weightism and the Sexes: What's Unfair is Unfair

While discrimination based on weight affects both sexes, women experience it more intensely than do men. In a survey of 10,000 young adults, heavy women reported household incomes averaging $6,170 a year less than average weight women.[7] Fat women are more likely to remain poor and are less likely to have the opportunity to "marry up," since men's social status is linked to the attractiveness of their wives.[8] Overweight women are 20% less likely to get married than normal weight women. In fact, a survey of college students found that they would prefer to marry an embezzler, drug user, shoplifter, or blind person than someone who is fat.[9]

Larger women have limited family support for their education and are also less likely to be accepted at elite colleges than are their thin peers with identical credentials. Slim women go on to earn more than their parents, while fat ones earn less.[10] In the mass media, large women generally appear only as objects of ridicule. In the retail world, fat people must shop in different departments, sometimes in different

"The women of Samoa tended to gain weight with each pregnancy, becoming increasingly larger over the course of their lives, until by middle age they were by our standards distinctly fat. But these large women dance without shame, for in their culture, there is no social stigma associated with being fat."
—Kim Chernin, author,
The Obsession

stores. As the industry begins to recognize this lucrative market, however, the "chubby" department is becoming less marginalized. Nonetheless, when fat people exercise, dance, or otherwise expose their bodies, they are often judged, mocked, and insulted. These realities contradict what the feminist movement has been telling girls for the past 20 years—that the world is wide open to them. Yet the message is, to be *more*, a female is expected to weigh *less*.

Men are not immune from weightism. In fact, a California jury recently awarded $1 million to man who was dismissed from his job at an auto parts store because he weighed 400 pounds. The state's Fair Employment Act, similar to the federal

Americans with Disabilities Act, guided the decision. Medical testimony about the significant genetic contribution to obesity resulted in the conclusion that this man's weight was a valid disability.[11] The courtroom may prove to be an important battle-field in the fight against weightism.

Weightism and Medicine: What You Don't Want to Know

The health care system treats fat women as poorly as do other American institutions. Obese women receive significantly fewer pelvic exams, despite their risk for endometrial and ovarian cancers. In a survey of 1,300 physicians, 17% said they would not perform a pelvic exam on an obese patient, and the other 83% stated they would be reluctant to conduct this routine procedure on a fat patient.[12] In the hospital setting, judgments and poor treatment of fat people abound. Physicians are typically unabashed about their intolerance. Some surgeons simply claim that they do not like to cut through so much adipose (fat) tissue because it makes their job more difficult.

Fat patients of both sexes are sometimes denied life-saving surgeries or other procedures. In studies of organ transplants, they have proportionally the same complications, spend the same amount of time in the hospital, are as likely to accept the organ, and demonstrate the same survival rate three years later.[13] Yet, transplants are often withheld because anti-fat prejudice is accepted even by the most educated and influential people in America. Inspired by weightism, physicians will readily prescribe pills and surgical procedures to women despite limited data about either short- or long-term safety or effectiveness, while denying other services essential to survival.

Absurd proposals to control the "problem" of fat flourish. Concerns about cost containment have even led some policy makers to suggest a "fat tax" on people of higher weights to cover obesity-related medical problems.

Schools: The Golden Rule and Big Kids

In school, fat kids face discrimination by faculty and students alike. In 1994, the National Education Association issued a report on weightism with the following conclusions:

"For fat students, the school experience is one of ongoing prejudice, unnoticed discrimination, and almost constant harassment. From nursery school through college, fat students experience ostracism, discouragement, and sometimes violence. Often ridiculed by their peers and discouraged by even well-meaning education employees, fat students develop low self-esteem and have limited horizons. They are deprived of places on honor rolls, sports teams, and cheerleading squads, and are denied letters of recommendation."[14]

> "I didn't do anything wrong. I am fat. And I am being punished for it because this society believes it isn't okay to be 16 years old, 5' 6" tall, and be fat. It isn't okay and it isn't fair."
> —16-year-old girl quoted in Parade Magazine, 11-4-90

Large kids who experience obstacles and prejudice from early childhood on fail to develop self-esteem. Lacking easy access to the educational or social experiences that build self-confidence and social skills, and accosted by persistent ridicule, they become fearful of trying new things, going places, and taking risks. Fat children will go to great lengths to be treated like human beings, even if it means dieting and self-deprivation. Girls are especially vulnerable because of our culture's obsession with the female body. Hoping for better treatment and a life free of discrimination, fat kids are easy targets for advertisers' products that glorifiy thinness.

STRATEGIES FOR CHANGE

The first step in overcoming prejudice is to assess your own fat phobic attitudes. Take a personal inventory of your weightism by completing the following "Size Acceptance Questionnaire" from the National Association to Advance Fat Acceptance. Be honest. You may be surprised by what you find.

SIZE ACCEPTANCE QUESTIONNAIRE

How often do you...

1. Make negative comments about your fatness.

2. Make negative comments about someone else's fatness.

3. Support the assumption that no one should be fat.

4. Disapprove of fatness (in general).

5. Say or assume that someone is "looking good" because s/he has lost weight.

---

6. Say something that presumes that a fat person(s) wants to lose weight.

7. Say something that presumes that fat people should lose weight.

8. Say something that presumes that fat people eat too much.

9. Admire or approve of someone for losing weight.

10. Disapprove of someone for gaining weight.

11. Assume that something is "wrong" when someone gains weight.

12. Admire weight loss dieting.

13. Admire rigidly controlled eating.

14. Admire compulsive or excessive exercising.

15. Tease or admonish someone about his/her eating (habits/choices).

16. Criticize someone's eating to a third person ("so-and-so eats too much junk").

17. Discuss food in terms of "good/bad."

18. Talk about "being good" and "being bad" in reference to eating behavior.

19. Talk about calories (in the usual dieter's fashion).

20. Say something that presumes being thin is better (or more attractive) than being fat.

21. Comment that you don't wear a certain style because "it makes you look fat."

22. Comment that you love certain clothing because "it makes you look thin."

23. Say something that presumes fatness is unattractive.

24. Participate in a "fat joke" by telling one or laughing/smiling at one.

25. Support the diet industry by buying their services and/or products.

26. Under eat and/or exercise obsessively to maintain an unnaturally low weight.

27. Say something that presumes being fat is unhealthy.

28. Say something that presumes being thin is healthy.

29. Encourage someone to let go of guilt.

30. Encourage or admire self-acceptance and self-appreciation/love.

31. Encourage someone to feel good about his/her body as it is.

32. Openly admire a fat person's appearance.

33. Openly admire a fat person's character, personality, or actions.

34. Oppose/challenge fatism verbally.

35. Oppose/challenge fatism in writing.

36. Challenge or voice disapproval of a "fat joke."

37. Challenge myths about fatness and eating.

38. Compliment ideas, behavior, character, etc., more often than appearance.

39. Support organizations which advance fat acceptance (with time or money).

Reprinted (edited) with permission from the *NAAFA Brochure Supporting the Physical and Emotional Health of Fat People Through Personal and Social Change*[15]

If you are a parent, teacher, or other important influence on children, recognize the messages you are passing along to them. Parents sometimes emphasize the importance of being thin because they want to protect their children from the pain of teasing and rejection, or because they believe that a svelte body will be an economic and social advantage, especially for their daughters. Teachers sometimes model weightism rather than acceptance of all children by ignoring, excluding, or otherwise subtly rejecting their larger students. Examine your own attitudes and behaviors that might reveal fat prejudice.

Also, educate the children and other people in your life about weightism. For example, when you watch television together, point out programs or commercials which make fun of fat people or promote misleading weight loss information. Challenge your friends who are on diets or who make derogatory comments about fat.

"Try as I might, I couldn't destroy my spirit. And try as I might, I couldn't change who I was. I was left with what to me seemed to be the most difficult option: loving myself just the way I am."
—**Camryn Manheim, actress, author,** *Wake Up, I'm Fat!*

Individuals, however, are not the only source of weightism. Pay attention to the treatment of fat people by companies, the media, and other institutions. When you see a prejudicial message, write or call to complain to the advertisers, publishers, or others who promote those views. The National Association to Advance Fat Acceptance (NAAFA) lobbied Hallmark to remove an offensive card which ridiculed fat people from their line of "Shoebox" cards. An initial letter-writing campaign did not succeed, but a boycott did.[16]

Check your local schools, libraries and hospitals to make sure they are supplied with the educational materials and resources listed here. Find a community organization to put on a Healthy Weight Week to promote size acceptance, an annual January event sponsored by the "Healthy Weight Journal."

Celebrate healthy weight at any size and challenge the prejudices, biases, and misinformation that promote size discrimination. Weightism is a serious social, political, and economic war against the human body. Fight it.

RESOURCES

Associations

National Association to Advance Fat Acceptance (NAAFA)
PO Box 188620
Sacramento, CA 95818
916-558-6880
800-442-1214
www.NAAFA.org

Association for the Health Enrichment of Large People (AHELP)
PO Drawer C
Radford, VA 24143
703-731-1778

Council of Size and Weight Discrimination, Inc.
PO Box 305
Mt. Marion, NY 12456
914-679-1209

Largesse: The Network for Size Esteem
PO Box 9409
New Haven, CT 06534-0404
203-787-1624

Largely Positive
PO Box 17223
Glendale, WI 53217

Publications

Healthy Weight Journal
Subscription Office:
Decker Periodicals, 4 Hughson Street South
PO Box 620 LCDI, Hamilton, ON, Canada L8N 3K7
800-568-7281

Editorial Office:
402 S. 14th Street
Hettinger, N.D. 58639
702-567-2646
www.Healthy Weight Network.com

Radiance: The Magazine for Large Women
PO Box 30246
Oakland, CA 94604

Books

Fat is a Feminist Issue
Orbach, S., New York, Berkley Books, 1978.

Such a Pretty Face: Being Fat in America
Millman, M., New York, W.W. Norton, 1980.

Am I Fat? Helping Young Children Accept Differences in Body Size
Ikeda, J., Naworski, P., Santa Cruz, ETR Associates, 1992.

Self Esteem Comes in All Sizes
Johnson, C., New York, Doubleday, 1995.

The Invisible Woman: Confronting Weight Prejudice in America
Goodman, C., Carlsbad, CA, Gürze Books, 1995

Great Shape: The First Fitness Guide For Large Women
Lyons, P., Burgard, D., Palo Alto, Bull Publishing, 1990.

One Size Does Not Fit All
Naidus, Beverly, Littleton, CO, Aigis Publications, 1993.

Shadow on a Tightrope: Writings by Women on Fat Oppression
Schoenfielder, L., Wieser, B., San Francisco, Aunt Lute Books, 1983.

Fat is Not a Four-Letter Word
Schroeder, C.R., Minneapolis, MN, Chronimed Publishing, 1992.

Eat Fat
Klein, R., New York, Random House, 1996.

Fat: A Fate Worse Than Death? Women, Weight, and Appearance
Thone, R.R., New York, Harrington Park Press, 1997.

3

Obesity

FACT OR FICTION?

"The evil view of obesity has come from four places: the insurance industry, the medical moralizers, the drug industry and the docile, unquestioning nutritionists who are too often dupes of the faddists and hucksters."
—George Mann, physician

Throughout history, as an exhibit featuring sixteenth century art will remind you, many eras have considered rounded body shapes beautiful and inspiring. As recently as the 1940's and 1950's, full-bodied figures such as Mae West and Marilyn Monroe were the standard for good looks and sex appeal. But today, those same bodies would be judged as overweight. What has changed? Is obesity really an ogre destroying our health, or is it an ordeal created by our thin-is-in mentality? Is it a disease, or a condition that we do not understand or accept?

Simplifying Obesity: Standardized Tables

In the early 1900's, a gaunt appearance was considered unhealthy and unattractive. A thin person was thought to have tuberculosis or another serious medical condition. But as immigration to the United States proceeded into the mid-twentieth century, a thin, chic body became a statement of moral superiority over stocky immigrants who had yet to prove themselves.[1] Once North America became more affluent, many of the health problems of earlier times abated. Today, thinness is no longer a marker of poor health or low socioeconomic status. In fact, it is the opposite!

"The fact is that the tables of 'ideal' or 'desirable' weights are arm-chair concoctions starting with questionable assumptions and ending with three sets of standards for body frames . . . never measured or even properly defined. Unfortunately, those tables have been reprinted by the thousands and are widely-accepted as the gospel truth."
—Ancel Keys, Professor Emeritus, University of Minnesota

Initial attempts to define "normal" weight and obesity were based on economic considerations. In need of criteria to screen applicants, life insurance companies developed standard height and weight tables.[2] Since weight is easily tracked without significant costs, companies began collating weight with mortality. Initially, tables were sex and age specific and, arbitrarily, people 20% above the average weight paid higher premiums.

In the 1940's, the New York Metropolitan Life Insurance Company published tables with "ideal," rather than average weights, and with no age adjustment, which meant adding pounds after age 20 was not allowed. Suddenly, obesity became "America's number one health problem."[3]

The MetLife tables were based on statistics from affluent whites of northern European descent living in the eastern United States. These tables imply that any increase in weight intensifies the risk of death. The tables have been revised several times, but still, mainstream propaganda maintains that thinner

"The establishment clings to the belief that weight causes disease and death just as people once insisted that the world was flat." **—Susan Wooley, co-editor,** *Feminist Perspectives on Eating Disorders*

is better. Certainly, trusting a graph of averages to determine an individual's optimal weight is an unethical and potentially dangerous practice, as these statistics omit race, ethnicity, body frame, composition, health status, and age, among other important factors. Age and gender alone are critical to body weight, as men and women age differently. Men tend to gain weight in their early 20's, women after menopause. Standards based on one particular age can be impossible to maintain with normal nutritional intake.[4]

The Body Wars industries simplify and scapegoat the issue of weight in order to promote dieting, but the myths they have promoted are far from the truth. Studies to determine the causes of obesity are often based on limited research and a blindness to obvious factors. For example, socioeconomic status is rarely examined, despite that obesity and poverty are closely linked in the US.[5] Non-obese Americans tend to be in higher economic strata, and are apt to be more educated and have greater access to dietary and health information, while obese people from lower socioeconomic groups have less access to such information.

One powerful stereotype implies that all obese people cause their own "weight problems" by uncontrolled eating. Research over the past 20 years has not confirmed this. In 12 of 13 studies reviewed by one author,[6] obese people ate the same amount or less food than non-obese people. Other studies have examined more specific eating habits and found no major difference in food choice, the amount of calories, carbohydrates, protein, or fat consumed, or other food related behaviors.

Obesity myths also ignore genetic contributions. Adopted children are more similar in weight to their biological parents than to their adoptive parents.[7] Set-point theory also suggests that genetics affect weight, distribution of body fat, frame, metabolism and appetite.[8] Contrary to popular opinion, weight is not a reliable measure of morality or character strength. It is a complex mix of biological, social and psychological issues as well as lifestyle influences. The simple truth about weight is that optimal body sizes cannot be found on standardized tables.

Thin Today, Fat Tomorrow

While most people worry about potential health risks associated with obesity, there is little agreement in professional circles about what these are, and even on a standardized definition of obesity. Some classify it as 20% to 40% above the average weight on the Metropolitan Tables, while others utilize the Body Mass Index (BMI), often considered a more objective and reliable standard, as it relates weight to height. (The BMI is calculated by multiplying weight in pounds by 700 and dividing it by the square of height in inches).

The cut-off points for obesity, however, are arbitrary and subject to change. On June 17, 1998, the government declared the previous BMI standards too lenient, and altered their recommendations. Without gaining a pound, millions of Americans, whose BMI's were considered normal on the 16th, woke up the next day to learn that they were in the danger zone. This instigated the New York Post to print the new charts along with the header, Government Mumbo Jumbo.[9]

Weight vs. Health

In a culture horrified by the sight of fat, motivation is mounting to reduce the increasing "problem" of obesity to a formula, and to prescribe a quick-fix cure. Yet, the precise biological, social, and psychological causes, risk factors, and related medical problems are unclear, especially when clouded by prejudicial attitudes and stereotypes about fat people. Despite this ignorance, the general consensus is that it is healthier to be thin-ner, whatever the costs. In fact, studies depicting no relationship between weight and health, or those correlating a high weight with health, far outnumber the thinner-is-better stud-

"The kinds of disease we see in overweight people are the same diseases we see in sedentary and unfit people of every weight. How can we be so sure it's weight that kills? Maybe it's just inactivity."
—Steven Blair, epidemiologist and exercise physiologist

ies.[10] Whether or not obesity ought to be tackled and "treated" is still unclear.

"Extra" weight can actually be an advantage against the onset and mortality associated with some diseases. For example, larger men and women have a lower risk for lung cancer (regardless of smoking) and osteoporosis. Studies repeatedly demonstrate that underweight people are most at risk for health problems.[11] This is not brand new, hot-off-the-presses research. In 1969, the American Cancer Society published a major study that discovered that weight loss, whether voluntary or involuntary, dramatically increases the risk of premature death by heart disease or stroke. This study followed 800,000 men and women ages 40-79 for six years and found no connection between weight gain and mortality. Only weight loss was associated with mortality.[12]

> "Can a century's worth of assumptions be wrong? Do millions of Americans risk premature death *unless* they lose weight or *because they lose weight?*"
> —Glenn Gaesser, author, *Big Fat Lies*

In truth, weight has limited value as a measure of health, except probably at both extremes. Many people struggle to stay thin by restricting their nutritional intake when, in reality, average or even above average weight coupled with physical fitness is the best assurance of health.[13] Prominent researchers in the field of eating disorders believe that starvation and malnutrition from dieting may actually cause the heart disease, arteriosclerosis, hypertension, and diabetes usually considered an outcome of obesity.[14] Since many obese people diet chronically, it is difficult to determine whether medical problems or obesity come first. When you add dieting to the equation, the cause-effect relationship becomes even more murky.

In fact, a reliable association does not exist between obesity and mortality. Numerous studies promote a connection between the two, having interpreted data to support erroneous assumptions. For example, the 1995 Nurse's Health Study[15] received considerable attention when it concluded that mild to moderate overweight increases the risk of early death. For a 5'5" woman, the risk increases slightly between 120 and 175 pounds, and then jumps dramatically for those at or above 190 pounds, according to this research. The study had a number of limitations: only a small number (4%) had died; of those a very small percentage was associated with cardiac disease; and, the researchers did not control for smoking, fitness, or dietary patterns. The conclusions and their far-reaching implications were not supported by appropriate data. Further, their data proved to be statistically insignificant. However, the popular press sensationalized the findings to suggest that any woman who veers even 10 pounds upward of standard weight charts should be getting her affairs in order.

"Even as scientific research has lifted some of the burden of shame from obese people, the medical war against the condition has escalated."
—Shawna Vogel, author,
The Skinny on Fat

There is more. An ongoing study of 10,000 men and 3,000 women ages 20-60 disproves the association between higher weight and premature death.[16] Research on 17,000 Harvard alumni followed regularly from freshman year in college through adulthood found the highest mortality rate in men who did not gain weight. Those who gained the most had the lowest death rate, while alumni with the lowest weight gain had a 29% higher risk in comparison.[17] Another longitudinal study found that higher weight contributed to mortality when men were at 190% of the average and women were at 210%.[18] In other words, they had to be at twice the average weight for build to be at risk for serious health problems.

Clearly, society's phobic attitudes towards higher weights have, for several decades, been based on "fat fiction." This has fueled the Body Wars of self-rejection, dangerous dieting, and body shame. Arm yourself with the "fat facts" and make a difference!

STRATEGIES FOR CHANGE

Learn as much as you can about your body and what you can do to keep it healthy, no matter what your size. Be sure to consider genetic and environmental factors. Make a commitment to trade in your worries about weight for a serious and realistic health assessment.

Change starts with you. How have you been swayed by anti-obesity propaganda? Can you challenge your beliefs about obesity? Take the following quiz, then commit to sharing what you learn with others to help destroy obesity myths.

OBESITY QUIZ — FACT OR FICTION?
True or False:

1. Weight is a reliable predictor of health and health risk.

2. Being slightly above average weight puts you at health risk.

3. There are significant differences between the eating habits of normal and obese people.

4. When it comes to weight, genetics may be more important than environment or learned behavior.

5. Being underweight presents no health risks.

6. The health problems associated with obesity may result from dieting.

7. The weights recommended by the Metropolitan Tables are reliable, universal standards for all people.

8. Weight should be stable after the age of 25.

9. It is more dangerous for women than men to be overweight.

10. Fat on the body is always a predictor of dangerous fat in the body, such as clogged arteries (atheriosclerosis).

Answers: 1. F, 2. F, 3. F, 4. T, 5. F, 6. T, 7. F, 8. F, 9. F, 10. F

Teach others about fat facts. For example, if your physician focuses on the weight tables, discuss what you have learned about fat facts. If you recognize misinformation printed in the newspaper or magazines you read, write the publication to request more extensive research before publishing articles. Explain the high costs, particularly to women, of living in an ignorant society.

Check the contents of the health curriculum in your school district. Specifically, look at how it describes the relationship between weight and health. Be sure that the information is accurate, as this may prevent future prejudice and its fallout.

RESOURCES

National Institute for Diabetes, Digestive and Kidney Disorders (NIDDK) is the branch of the National Institute of Health responsible for obesity research. They fund research to promote the understanding and treatment of obesity, including how the body stores and uses fat. They maintain a National Task Force on the Prevention and Treatment of Obesity which includes the leading experts and lastest information on obesity research. NIDDK also distributes information on obesity and weight control through:

WIN (Weight Control Information Network)
1 Win Way
Bethesda, MD 20892-3665
301-984-7378
800-WIN-8098
win@info.niddk.nih.gov

The Obesity Law and Resource Center
Represents morbidly obese people in personal injury and civil litigation, especially related to employment discrimination, insurance coverage, and denial of medical treatment.
3160 Camino del Rio South, #312
San Diego, CA 92108

619-516-3939
www.obesitylaw.com

The Association for the Study of Obesity in Great Britain
Publishes the International Journal of Obesity and sponsors an information center to promote understanding of obesity.
Obesity Resource Information Center
40-42 Osnaburgh St
London NW1 3ND England
0171-465-0130
www.aso.org.uk.oric.frame2html

Books

Big Fat Lies: The Truth about Your Weight and Your Health
Gaesser, G., New York, Random House, 1996

Transforming Body Image: Learning to Love the Body You Have
Hutchinson, M. G., Trumansburg, NY, Crossing Press, 1985.

200 Ways to Love the Body You Have
Hutchinson, M. G., Trumansburg, NY, Crossing Press, 1999.

Such A Pretty Face
Millman, M., New York, Norton, 1990.

Fat is Not a Four Letter Word
Schroeder, C. R., Minneapolis, MN, Chronimed, 1992.

Never Too Thin: Why Women are at War with their Bodies
Seid, R., New York, Prentice-Hall, 1989.

4

Dieting
DECEIT, DANGER AND DEATH

"The history of the diet industry in America (as yet unwritten) probably represents one of the most astounding triumphs of the twentieth century capitalist enterprises."
—Joan Brumberg,
author of *Fasting Girls*

Apparently, Moses added another commandment: Thou shall not be fat. Today, eating and morality have become so intertwined that women attack their bodies with a religious zeal rarely applied elsewhere. Now, when a woman says she has cheated, she usually means she ate a chocolate, not that she has copied answers during an exam or been untrue to her partner. Dieting has become a moral imperative of utmost significance; many who fail to lose weight feel they have failed at life.

How did this happen? To find the answer, we must challenge our cultural values of self-determination, self-reliance, and the belief that, with sufficient self-control, one can reach any goal. We tend to believe that we can control all aspects of life and, therefore, that people get what they deserve. Consequently, overweight people are seen as morally inferior and lazy. Particularly for women, fat is no longer a size; it is a symbol of weak character. Dieting has become a form of redemption.

Although the exact number of people dieting at one time is unknown, most studies show that women are at least twice as likely to diet as men. White and Hispanic men are more apt to diet than black men,[1] while women of all different races, ethnicities, and educational levels are likely to dislike their bodies and to restrict food intake in hope of losing weight. A 1978 Nielsen survey of 24-54 year old women found that 56% were dieting. The same survey, repeated in the late 1980's, revealed that 72% were dieting.[2]

"Marketers' most ingenious lightbulb blinked on when they apparently realized that the way to REALLY guarantee profits forevermore was to cast the standard of bodily perfection at lower and lower weights, until the "ideal" actually became unattainable for about 95 percent of female body types."
—Terry Poulton, author,
No Fat Chicks

Despite all of the food-related rules and restrictions that have flourished in the past 20-30 years, as a nation we have become fatter. Between 1960 and 1980, one out of four American adults was overweight. By 1990, this statistic increased to one of every three. In the same time period, childhood obesity increased by 50%.[3] Dieting has proven to be counterproductive, and it has stolen our self-esteem, energy, and freedom.

Oddly, most people who diet are not obese to start with.[4] One study found that 64% of normal-weight women and 23% of normal-weight men without a history of weight problems were dieting.[5] Some dieters know they are not fat but are driven to limit what they eat by fear of weight gain, while others, average in weight, overestimate their body size. According to one study, 20% of underweight adolescent girls actively diet.[6] These Body Wars have indeed become a cultural norm.

Capitalism at Work

The diet industry is a capitalist dream come true, with its self-generating market, widespread target audience, and high failure rate. Check the bestseller list to see the latest fad diet books. Entire sections of bookstores and even greeting cards are dedicated to weight loss. A myriad of magazines devote themselves to weight loss and body shape. Special "diet" foods, such as frozen meals, crackers and cookies, and meal replacement bars and drinks, once only available in health food stores, are now mainstream. Additionally, weight loss clinics, no longer reserved for severe weight conditions, populate most cities. Infomercials touting the latest diet products infiltrate late night and weekend television. Herbal weight loss products are advertised on daytime television using models slim enough to grace the pages of fashion magazines. Due to the diet industry's insidious and pervasive influence, most of us are not even aware of the harmful messages we take in from the culture.

The dieting Body Wars are great for the economy, as the majority of discontented dieters repeatedly invest their resources in shedding pounds. Figures from the late 1990's showed that Americans spent $50 billion annually on diet products.[7] This exceeds the projections for the entire federal Education, Training, Employment and Social Services budgets by five to ten billion dollars.[8] In fact, this figure is the equivalent of the gross national product of Ireland.[9] The price per pound lost is enormous, with one study of Optifast dieters reporting the cost to be $180 per pound.[10]

A Set-up for Failure

After all of the elaborate planning, garnering of resources, and emotional investment in weight loss, dieting still rarely works. Of those who lose 25 or more pounds, 90% will regain those pounds within two years, and 98% will regain the weight within five years. In fact, many regain more weight than they lose.[11] Most diets do result in an initial weight loss, but long-term maintenance is unusual.

Diets fail for emotional, physical, and cultural reasons that have nothing to do with the will of the dieter, and the weight loss industry relies on such failures to keep the American public hooked on its products. First, dieting leads to binge eating, the body's natural response to deprivation. Second, external diet plans do not address the emotional issues underlying the compulsion to eat. Also, diets dissociate the dieter from body cues, such as hunger and satiety. The inefficacy of weight loss diets relates to set-point theory, which argues that each body has a natural, preprogrammed weight range that it fights to maintain.[12] When we eat too little, our metabolism slows down to conserve energy. Conversely, when we eat too much, our metabolism speeds up to use energy and to keep our weight within its set-point range. After a period of semi-starvation (most diets require a caloric intake consistent with starvation), our bodies store fat to protect us from future famine. In this way, dieting distorts set-point and creates more weight problems.

The Dangers of Dieting

Despite a poor track record, the weight loss industry does not warn its customers about the negative outcomes or the potential risks of most weight loss attempts. The following list includes some of the medical problems associated with severe dieting:

> hypertension
> fainting
> gallstones
> diarrhea
> constipation
> aching muscles
> weakness
> fatigue
> increased serum cholesterol
> slow or irregular heartbeat
> abdominal pain
> anemia
> headaches
> nausea
> death[13]

Fasting or semi-starvation can lead to cardiovascular, metabolic, gastrointestinal, neuromuscular, and renal problems. The very low calorie diets (VLCD) such as the popular liquid supplements do not provide enough calories or protein to keep the body from eating its own muscles and organs. Consequently, they can boast of a death rate 40 times that expected in the general population. Numerous deaths have been associated with products as seemingly safe as diet teas. Used excessively, these ostensibly benign drinks can cause cardiac arrhythmias, just like any other laxative.[14]

The medical risks are even higher for surgical techniques. Intestinal by-pass surgery may lead to progressive liver failure and death. Stomach stapling can result in liver failure, brain and nerve damage, ulcers, hernias, cardiac arrhythmias, infections, anemia, vitamin deficiencies, osteoporosis, diarrhea, constipation, vomiting, malnutrition, stomach cancer, and death. Two to four percent of patients die within days after surgery, and undergoing this procedure increases mortality risk nine times. Despite these dangers, physicians perform 15,000 weight reduction surgeries, about 85% on women, each year in the U.S.[15]

"Body fat is not intrinsically unhealthy. Dieting is."
—**Glenn Gaesser, author,** *Big Fat Lies*

Mounting evidence suggests that the medical problems commonly associated with obesity may be due to drastic attempts to lose weight. For example, animal studies reveal that repeated periods of restricted eating are associated with high blood pressure.[16] One 32-year study found that weight fluctuations correlate with increased risk for heart disease and death.[17] When compared with non-dieters, yo-yo dieters—those who cycle up and down in their nutritional intake and weight—double their chances of developing diabetes, cardiovascular disease, hypertension, and coronary heart disease. These studies indicate that it is safer to be large than to subject oneself to low calorie diets.[18]

Magic Pills

In 1996 in the United States, millions of prescriptions were written for diet pills, mostly for women. Despite the possibility of pulmonary hypertension (an often fatal condition), and very little research on their long-term use,[19] diet drugs have become the latest weight loss propaganda.

Fenfluramine (marketed as Pondimin by Robbins) and Dexfenfluramine (marketed as Redux by Interneuron and Wyeth-Ayerst) are appetite suppressants which act on the serotonin in the brain. Phentermine (also known as Adipex, Fatin, Ionamin, by Smith Kline Beecham and Didrex by Upjohn) is a stimulant that suppresses appetite by releasing catecholamine, norephinephrine, and dopamine from neurons.[20] These two drugs ("Fen/phen"), in combination, gained overnight popularity, despite little research on their effectiveness or safety.

"The so-called clinical research in this field has been largely paid for by the formula and drug companies."
—**C. Wayne Callaway, M.D., author, *The Callaway Diet***

In the past, appetite-altering drugs were prescribed only for

48

short-term use, often to enable the patient to acclimate to a lower caloric intake. But greedy pharmaceutical companies "realized that considerably more profit can be made selling a drug that must be taken for a lifetime."[21] Even used briefly, these medications are extremely risky and addictive. One patient died from pulmonary hypertension after taking fen/phen for only 23 days.[22] She reportedly wanted to lose weight before her wedding.[23] Her family has filed a wrongful death suit against the drug company.

In 1997, the Food and Drug Administration requested pharmaceutical companies to issue more stringent warnings to physicians and consumers of weight loss drugs.[24] That year an editorial in the New England Journal of Medicine urged a "moratorium" on the use of diet pills for cosmetic weight loss. The editorial declared that "the only justifiable medical use" of such drugs is for seriously obese patients who already have obesity-related medical problems, and that use must be closely monitored.[25] Despite such compelling arguments, the CEO of a corporation called Medical Weight Loss Centers stated that clients still seek these medications because they believe the benefits of weight loss "outweigh the risks."[26] Yet, 25-30% of the six million otherwise healthy people who fearlessly used fen/phen ended up with leaky heart valves[27] and will expend endless money, time, and emotional energy as they endure echocardiograms, valve replacements, and related medical visits.

On September 15, 1997, the FDA removed fen/phen from the market. However, weight loss "professionals" and consumers immediately began to experiment with other medications and herbs. Soon after the legal removal of fen/phen, despite the limited research and the drug's associated risk of increased blood pressure and heart rate, the FDA approved Knoll Pharmaceutical's Meridia. Studied for just one year, long-term use is not recommended and, when the drug is stopped, the "loser" gains weight.[28]

"Imagine what you could avoid eating."
—ad for Meridia, August 1999

In light of the modest weight loss and considerable risks associated with weight reduction medications, the National Task Force on the Prevention and Treatment of Obesity warned that drug therapy is not recommended for routine use in obese individuals. The Task Force reviewed 20 controlled studies of appetite suppressant drugs and warned that "off-label" use (prescribing other than as approved by the FDA) is the norm when it comes to weight loss.[29]

In desperation, many people turn to "natural" products that can be equally dangerous. In the U.S., between five and seven billion dollars are annually spent on these supplements.[30] Positioned as the natural alternative to fen/phen, a product called Ephedra is especially dangerous. In many products, this stimulant is associated with cardiac irregularities, high blood pressure, tremors, anxiety, headaches, seizures, heart attacks, stroke, and death. In 1994, the FDA received over 800 complaints about Ephedra.[31]

Food and Mood

Dieting creates mood swings and emotional distress, notably feelings of hopelessness and worthlessness. Subsequent to ineffective diets, some women become clinically depressed, even attempting suicide. For others, the deprivation of dieting, the rigid rules and eating constraints, and the connection between self-esteem and food can lead to eating problems. Up to 35% of normal dieters will progress to pathological dieting and, of those, 20-25% will progress to partial or full-blown eating disorders.[32] Since eating disorders can turn deadly, with a mortality rate between 5 and 20%,[33] these statistics are alarming.

> *"Each penny we pay to the reducing industry increases its power over us."*
> —**Vivian F. May,**
> in *Shadow on a Tightrope*

Many people seek out weight loss programs even when their primary problem is not weight. Often, poor body image and feelings of inadequacy or depression prompt the desire to diet. Studies of commercial weight reduction programs show that between 15% and 50% of those seeking weight loss suffer from depressive symptoms.[34] Depression can lead to impairments in all areas of life, and losing weight is an attempt, however misguided, to improve one's situation.

Individuals struggling with self doubt, stress, and feelings of inadequacy are easy prey for Body Wars. In light of this, weight loss clinics should screen for symptoms of psychological disturbances. People who are dissatisfied with themselves, or who are depressed, need more sensitive interventions, not less food. Starvation and failed dieting only exacerbate depression.

History Teaches Nothing

Warnings about the dangers of dieting have been issued many times. In 400 B.C., Hippocrates advised that "dieting that causes excessive loss of weight is beset with difficulties."[35] In the 1920's, physicians discussed the dangers of female dieting in the preventative medicine program of the Progressive Era. The first anti-diet book, *Diet and Die*, by Carl Mamberg, was published in 1935.[36] Between 1983 and 1993, 15 comprehensive studies found that weight loss increases the risk of premature death by 260%. Only two studies during that time found any decrease in mortality associated with weight loss. One showed an increase of 11 hours of longevity for each pound lost. At that rate, to gain a year of life, 796 pounds would have to be lost.[37]

The following chart summarized how dieting backfires.

WHAT REALLY HAPPENS WHEN WE DIET

How We Diet	This Is What *Really* Happens
Skip meals or decrease calories	We lower our metabolism and we store fat more easily from fewer calories.
	The body's need for fuel causes rebound "munchies," usually for high fats and sugars.
	Hunger causes poor attention span, irritability, fatigue. Muscle may be lost.

Cut out starches	Your body loses a source of stable energy, so you'll be more likely to feel moody and tired.
	You eat higher fat and sugary foods to satisfy munchies.
Cut out meats	You may risk iron deficiency leading to fatigue.
	Energy from meals does not last as long, so you are more hungry between meals for high fat, high sugar foods.
Go on preplanned meal replacement diet or liquid diet	You have a 95% chance of regaining any weight you lose in 1 to 2 years.
	You lose muscle mass along with fat and lower your metabolism, making it easier to store fat on fewer calories.
	This is a "quick-fix" and doesn't teach you how to eat healthy.
	And, it's very expensive.
Fasting	The weight loss is primarily water.
	Muscle mass decreases, lowering metabolism resulting in fat gain.
	It is medically dangerous.

Why We Diet	This Is What *Really* Happens
To be slim	Slimness is temporary.
	Over the long run, 95% of dieters regain the weight and then diet again, with similar results.
	This diet cycling, or yo-yo dieting, can lead to obesity.
To be healthier	Diet cycling increases health risks.
	There is no evidence that being plump is unhealthy, but there is evidence that being too slim is unhealthy.
	Dieting can decrease muscle mass. Muscles are necessary for good health.
	Diets are unhealthy.
	Your body and mind don't run well when you restrict calories.
	You become moody, irritable, and obsessed with food, which is a physiological response to starvation, not a lack of will power.
To be more attractive	Ask yourself these questions: What attracts you to someone else? Do you want your friends to like you for your body or yourself? What are long term relationships

based upon? If you are dieting, are you any fun to be around? Does dieting really make you more attractive or just more self-centered?

Adapted from information prepared by the Nutritionists from Boundary Health Unit.[38]

In 1992, in response to the broadening demographics of obesity, the National Institute of Health convened a meeting to explore the safety and effectiveness of dieting. A panel of academics, physicians, and public health experts listened to testimony from leading obesity specialists, many of whom supported the very low calorie diets (VLCD's). No anti-dieting advocates were invited. Still, the committee concluded that most diets do not work, that there is little evidence that weight loss prolongs life, and that we have no clear definition of "overweight" due to the diversity of body shape and size in healthy Americans.[39]

The committee did underscore that poor eating habits, whether eating too much or too little negatively affect health. They affirmed that adequate, balanced meals and snacks, in combination with an active lifestyle, are ingredients of optimal health.

STRATEGIES FOR CHANGE

As always, the first step to changing your relationship with your body involves assessing your own attitudes about fitness and fat. If you feel pressure to lose weight, talk about your concerns with friends, loved-ones, or a professional who is knowledgeable about weight issues. Remember that people come in all shapes and sizes. Recognize disparaging comments about body size. With the knowledge that dieting is often a frustrating and futile endeavor, love your natural body.

If, after careful consideration, you do choose to enhance your activity level and to eat a more balanced diet, find a nutritionist and a physician to work with you. Choose your support system with care. Even healthcare professionals are influenced by our cultural obsession with dieting, and may know very little about the complexities of weight management, metabolism, and health. Health, rather than weight, must be your primary impetus. Since weight and eating issues often coincide with complex psychological issues, consult a mental health professional to better understand your eating patterns, thoughts and feelings. Before prescribing weight loss for yourself or for anybody else, scrutinize your own attitudes and beliefs about fat and food, and read, "Weight Control: Facts, Fads, and Frauds," in *The Health Robbers*, by Stephen Barret and W.T. Jarurs, published by Prometheus, 1993.

Ask organizations like your National Organization of Women (NOW) to sponsor programs on healthy body image and the dangers of dieting. Or, ask other women's organizations to write a position paper, educate women, and demonstrate the connection between women's power and the time, energy and drive lost in the pursuit of a thinner body. Starving women will never achieve equality or their rightful position in any culture.

Since consumer dissatisfaction and fraud are highest in the

diet industry,[40] lobby the government to actively regulate diet programs. Connecticut is a positive example, as its legislature passed a bill requiring truth in advertising for weight loss programs. You can also urge the Federal Trade Commission or the Food and Drug Administration to substantiate claims in advertising, ensuring that potential weight-loss customers are informed of the grim statistics and potential risks of the various weight loss methods.

Join a nationwide campaign to raise consciousness about the damaging impact of beauty ideals. Help your peers to realize that the media's model of thinness is not an appropriate goal for most of us, and that dieting does more harm than good. National organizations dedicated to the primary and secondary prevention of eating disorders promote this message through a variety of programs and campaigns. For instance, annual "Fearless Friday" sponsored by Eating Disorders Awareness and Prevention (EDAP) is a day when people are encouraged to eat without fear or imposed restrictions.

Likewise, "No Diet Day," founded by Mary Evans Young, the British leader of the anti-diet movement, is designed to increase awareness of the futility of dieting, and to emphasize the difference between healthy and disordered eating. Posters, buttons, and literature are available to promote the event and its positive message year-round.

The size acceptance movement uplifts people of all shapes and sizes. Respect for all bodies removes thinness from its pedestal and alleviates the pressure to diet. Support organizations that work towards this goal with both your time and resources.

TOP TEN REASONS TO GIVE UP DIETING

#10: Diets don't work. Even if you lose weight, you will probably gain it all back, and you might gain back more than you lost.

#9: Diets are expensive. If you didn't buy special diet products, you could save enough to get new clothes, which would improve your outlook right now.

#8: Diets are boring. People on diets talk and think about food and practically nothing else. There's a lot more to life.

#7: Diets don't necessarily improve your health. Like the weight loss, health improvement is temporary. Dieting can actually cause health problems.

#6: Diets don't make you beautiful. Very few people will ever look like models. Glamour is a look, not a size. You don't have to be thin to be attractive.

#5: Diets are not sexy. If you want to be more attractive, take care of your body and your appearance. Feeling healthy makes you look your best.

#4: Diets can turn into eating disorders. The obsession to be thin can lead to anorexia, bulimia, bingeing, and compulsive exercising.

#3: Diets can make you afraid of food. Food nourishes and comforts us, and gives us pleasure. Dieting can make food seem like an enemy, and can deprive you of all the positive things about food.

#2: Diets can rob you of energy. If you want to lead a full and active life, you need good nutrition, and enough food to meet your body's needs.

> *And the number one reason to give up dieting:*
>
> **#1: Learning to love and accept yourself just as you are will give you self-confidence, better health, and a sense of well-being that will last a lifetime.**
>
> © 1994 Council on Size & Weight Discrimination, Inc. For more information, write: International No Diet Coalition, P.O. Box 305, Mt. Marion, NY 12456, or call 914-679-1209. Copying permitted (with copyright intact).

RESOURCES

Better Business Bureau
Listed in the white pages of your phone book. Most states also have an office of Consumer Protection found in the government section. Or, consult *The Consumer Bible* by Mark Green and Nancy Youman published by Workman, 1998, which lists all of the state consumer offices including phone numbers, addresses and websites.

EDAP (Sponsors of Fearless Friday)
603 Stewart St. #803
Seattle, WA 98101
206-382-3587
www.edap.com

The National Center for Overcoming Overeating
315 W 86th St. #17-B
New York, NY 10024-3111
212-874-6596

The Federal Trade Commission (FTC)
In conjunction with the FDA and the National Association of Attor-

neys General, have produced a document called, *The Facts About Weight Loss Products and Programs,* to help the public evaluate the claims of diet programs and industries. Another helpful brochure is titled, *The Skinny on Dieting.* Both are available through:
Federal Trade Commision
Public Affairs Branch, #130
6th St. & Penn Ave. NW
Washington, DC 20580
www.ftc.gov

Food & Drug Administration(FDA)
5600 Fisher's Lane
Parklawn Bldg.
Rockville, MD 20857
888-INFO-FDA

For information on No Diet Day, contact:
Miriam Berg
PO Box 305
Mt. Marion, NY 12456
914-679-1207

Melpomene Institute for Women's Health Research
1010 University Ave
St Paul, MN 55104
612-642-1951

National Organization for Women
1000 16th St. NW
Washington, DC 10021
202-628-8669

Books

The Dieter's Dilemma
Bennett, W., Gurin, J., New York, Basic Books, 1982.

Losing It: False Hopes and Fat Profits in the Diet Industry
Fraser, L., New York, Penguin Putnam, Inc, 1998.

Fed Up!
A Woman's Guide to Liberation from the Diet/Weight Prison
Garrison, T., New York, Carroll & Graf, 1993.

Making Peace with Food
Kano, S., New York, HarperCollins, 1989.

The Don't Diet, Live-It! Workbook
LoBue, A., Marcus, M., Carlsbad, CA, Gürze Books, 1999.

Breaking Free from Compulsive Eating
Roth, G., New York, Bobbs-Merrill, 1984.

Never Satisfied: A Cultural History of Diets, Fantasies, & Fat
Schwartz, H., New York, The Free Press, 1986.

Food & Mood: The Complete Guide to Eating Well and Feeling Your Best
Somer, E., New York, Henry Holt and Company, 1995.

Intuitive Eating: A Recovery Book for the Chronic Dieter
Tribole, E., Resch, E., New York, St. Martin's Press, 1995.

5

The Pursuit of Beauty

EMPOWERING OR DISEMPOWERING?

> *"Beauty is a very tangible asset in these days of fluctuating values. If your face isn't your fortune today, who knows that it may not be tomorrow—and what kind of fortune is it going to amount to?"*
>
> —Elizabeth Arden ad 1932

One dictionary defines beauty as that which "stirs the senses and mind at the highest level."[1] Another states, "a quality that is present in a thing or person giving intense aesthetic pleasure or deep satisfaction to the senses or the mind." Such abstract definitions stimulate us to think about beauty in a spiritual, expansive way. But not for long! The next entry reads: "an attractive, well-formed girl or woman."[2]

In contemporary America, beauty is an asset, a sign of one's value. Or, in the words of writer Naomi Wolf, "Beauty is a currency like the gold standard."[3] In fact, we spend over $20 billion each year on beauty products![4] That much money could fund for a year: 400,000 four-year university scholarships; 20 million airline tickets around the world; one million well paid home health aides for homebound elderly; 75,000 women's music, art or film festivals; 33,000 battered women's shelters.[5]

Appearance and status have gone hand-in-hand for a long time. Technological and medical advances, however, have made "beauty" the serious business it is today. The beauty industry thrives off of women's traditional role to please others, to do well for their men, and to be as attractive as possible. Sadly, American women feel more negatively about their bodies than their counterparts in any other culture.[6] In America, women repent for their flaws by engaging in Body Wars with religious zeal. But the time and money invested in the pursuit of beauty, which appears to promise them power, is actually a tenuous, disempowering affair.

> *"The more legal and material hindrances women have broken through, the more strictly and heavily and cruelly images of female beauty have come to weigh upon us."*
> —Naomi Wolf, author,
> *The Beauty Myth*

A Bit of History

Before the Industrial Revolution, both sexes pursued personal adornment to an equal degree. Once men began working in factories, however, they had to dress plainly, avoiding ruffles, cuffs, or other items that might get caught in the machines. After industrialization, men could accumulate wealth and social status through capitalistic endeavors, but they could no longer publicly demonstrate success through their own appearance. Image became less important, although male social standing was still enhanced by a beautiful wife.

By the late 1800's, beauty had become the domain of women and evolved from its spiritual and aesthetic dimensions into, as noted by Karl Marx, a concept related to gender, power, and economic status. This political economist suggested that a culture's progress could be measured by the social position of plain-looking women![7] Still, how a woman measured up in the beauty arena could either significantly enhance or diminish her value to the men who had power, money, and influence. As a result, women were increasingly drawn to Body Wars to achieve "beauty" for themselves and status for their men—a sad and misguided path to empowerment.

Beauty is Destiny: Being Female in the New Millennium

Sex-stereotyped messages about appearance start early in America. When a group of parents were asked to describe their infants 24 hours after birth, significant differences emerged. Although the babies were equal in height, weight, and responsiveness, girls were consistently described as beautiful, pretty, delicate, soft, and cute. In contrast, the boys were described as large, hardy, well-coordinated, firm and strong.[8]

Beginning at birth, aesthetics, appearance, and beauty are emphasized for girls, while strength and physical skills are stressed for boys. Girls, therefore, tend to be more sensitive to messages about appearance and more responsive to the latest cosmetic product, practice, or trend. Their feelings of self-esteem and happiness are often determined by how closely they conform to current standards of beauty. In contrast, boys are far less likely to connect their physical appearance with their self-worth. These gender-based differences only increase as children's bodies mature into adolescents and adults.

Consider the things we say: "She looks like a million dollars." "Her body is first class." "Her face is worth a fortune." "Those legs should be insured by Lloyds of London."

English is one of the few languages that has separate tems for male and female beauty. For example, while a woman is "as pretty as a picture," for men, "handsome is as handsome does."

The requirements for obtaining a "beautiful" appearance have become more stringent as fashion magazines promote new ideas, new products, and new rules, primarily to women. Many spend nearly as much time on "looking good" as they do working.[9] Naomi Wolf writes that women today work three shifts: one at their job, one taking care of the home and family, and the third trying to meet the beauty standards of our culture.[10] Sadly, women continue to be judged more by their image than by their accomplishments.

Advertising Beauty

Every type of product imaginable is advertised to help women attain the impossible beauty paragon. Just pick a body part:

Faces get toned, sloughed, peeled, massaged, lifted, moisturized, creamed, powdered, painted, blushed, waxed, and even pierced. Ears are pierced or surgically altered. Lips are lined, covered, pumped with silicone or made smaller. Teeth are straightened, capped, bleached, bonded, and removed. Eyes get a lot of attention. Brows are tweezed, penciled, dyed and waxed. Lashes are curled, coated with mascara, or false ones are glued on. Lids are lifted, lined, and shadowed. Eye color can be changed with contact lens. Hair is cut, curled, straightened, dyed, conditioned, sprayed, and teased. Nails are pedicured and manicured, or new ones are glued on. Body hair is tweezed, shaved, waxed, or removed via electrolysis, depilatories, or lasers. Fat is sucked out of "problem areas" to make them thinner and sometimes injected elsewhere to create a fuller feature. Bones can be removed or reshaped so the beauty can just shine on through!

Approximately 50 cents of every dollar we spend on cosmetics is put back into advertising.[11] The sad result is that we continue to believe we need to cover-up, rather than expose, our true beauty. Although cosmetic companies have recently developed product lines and marketing campaigns for men, women remain the overwhelming majority of customers.

We are living in harsh times as a barrage of criticism is projected onto our bodies, beginning with the tone and texture of our skin. Before the 1900s, in contrast, there was no opportu-

66

nity to find fault with complexion. But when the mirror became a popular household item in the early 20th century, normal variations in the skin, such as lines or wrinkles, could be noticed and considered pathological. Pimples, once accepted as natural, became significant medical and cosmetic problems in this era of Body Wars. Today, more than 2/3 of American girls between the ages of 12-15 buy over-the-counter medicines for acne. Some will go further, using powerful drugs such as Retin-A or Accutane, associated respectively with increased photosensitivity to sunlight and birth defects. The latest products for these young people now include anti-aging chemicals.[13] What a hoax! To help kids cope with the normal adolescent condition of acne, the agents of Body Wars instill early fears of wrinkles.

Every minute Americans buy: 1,484 lipsticks ($4,566); 1,324 eye products (liner, shadow, mascara, at $6,849); and 2,055 jars of skin cream ($12,785).[12]

Advertising campaigns for cosmetics are creative and powerful. Written in pseudo-scientific language, they tempt and intimidate us by their authority. For example, the claim that topical creams "fight environmental damage" elevates skin care to a concern of the Environmental Protection Agency! Meanwhile, the cosmetic industry is basically unregulated, even though it is notorious for false advertising. According to a spokesperson for dermatologists, "Essentially none of this stuff works."[14]

The Federal Trade Commission (FTC) and the Food and Drug Administration cannot investigate for misleading advertising until a consumer, a competitor, or another agency files a complaint. Unlike drugs, cosmetics do not have to prove their safety by the FDA. Only 500 of the 10,000 chemicals used have ever been tested, yet we absorb them through our skin. For example, the average woman who wears lipstick will swallow 10 pounds of it over 40 years; an ingredient in sunscreen impairs the immune system and is associated with cancer in mice.[15] Maybe we should all think a bit more about spreading on our bodies chemicals whose safety is unknown.

Not-So-Blind Allegiance to Beauty

Beauty is a trap door for women. Although "a potentially profitable tool,"[16] it does not have a long shelf life. The pursuit of perfection is, in truth, an empty, endless cycle that leaves women emotionally and spiritually bereft, as a preoccupation with external appearance undermines inner beauty. Yet, women continue to rotate through this revolving door, motivated by tantalizing rewards. In one study, 86% of women report that beauty bestows them with self-confidence.[17] Albeit temporary, the quick confidence boost appears to be worth the struggle to women who, unknowingly, collude in their own oppression.

As gender roles have changed dramatically in recent decades, most women today work outside of the home. Their bodies, thus, are now more public than ever before. The aesthetic standard has also become more rigid and arbitrary. Sadly, beauty is often a determining factor in a woman's success. In the past, only a few professions based their inclusion on looks (i.e. act-ing, dance, and modeling), whereas today, most occupations come with expectations and judgments about appearance. In fact, the criteria for beauty seems more powerful as women challenge old notions regarding their societal roles and the essence of femininity.

Despite Title IX of the Civil Rights Act banning sex discrimination, some court rulings allow employers to terminate women who are "too ugly," "unfeminine," or who do not "dress right."[18] After a female television commentator was fired and two juries found sex discrimination, a judge overturned the decision. According to his justification, market logic allows a network to base employment on appearance or attractiveness.[19] Routinely, women are coerced into wearing make-up or dressing a certain way just to keep a job. Most female employees do not question this; they are accustomed to being judged by their looks. It is no wonder that when it comes to financial reward, only women who use their bodies for income have overcome the pay inequities between the sexes. Models and prostitutes are the two female occupational groups that outearn men.[20]

> *"It's important to remember that because beauty ideals are learned, and vary across culture and time, there is really no such thing as a 'natural' beauty. Given the right time period and the right culture, all of us could enjoy a place on the pedestal of a culture's beauty ideal."*
> —**Joni E. Johnston, author, *Appearance Obsession***

A woman's beauty allows her to "succeed" without competing with or offending men. It compensates for the economic disparity between the sexes by attracting men, especially the wealthy ones, and by providing status, a false sense of security, and power for as long as "the look" lasts. Until women have real power, the deceptive promises of artificial and superficial beauty will continue to hook them.

Beauty vs. Power

What are we to make of the impulse to cover women up, change them, and render their self-value dependent on the mirror's reflection, so often distorted? In the past quarter century, women have heeded the empowering messages of the feminist movement to incorporate new experiences, widen their influence, and take up more space in the world. While women's presence in the public sphere has expanded, however, the ideal female body has been shrinking.

"Putting on make-up, styling hair, and so forth are conceived of only as free play, fun, a matter of creative expression. This surely they are. But they are also experienced by many women as necessary before they will show themselves to the world, even on a quick trip to the corner mailbox"
—**Susan Bordo, author**
Unbearable Weight

The 1990's witnessed a return to thin, waif-like models who appear powerless. Models today are 13-19% thinner than the average weight for women of the same height and age.[21] One criteria for anorexia nervosa is weight loss of 15%, or failure to gain more than 85% of expected weight. Thus, attempting to look like a model may cause a woman to develop a serious medical condition. While beauty has always come at a price, this "bare-bones" standard is particularly costly. Few people can maintain such a low weight and still be healthy. Even fewer can exert real power while constricting their appetites, starving their bodies, and pursuing "the look." Judging by the small size of this cultural corset, women's potential, if freed from Body Wars, is staggering.

Think of the stereotypes assigned to women who have shown more interest in power and fairness than in beauty. People ridicule feminists, lesbians, and other "liberated women" for mini-rebellions like not shaving their legs or not wearing make-up. By judging an entire sex by their willingness to conform, these attitudes belittle and disempower all women.

Our preoccupation with a narrow definition of female beauty renders women subordinate, insecure, powerless, and fighting Body Wars instead of living full lives. Let us return to the real definition of beauty—those things that "stir the senses or the mind at the highest level"—and stop reducing the value of females to physical appearance. It is time to quit trivializing and discounting women's accomplishments and worth and to declare an end to Body Wars. It is time to allow women to have real power.

STRATEGIES FOR CHANGE

Observe the power of the "beauty myth" in your own life. Do you judge the value of girls or women based on how they adhere to the current standards of beauty? Do you think negatively about a woman "who doesn't keep herself up?" Or do you distrust a woman whom you see as too attractive? Become aware of how your perceptions, beliefs, and interactions are tainted by a woman's appearance.

Consider how you handle pressures to appear a certain way, and the premium you attach to appearance. Do you spend more time criticizing and changing your body than you do reading poetry, appreciating nature, talking to friends or loved ones, or doing other things that will "stir your senses?" If having a pedicure will satisfy your soul, then do it, but also find other ways to achieve self-care.

"If you talked to your friends the way you talk to your body, you'd have no friends left at all."
—**Marcia Hutchinson, author,** *Transforming Body Image*

If you are a man, examine how women's lives are complicated by the pressure to please others. Do not criticize a woman for her concern with how she appears; instead, communicate what you find beautiful and valuable.

If you are involved with children, be aware of the messages you may inadvertently communicate about physical appearance. Help them to realize their inner value and self-worth. Allow them to see the beauty in every body, face, race, or ethnicity. Teach kids about the changing norms for appearance. Show them family photos of your generation, as well as their grandparents and previous generations. Point out the trends for beauty, body size, and appearance. Visit an art museum to show them how beauty symbols are not constant or universal, but are dynamic, multifaceted, and reflective of the expectations of a particular era or culture.

As a culture, we must address the inequalities that still exist between the sexes. So long as women earn considerably less for equal work, females will feel chained to the beauty rituals that promise status, recognition, or power. Gender inequities support many of our Body Wars.

Investigate the institutions you support—churches, schools, businesses, community groups, your workplace. How do these organizations treat women? Are women seen as equal or subordinate? Is their value or role often based on their appearance and their "PBQ" (professional beauty qualification)?[22] How much do these organizations use women for display rather than providing opportunities for meaningful work and access to advancement? If you are affiliated with an institution that limits and devalues women based on beauty, withdraw your support or your business. Communicate to those in control about why you are investing your money elsewhere. Consider writing a letter to the editor of your local paper to expose the problem.

Anything you do that promotes gender-equity will help to diminish the Body Wars of the beauty industry. Do something!

RESOURCES

When contacting cosmetic companies, do not simply use the address on the packaging; letters directed to customer service will go nowhere. In order to make your complaint heard, you must contact the person in charge of advertising, usually through the publicity or marketing department. The following are all divisions of *Cosmair*. Each is a separate entity, with its own advertising department. Send letters accordingly.

Clinique & Estee Lauder
Estee Lauder
767 5th Ave.
New York, NY 10153
212-572-4200

Elizabeth Arden
1345 Avenue of the Americas - 35th Floor
New York, NY 10105
212-261-1000

Lancome
304 E. 45th St.
New York, NY 10017
Publicity: 212-370-1313, ext. 613

L'Oreal
575 5th Ave.
New York, NY 10017
212-984-4916

Maybelline
Consumer Affairs
PO Box 1010
Clark, NJ 07066-0101
212-984-4626
800-944-0730

Max Factor
11050 York Rd.

Hunt Valley, MD 21030
410-785-3330

Redken
575 5th Ave. 19th Floor
New York, NY 10017
212-984-4360

Revlon, Almay, Ultima II, The Ritz
Plus-size model Emme is a spokesperson for Revlon, which indicates
their willingness to embrace size acceptance. Let them and other manufacturers of beauty products know that you support size diversity in
advertising.
Att. Advertising Dept.
625 Madison Ave.
New York, NY 10022
800-473-8566 (consumer information center)

Books and Articles

The Cosmetics Trap: When Truth is Only Skin Deep
An investigative report by the New York City Department of Con-
sumer Affairs, published in June 1992. Available through:
NYC Dept of Consumer Affairs
42 Broadway
New York, NY 10004

Don't Go to the Cosmetics Counter Without Me
Paula Begoun (Beginning Press, 1993) To understand more about
what you are buying, or subscribe to her newsletter, Cosmetics Counter
Update, for $25 a year. Write to:
5418 South Brandon St.
Seattle, WA 98118
800-831-4088

True Beauty: Positive Attitudes & Practical Tips from the World's Leading Plus-Size Model
Emme with Daniel Paisner, New York, G.P. Putnam & Sons, 1996.

The Safe Shopper's Bible: A Consumer's Guide to Nontoxic Household Products, Cosmetics, and Food
Steinman, D. and Epstein, S., New York, McMillan, 1995.

The Body Project: An Intimate History of American Girls
Brumberg, J.J., New York, Random House, 1997.

Real Gorgeous: The Truth about Body and Beauty
Cooke, K., New York, Norton, 1996.

Backlash: The Undeclared War Against Women
Faludi, S., New York, Anchor Books, 1991.

Body Love
Freedman, R., New York, HarperCollins, 1988.

The Power of Beauty
Friday, N., New York, HarperCollins, 1996.

Down from the Pedestal
Harris, M., New York, Anchor Books, 1994

Face Value: The Politics of Beauty
Lakoff, R.T., Scherr, R.L., Boston, Routledge, 1984.

Body Traps
Rodin, J. New York, William Morrow, 1992.

The Beauty Myth
Wolf, N., New York, William Morrow, 1991.

6

Advertising

GUERRILLA WARFARE

"Bean lean, slender as the night, narrow as an arrow, pencil thin, get the point?"
—Bloomingdales ad

Contemporary Americans live in an "Adcult," a culture immersed in the messages and media of advertising.[1] More than $130 billion is spent on advertising annually; some of us experience as many as 1500 ads per day.[2] By high school graduation, the average American teenager, conservatively exposed to 300-500 ads per day, will have been bombarded by as many as 350,000 commercials.[3]

Everyday our "adcult" produces:

- more than 184 billion classified ads and more than 12 billion display ads in newspapers
- 6.6 billion magazine ads

- 2.6 billion radio ads
- 330 million TV ads[4]

Overall, advertising consumes 60% of newspaper, 52% of magazine, 18% of radio, and 17% of prime time television space.[5]

This advertising onslaught, with its surprise tactics, control of our communications, and constant attack on our senses has become a form of guerrilla warfare. If we expect to make peace with women's bodies, we must confront its toxic messages with committed counterattacks.

Inequality in Advertising

A United Nations report on the status of women named advertising the worst offender to women's well-being. According to the critics, the female body has been consistently degraded and sexualized, rendering women inferior.[6] The truth is startling: 97% of print ads portray women in powerless positions, as victims, sex objects, or other female stereotypes.[7] Women are objectified and trivialized, as evident by print ads featuring a woman's full body, although often headless, but only the upper body of a man. Females are also more likely to be displayed lying down or bending over, while males stand erect.[8]

The first major analysis of the portrayal of men and women in magazine ads, conducted in the early 1970s, found considerable gender bias. The research revealed four consistent stereotypes: a woman's place is in the home; women do not make important decisions; they are dependent and need male protection; and men regard women as sex objects primarily.[9] Repeated studies have produced nearly identical results, except that now women are portrayed in the workforce.

Relative to a decade ago, women today are more sexualized in magazine ads. The amount of body exposure and partial nudity has increased, with 52.9% of black women and 61.6% of white women scantily clad, often in bathing suits or underwear. Male body exposure is comparatively minimal, as only 25% of ads reveal male bodies. In over 17% of the ads reviewed, white women are displayed in lower status positions, such as on their knees or on the floor. Meanwhile, black women are often pictured in animal prints, in sexualized, predatory poses.[10]

Untruth in Advertising

Unfortunately, advertising campaigns that objectify and trivialize women are the norm, not the exception, despite the advent of women's rights, gender equity and feminism. Women's bodies are used to sell all kinds of products, even when there is no evident connection between the ad's images and the commodity.

> "Am I saying the billion-dollar brainwash is really a conspiracy? Yes. Absolutely. The same kind of de facto, unorganized, indefinable conspiracy that kept women from voting for so long, and keeps us from achieving economic and political equality today.
> —Terry Poulton, author, No Fat Chicks

In an ad for Calvin Klein's *Obsession* cologne, a naked Kate Moss appears powerless, with sunken, vacant eyes and a slight frame. The Gap spotlights waif-thin young women to sell its clothing to an impressionable market. Reef

Brazil, a Southern California sandal company, is known for their "butt girls," usually teens, who wear thong bikinis in their magazine and print ads to sell products mainly to males.

The list goes on and so does the impact. After exposure to manipulated images of the ideal such as these, men systematically rate the beauty of average women more critically.[11] One researcher found that children living without television had fewer gender biases, but once exposed to TV, their attitudes and beliefs became prejudiced.[12] Another study revealed that men interviewing female job applicants after seeing sexist television commercials judged them harsher, and remembered less biological information and more about their appearance than men not exposed to these ads.[13]

> "Advertising often reduces the political to the personal. . .We must constantly perfect and change ourselves, working for self-improvement rather than societal change. The wider world of discrimination, poverty, and oppression simply doesn't exist in advertising. . . If we are unhappy, there is something wrong with us that can be solved by buying something."
> —Jean Kilbourne, author, *Deadly Persuasion*

An integral part of contemporary life, advertising convinces us to believe its images and promises. More often than not, however, the images in ads are far from real. Instead, they have been airbrushed, touched up, elongated, or otherwise distorted. Multiple models or computer images may be used in the same ad. Photo retouching is so extreme that one supermodel claims that sometimes she recognizes herself only because of her distinctive mole.[14]

Many of these ads seem trivial, but their cumulative effect is not. In the long run, we are programmed to believe that the bodies in ads, no matter how unreal, unattainable and unhealthy, are ideal. As a result, women often become contemptuous of their own bodies; they may perceive imperfections as limiting their power and nullifying their achievements. These ads also make women envious of and competitive with one another.[15] Deluged by stereotypical images, women succumb to buying products which they hope will alleviate feelings of inferiority and improve their social status.

> *"Isn't it about time that someone told you that your body is all right, just the way it is?"*
> —**Marcia Hutchinson, author,** *Transforming Body Image*

Advertising and Health Dangers

In addition to emotional and psychological damage, advertising can also instigate serious health risks. At one time, laxative ads featured elderly people who often have slower gastrointestinal systems that may benefit from laxatives. Now they feature slim young women, an irresponsible ploy that instills erroneous ideas about methods for achieving thinness. Also, ads for cigarettes often link thinness to smoking as a lure for sales. As early as 1928, a Lucky Strike ad stated: "To Keep a Slender Figure . . . Reach for a Lucky Strike Instead of a Sweet."[16] Exploiting women's weight consciousness, the tobacco industry targets women's magazines in particular, spending $3 billion or more per year, or $100 a second, to hook them. More female adolescents smoke than males (2 to 1), and lung cancer poses more of a mortality risk for women than breast cancer.[17] One quarter of female smokers will die because of this habit. The good news? Their corpses are four pounds lighter than their living nonsmoking peers.[18]

STRATEGIES FOR CHANGE

We can put an end to the advertising industry's guerrilla tactics. It is time for irresponsible advertisers to recognize their contribution to Body Wars. Each of us can make a difference. However, these changes are not going to come from the advertisers. By developing a critical perspective and choosing what messages to take in, you can change the impact of advertising.

Become more **Active**. Pay attention to the **Advertising** messages that bombard you daily. **Acknowledge** their impact on you. How do these images affect your feelings about yourself, your body image, and how you treat yourself? Use the following questions to increase your awareness as a consumer.

Keep a media journal where you write your impressions and responses to these questions. Doing this with a friend or small group can be even more interesting, as media images affect us differently. You will find some common ground and some reactions that are yours alone. Then decide whether you want to share your reactions with the company creating the ad.

ACTIVE ADVERTISING ACKNOWLEDGMENT

What product is this ad advertising?

What other messages and feelings are part of this ad?

How is this ad getting your attention, and how is it try-ing to convince you to buy this product?

Are the people in the ad realistically depicted? How di-verse are they?

What do you like about this ad?

What turns you off?

Will the ad influence your decision to buy the product?

What would you change in the ad if you were in charge?

Do you think your opinion, positive or negative, would make a difference to the company? Consider sharing it with the people in charge.

Boycott, or refuse to buy, products whose advertising cam-paigns promote Body Wars. "Buycott," or support, companies who promote acceptance of all body sizes, such as The Body Shop. One woman suggested that the 33 million women in the U.S. who occasionally drink beer should target a beer company that uses offensive ads. If each woman were then to drink three fewer beers a year from that company, there would be 99 mil-lion bottles more on shelves and a new ad campaign.[19] Could your sorority or club organize such a campaign?

Some public campaigns have attacked and defeated specific ads. A cigarette called UPTOWN, marketed to African-American youth, was removed from stores after a strong negative community response. Since then, the surgeon general has called for restrictions on ads for alcohol and cigarettes.[20] Hersheys removed an ad for a chocolate bar that used the marketing slogan, "You can never be too rich or too thin" after complaints from eating disorder organizations.[21] In 1993, a group from Massachusetts called Ban Anorexic Marketing (BAM) hounded Sprite to withdraw an ad campaign that featured a model called "The Skeleton."

A group led by Michael Levine, a past president of Eating Disorders Awareness and Prevention (EDAP) and an expert in media literacy, successfully protested an ad by Hormel for "Light and Lean 100" hot dogs. The ad featured a young girl questioning her mother about calories, then choosing to refuse a slice of birthday cake because it will "go straight to my hips." Although initial letters of protest only resulted in acknowledgment from Hormel, after two weeks a follow-up letter signed by 30 professionals instigated them to withdraw the ad.[22] With e-mail, the internet and chatrooms, making our voices heard has become easier than ever.

Work with your educational system to develop or implement media literacy programs in the schools to prepare the next generation running the country to be more critical, informed media watchers. Use the Active Advertising Acknowledgment exercise with older children, adolescents and college students. The tobacco and alcohol industries have been targeted. Now we must focus on industries like fashion and diet companies.

You can make consumer complaints about advertising in a variety of ways. Write to the company's customer relations department or the Chief Executive Officer (CEO). Send a copy to your local Better Business Bureau and State Department of Consumer Protection. To get the names and address of CEOs for the leading consumer companies, check The World Almanac Book of Facts at your library, or call the company directly.

If the ad in question was in a magazine or newspaper, send a copy of your letter to the editor and to the advertising sales department asking them to cancel the ad, or lobby with you to change it. You can also send it to a features writer or radio talk show host in your local community. Volunteer for an interview to discuss your feelings and bring attention to the issue.

In response to television ads that you find offensive, write or call the Audience Relations Department or the Office of Broadcast Standards and Practices of the Network. Specify the product, the company, the ad, and what you found offensive. The addresses and numbers for the major networks are:

ABC
Audience Relations Department
147 Columbus Ave.
New York, NY 10023
212-456-7777

CBS
Audience Relations Department
555 West 57th Street
New York, NY 10019
212-975-4321

NBC
Standards and Practices Department
30 Rockefeller Plaza
New York, NY 10020
212-664-4444

FOX Broadcasting Network
Viewer Comment Line
PO Box 900
Beverly Hills, CA 90213
310-369-1000

Arts & Entertainment
555 5th Ave.
New York, NY 10020
212-210-1400

CNN and TNT
1 CNN Center
PO Box 105366
Atlanta, GA 30345-5366
404-827-1500

Cinemax and HBO
1100 6th Ave.
New York, NY 10036
212-512-1000

MTV and Nickelodeon
1515 Broadway
New York, NY 10036
212-258-7500

ADVERTISING

Showtime and The Movie Channel
1633 Broadway
New York, NY 10019
212-708-1600

USA Network
1230 Avenue of the Americas
New York, NY 10020
212-408-9100

RESOURCES

Media Watch
An organization dedicated to attacking sexism in advertising. In their quarterly newsletter, they sometimes include postcards or letters to advertisers who have been running offensive campaigns.
PO Box 618
Santa Cruz, CA 95061-0618
408-423-6355

The Media Foundation
An active media critic, producing educational materials, a video called "Culture Jamming," and an innovative magazine, *Adbusters.* They hope for a revolution and want your help.
1243 West 74th Ave.
Vancouver, BC V6H 1B7 Canada
604-736-9401
www.adbusters.org

About-Face
(Formerly the Stop Starvation Imagery Campaign) Questions, satirizes, and attempts to change negative images of women. Its website gives you access to many resources that promote media literacy and healthy self image, as well as suggestions on how to hold companies accountable for their advertising.
PO Box 77665
San Francisco, CA 94107
415-436-0212
www.about-face.org

The Center for Media Literacy
Has multiple resources for families, teachers, and all concerned about the impact of advertising, violence, and other media influences. It promotes media literacy education as an alternative to censorship.
4727 Wilshire Blvd
Suite 403
Los Angeles, CA 90010
213-931-4177
www.medialit.org

Eating Disorders Awareness and Prevention (EDAP)
Has several media advocacy projects in progress.
603 Stewart Street
Suite 803
Seattle, WA 98101
206-382-3587
www.edap.org

The Body Shop
Demonstrates that a company with corporate consciousness can succeed. Anita Roddick, its founder, has been committed to challenging the culture of the beauty industry and to celebrating women's bodies rather than exploiting their insecurities. The Body Shop ad campaigns

and products uphold this philosophy. Contact them to request a copy of Full Voice, a pamphlet that includes statistics about dieting and ideas to promote self-esteem and graceful aging.
The Body Shop
full_voice@bodyshop.co.uk
www.the-body-shop.com

Killing Us Softly and *Still Killing Us Softly: Advertising's Image of Women*
Videos by Jean Kilbourne, available through:
Cambridge Documentary Films
PO Box 385
Cambridge, MA 02139
617-354-3677

Slim Hopes
Video by Jean Kilbourne, available through:
Media Education Foundation
26 Center Street
Northamptom, MA 01060
800-897-0089 or 413-584-8500
www.igc.org/mef

Book

Deadly Persuasion: Why Women and Girls Must Fight the Addictive Powers of Advertising
Kilbourne, J., New York, The Free Press, 1999.

7

Magazines
PROPAGANDA MACHINES

"I open a magazine and a supermodel stares back at me, her waist the size of a lifesaver. An article accompanying the picture constantly mentions how beautiful she is. I immediately drop the magazine and start doing sit-ups. Can you blame me?"

—Sarah, from K. Cooke's *Real Gorgeous*

Mainstream women's magazines have been an active media force promoting Body Wars for decades. They advocate and glamorize what the social structure needs: to hold women back by cultivating self-doubt and body preoccupation. Today, from the racks at almost every grocery store, magazine covers taunt with misleading claims, such as "Lose Ten Pounds in Ten Days," "Look Great Naked: Build A Ready-to-be-Bare Body," "Burn Fat, Tighten Your Butt Fast," and "From Fat to Firm: Get Real Results in 10 Minutes A Day." In page after page of thin figures, they tease us with recipes for happiness and success, urging us to buy products and to change our bodies to meet this month's beauty standard. Magazines imply that we are not acceptable as we are; and each month, millions of Americans buy them, looking for a transformation.

A Bit of History

During the past two centuries, women's magazines have been a powerful influence on women's expectations, aspirations, and roles. With confusing but captivating messages, they connect women to the dominant cultural values. Ironically, magazine growth has coincided with, contributed to, and contradicted women's progress.

Early periodicals, filled with Victorian values, stressed women's domestic roles and duties, and promised to maintain, rather than challenge, the status quo. The editor of one of the first women's periodicals, *Ladies Magazine*, published in Boston in 1828, assured men that nothing in its pages would encourage a wife "to be less assiduous in preparing for his reception or encourage her to usurp station or encroach upon prerogatives of men."[1]

In the last 100 years, as women have obtained educational and financial resources in traditional institutions, magazines shifted their emphasis to consumerism. Initially, print spreads focused on women's household needs, promoting products for each domestic duty. As technology gradually made housework less demanding, however, magazines began to emphasize beauty and appearance.[2] Women might have been free from some limitations, but were soon to be enslaved to others: the precursors of Body Wars.

As the 20th century unfolded, women participated more in the world outside the home, especially during World Wars I and II. Magazines reflected this increasing social awareness, but powerful messages appeared between the lines which stressed the importance of maintaining traditional femininity and beauty. For example, cosmetics ads and complementary copy sometimes subliminally implied that World War II was necessary to preserve women's right to be feminine and beautiful.[3]

After World War II, the pendulum swung back to an emphasis on being a good wife, mother, and homemaker. This answered several needs. Manufacturers needed to replace their war contracts, so the production and marketing of consumer goods escalated. Also, men needed jobs and the economy needed women to spend money. Magazines spearheaded this campaign by stressing women's traditional domestic roles of homemaking, striving for beauty, and consumerism.

"Women's magazines, with their glossy pages of advertising, advertorials, and beauty advice, hold up an especially devious mirror. They offer to "help" women, while presenting a standard nearly impossible to attain."
—**Sharlene Hesse-Biber, author,** *Am I Thin Enough Yet?*

When the feminist movement gained strength in the late 1960's, magazines responded once more. While the economy and social structure still needed women to be consumers, editors started to weave pro-feminist content about how to control one's life, become assertive in relationships, and manage a career, family, and finances, with articles and ads about beauty. While on the surface a liberating trend, women soon became increasingly enslaved by Body Wars. In the ultimate mixed message, women's magazines managed to popularize feminism more than any serious feminist publications, while instilling a paralyzing degree of self-consciousness and anxiety about weight and appearance.[4]

Magazines continue to function as agents of social control, defining the acceptable role for women, and rendering them dependent on "expert" advice. Clearly, the messages from women's magazines are dichotomous and double binding. While they have helped women to embrace their sexuality, they also have robbed them of self-esteem. Filled with fashion do's and don'ts, even accomplished, powerful, "liberated" women turn to magazines looking for direction about womanhood. Instead of bolstering female confidence, women's magazines have encouraged women to view their bodies as a war zone.

Selling Self-Improvement—The Self-Esteem Enigma

The desire for self-improvement is healthful, but many are misguided in this quest by magazines which define "improvement" almost exclusively through the external lens of appearance. The truth is that magazines promise what they cannot deliver. Tampering with your natural body only results in superficial self-esteem, which falters as the pounds are put back on, or until next season's fashion trend emerges with a new set of dictates. A focus on outer beauty is usually at the neglect of one's emotional life, and not a firm foundation for lasting self-esteem.

Women read magazines to feel part of the dominant culture and to connect with other women. They are led to believe that others will find them more worthy if they subscribe to the advice provided. Traditionally, women are taught to "be good" and comply, rather than to question and defy, so they often accept the dictates of magazines without thinking critically. Although magazines claim to promote self-esteem, this mission backfires. Until a woman learns to accept herself exactly as she is *right now,* she will never be satisfied. In the end, she has wasted precious time and money, and likely damaged what self-esteem she had in the first place.

Not-So-Subliminal Messages—The Cover Story

The cover of a magazine is a powerful medium. Publications that target women consistently broadcast messages that focus on beauty, appearance, weight, and sex appeal. The more "real" she is, the less likely she is to host the cover, a sad statement in an era of so many accomplished women.

Women's magazines are not the only publications that confine women to image. In 50 years, *LIFE* has featured only 19 women who were not actresses or models on its cover.[5] That is 19 out of 2,600 potential shots, or about 3%—not a great batting average. The message is that a woman is considered successful only if she ranks as beautiful.

Additionally, people of color are rarely seen on the pages of magazines, except for those devoted exclusively to them. A special edition of *Ladies Home Journal* called "Women of The Year"[6] exemplifies the white-skinned journalism. Highlighting "The Most Unforgettable Women of 1995," the cover featured seven women. No African Americans were among them and only one face had any remote color—that of newscaster and television personality Connie Chung. In the entire magazine, with photos of hundreds of women, only five non-whites are mentioned and three of them were connected to the O.J. Simpson murder case. Only four large women were profiled. Although 30% of high school students in the United States are non-white, racial minorities are represented in less than 10% of magazine photos and articles.[7] This journalistic slant reflects and encourages our society's preferences: white skin and a thin body.

> *"The slim and flawless cover girl is an icon created by capitalism for the sake of profit. Millions of women pay it homage."*
> **—Sharlene Hesse-Biber, author,** *Am I Thin Enough Yet?*

Even magazines devoted to "health" have succumbed to Body Wars. The articles recently featured on the cover of *American Health* included, "15-minute Super-Sculpting Workout," and, "Forget the Fat." *Health* featured "Changing Your Shape-Whatever Works," "The Best Way to Lose Weight," and, "Look Younger in 5 Minutes." *Country Living's Healthy Living's* cover attraction was "Helen Gurley Brown: Fab & Fit at 77 and How She Does It." Thus, even the publications whose mission is health too often encourage us to battle our bodies instead of respect them. Unfortunately, that is the most frequent cover story.

Reporting or Advertising?

Open most popular magazines, from *Cosmopolitan* to *Elle*, *GQ* to *Vanity Fair*, and even the health-oriented genre like *Prevention*, and you might think you're perusing a mail order catalogue. Regularly, one-third to one-half of the space is devoted to ads, with some surveys indicating a 70/30 ad/copy ratio.[8] With women making at least 85% of the purchases in the United States,[9] advertisers pour billions of dollars into women's magazines.

The competition for magazine sales is so high that publishers do whatever it takes to stay afloat. This can mean encouraging their readership to buy the advertiser's products, even if these products are not the best value. Many companies will not advertise if their ad is placed next to controversial copy, such as an article on abortion or gay rights, which further limits an editor's ability to present honest, informative material. Whereas men's magazines do not experience such pressures from advertisers, women's magazines are often forced to forgo usual journalistic or ethical standards.[10]

Teenzines

Unfortunately, mature women are not the only ones targeted by the money-hungry world of magazine publishing; preteens and teen-age girls are also in the firing line. "Teenzines" are slick periodicals that recognize the purchasing power of kids, and create and then prey upon their insecurities. A highly-desired consumer group, teenage girls spend upward of $34 billion a year.[11] As in adult magazines, ads generally comprise one-third to one-half of the pages, interspersed with fashion plates, prepubescent models, and scores of "beauty" tips. While many of the advertised products are the same as those in adult magazines, the use of younger models captures readers as young as 10 years old.

In an extensive review of teenzines, less than 20% of the pages were devoted to articles, and most of these focused on how to "relate" to boys and on attractiveness. One issue even mocked virginity with a quiz for "The Hymenally Challenged."[12] A survey of teenzines found less than 3% of copy devoted to educational or career issues, but more than 20% to beauty.[13] In the 30 periodicals reviewed, only two articles focused on practical tips for college, and the career most often discussed was modeling. Articles on health and nutrition all focused on weight reduction or control. Little, if any, space was devoted to political, social, intellectual, or athletic concerns.

> *"Searching through catalogues you wish you could order the bodies, not the clothes."*
> **—Jessica Bullman, age 17,** *in Ophelia Speaks*

Too many teens buy and read popular magazines for us to ignore the power that their editors possess. At least half the teenage girls in America regularly read teen magazines, such as *Seventeen*, *YM*, and *Teen*, and adult publications such as *Glamour* and *Vogue*.[14] Developmentally, this target market is at a time of peak social comparison, low self-esteem, and negative body image. Since identity formation is one of the most important developmental tasks of adolescence, socialization by these magazines is troubling. Magazines typically promote the idea that women can attain self-definition, power, and control by changing their bodies. Taking a risk is often defined as doing something as daring as changing hair color or getting a tattoo—far from bold actions aimed at promoting broad-based social change.

The New Ideal: Superwomen for the Millennium

Over the past 25 years, the ideal for women has become even more svelte, a shape most women cannot attain unless they develop an eating disorder. Mainstream magazines rarely feature photos of full-bodied or even average-sized women, and the ads and fashion photos regularly present abnormally thin bodies, as if they are standard. To help women achieve these impossible goals, diet and exercise articles increased dramatically between the late 1950s and the late 1980s.[15] By the 1990's, women's magazines boasted eleven times as many diet ads and articles as found in men's magazines.[16]

In addition to cropping, airbrushing and revamping the complexion and contours of models featured in magazines, editors now touch up the photos of ordinary people in print. Hence, viewers are not exposed to any images of a real body. When pressed to explain the rationale for these ridiculously thin models, the readers' services representative at *Vogue* expressed exasperation. Although she agreed that the models really are too thin, the only solution she offered was for teens to avoid her magazine. "What are we supposed to do?" she asked. "Nobody wants to see fat women in magazines. Very thin women are better clothes hangers." Sooner or later, we have to admit that the unreal images in magazines have damaged the health and well-being of far too many young women.

Magazines can have a tremendous impact on self-esteem and body image. In a study of female students at Stanford University, nearly 70% reported feeling worse about their bodies after looking at magazines.[17] Many people must stop buying magazines to feel comfortable with their weight, their appearance, and their need for food. For some, canceling subscriptions can be a critical turning point in self-acceptance.

The contemporary standard for a Superwoman is not just a woman who is accomplished and successful at work and in her community, invested in fulfilling relationships, healthy, strong, and vibrant. She must *also* be thin and attractive. If she does not possess all of these attributes, at best she will feel inferior, at worst she will feel like a failure.

"Women's magazines reinforce their anxiety that life only exists in this moment. Get yourself looked at now, because only obscurity lies ahead."
—**Nancy Friday, author,** *Our Looks, Our Lives*

The awesome power of mainstream magazines could help us develop a healthier ideal for the Superwoman of the Millennium. This female image should be presented as a woman with a natural body, complete with imperfections and unique style. She is any color and any weight. She feels innately beautiful. This ideal woman engages in gratifying activities (not just shopping or dieting) is influential in our society, and is taken seriously. Imagine her potential.

STRATEGIES FOR CHANGE

What are your magazine habits? Are you a junkie looking for the perfect body and external happiness on the pages of magazines? Do you read popular print despite your awareness of its negative messages? Take some time to understand how the magazines you read make you feel about yourself, and consider some changes.

Educate the girls in your life about the magazine business. Explain that magazines stay afloat as a result of ad sales, and that stories are frequently written to please advertisers. Point out to young readers that what they see is not real; photo manipulation—through lighting, makeup, computer-generated cyber images, and other tricks of the trade—helps editors achieve flawless renditions far from the real thing. Read and view magazines with young people with a critical eye, and let them know that fashion magazines, like other forms of media, should be seen as a form of entertainment, not as a mirror for self-scrutiny.

Consider other strategies

Purchase a wider range of publications; the variety available has never been as plentiful. Topics now include: current events, science, arts, crafts, fiction, sports, and adventure travel, just to name a few.

Send magazines with offensive ads, articles, covers, or other messages back to the editor with postage due, and a request for a refund. Mark the offensive material, and explain exactly what bothered you. See the following resources for tips on how best to contact your target publication.

Buy only magazines that respect women. If you cancel a subscription, contact the editor to explain your reason. Do not write on the renewal card; the subscription department has nothing to do with editorial. Let editors know in detail what kinds of articles you want. Be specific. Give them the opportunity to keep or to lose you as a customer. If they do not comply, let them know why you have stopped buying their product.

Review the magazines in the waiting rooms you frequent. If they are offensive to you, discuss this with the office manager, educating her/him about the subliminal messages within. Then, offer alternatives.

Do not allow your pre-teen and teen-age girls to purchase inappropriate materials. Educate them, explaining why they may be unable to view the layouts objectively. Talk, talk, talk to them about what is and is not normal for female bodies.

Recognize and accept that *haute couture* has become entertainment. Change your perception of the photos. Commit to viewing them with an objective, artistic eye, or not at all.

RESOURCES

Conde Naste
Conde Naste is the parent company of many publications that publish offensive beauty advertising and copy. The following list will provide you with phone numbers for each magazine. It is recommended that you send a copy of your letter to the publisher with a "c.c." to the

executive editor. Since publishers and editors frequently turnover, check the masthead of a current issue, or phone the publication, to be certain you have the correct names.

Conde Naste
350 Madison Ave.
New York, NY 10017

Allure
212-880-2341
Bride's Magazine
212-880-2518
Women's Sports & Fitness
212-880-7979
Glamour
212-880-8062
Mademoiselle
212-880-8627
Self
212-880-6700
Vanity Fair
212-880-8180
Vogue
212-880-8979

Cosmopolitan
224 W 57th Street
New York, NY 10019
212-649-2000
Fax: 212-307-6563 (Editorial Content)
Fax: 212-265-1849 (Advertising)

Harper's Bazaar
1700 Broadway
New York, NY 10019

MAGAZINES

212-903-5086
Fax: 212-262-7101

Sassy
437 Madison Aveenue, 4th Floor
New York, NY 10016
212-935-9150
Fax: 212-935-0457

Woman's World
270 Sylvan Ave.
Englewood Cliffs, NJ 07632
201-569-0006, X220
Fax: 201-569-3584

Family Circle
110 Fifth Ave.
New York, NY
Fax 212-463-1808

New Woman
215 Lexington Ave.
New York, NY 10016
212-251-1500
Fax: 212-251-1590

A list of publications follows that are doing a good job of helping women and girls develop a positive sense of self. Writing to editors of magazines who are publishing healthy copy and advertising is just as important as writing letters to editors of magazines with offensive ads.

Ms.

Ms. is published without advertising! Their readers pay more ($5.95 per issue), and the magazine is still thriving.

Ms.
20 Exchange Place, 22nd Floor
New York, NY 10005
212-509-2092
800-234-4486 (Subscriptions)

New Moon: The Magazine for Girls and Their Dreams

Devoted to children, celebrating girls. It is written for and by 8 to 14-year-old girls, assisted by adults as managing editors, staff, and the publisher. The goal is to explore the passage from girlhood to womanhood, to build healthy resistance to gender inequities, and to help girls stay true to themselves as they journey confidently into the world. The magazine, with a distribution of 25,000, offers a companion publication for adults who want to promote the same goals. Contact:
PO Box 3587
Duluth, MN 55803-3587
800-381-4743; 218-728-5507

Teen Voices

Publishes articles written by girls, targeting 13 to 20 year-olds, and focuses on issues such as racism, sexual assault, adolescent parents, careers, self-esteem, and relationships. "Because you're more than just a pretty face" is their message.
515 Washington St., Floor 6
Boston, MA 02111
888-882-TEEN; 617-426-5577
www.teenvoices.com

Blue Jean Magazine: For Teen Girls Who Dare

Written by teenage and adult women, and focuses on activism, careers and women's history.
716-654-5070

YSB

Although similar to the standard teenzine, is written for African American boys and girls, and focuses on serious issues such as self-esteem, education and job strategies. Contact: 800-888-0488

MODE

Mode is devoted to adult women and emphasizes style, not size. Still a fashion magazine, the message is definitely refreshing: Love your body no matter what you weigh. They have developed a magazine for teens called *GIRL*, promoting "Beauty for Every Face. Fashion for Every Body." Hoping to respond to the needs of its young readers, *GIRL* includes a survey asking readers for input, and has a *GIRL* council for this purpose.

22 East 49th Street
New York, NY 10017
MODE
888-610-6633
modemag@aol.com
GIRL
888-419-0427
girlpub@aol.com

JUMP

JUMP is a new teenzine, "for girls who dare to be real." The all-female staff is dedicated to developing a magazine that is both "cool and fun," but also "encourages you to follow your heart—not the herd."

21100 Erwin Street
Woodland Hills, CA 91367
letters@jumponline.com

8

Fashion
REAL WOMEN HAVE BELLIES

"Fashion that distorts the human body, or rejects it entirely, and is displayed on a starved child or a fantasy creature who can't move... That's fashion-forward."

—L. Gould,
New York Times Magazine
January 1997

Most women have bellies that tend to be convex, not concave. But bellies have vanished from the pages of the *Sports Illustrated* Swimsuit Issue and Victoria's Secret Swimsuit Edition. Is there something wrong with the majority of women or is the fashion industry intentionally fostering body insecurity?

Swimsuits hold special meaning for many of us who spend time in the water each summer. Putting on a swimsuit can bring us back to joyous childhood experiences of family fun and the exhilaration of water sports and sunshine. As adults, we deserve to feel free in our bodies, comfortably exposed to the elements. Yet, every suit in the Victoria's Secret Catalog does something artificial: underwire, push-up, padding, control panels on the side, back or stomach. The message we receive is that our bodies are not okay, and that these suits, and endless other products, will offer much needed help. Women across the country wonder every spring, "Should I do some exercises, go on a diet, buy that exercise equipment,

"All year long you've been judged by your efficiency, your creativity, your managerial talent—and suddenly, when you enter that fitting room, the only operative criteria are tilt of breasts, firmness of thighs. There should be warning labels on every suit: this product may be dangerous to your self-esteem."
—B. Ehrenreich,
Time Magazine, July 1996

take these pills, invest in some armor and weapons before I buy my bathing suit?"

Fashion and Sexism is "Fashism"

The demands of fashion for women reveal sexism, for men experience much less pressure to conform to clothing trends. While they are not totally immune, the basics do not change for them—suit and tie, pants and a shirt. Casual clothes can be very simple as well, with little attention to fashion "shoulds." Women's fashions, on the other hand, change constantly, and many risk being judged and in some arenas ostracized for not staying current. For women, casual clothes are rarely casual. To feel socially acceptable and succeed at being a "real woman," keeping up with fashion trends is a requirement at all times.

Fashion exerts control over women by defining the current standard of femininity and each era has had its own method for keeping women anxious, uncertain and dependent. But today, sexism in fashion is dictatorial, unforgiving, and oblivious to individual variations in body type, weight, or preferences. Although the buying and selling of status and self-worth reflect the basic American values of democracy, materialism, and opportunity, taken to the extreme as it has in the fashion industry, it can destroy a woman's freedom, creativity, self-esteem, and health, no apologies offered. Let's call it "fashism."

Fashion History

In 19th century America, the Protestant work ethic and the spirit of capitalism merged with females' economically dependent roles and limited opportunities. Women internalized the values of hard work, diligence, sacrifice, and, without other avenues available, poured this dedication into appearance and fashion. One promotion of the corset in Victorian times suggested, "If you want a girl to grow up gentle and womanly in her ways and her feelings, lace her tight."[1] By the 1960s, as body shape shifted to a more constricted, narrow type, tight lacing was no longer needed. With Twiggy and other

"Every generation laughs at the old fashions, but follows religiously the new."
—Henry David Thoreau

sylph-like figures as the fashion ideal, representing self-control and the "proper" way to present oneself, "tight lacing" became internal. Mothers were advised in the *Ladies Home Journal*, "Appearance plays too important a part in a girl's life not to have her grow up to be beauty-conscious."[2]

In the 1920's, when ready-to-wear clothing was born, a new era emerged. Previously, dressmakers individualized their work. Now, women had to fit into standard sizes. This shift brought a significant increase of anxiety about shape, weight, and dimensions. Women began to feel, on a deeply individual level, that the problem was their body rather than their clothes. To add insult to injury, they had to pay for alterations, while men did not![3]

By the mid-20th century, the commercialization of female beauty fueled the explosion of a fashion industry like no other. This was largely due to the evolution of modern advertising and its accompanying weapon, fashion photography. In earlier eras, women's decisions about clothing and appearance were a personal, rather than a media-driven, pursuit. Clothing was seen and felt, unlike the illusive images on screens, magazine pages, and billboards. But the onset of fashion photography bred body dissatisfaction. Slimmer models became the chosen ones in order to make up for the camera's distortion, and to promote the belief that clothes look best on thin frames. Previously, artists and photographers focused on the face, but now fashion photography emphasized the body.[4] This helped to create the distressing comparisons between the self and the ideal that fuel Body Wars.

Feminism and Fashism

Women follow fashion demands because, in a world belonging to men, fashion is "the most direct path to a sense of superiority and importance for women."[5] The "before and after" shots in fashion magazines demonstrate a means to that end by implying that if you exert the effort, you too can look acceptable, if not fabulous. Also inferred in these illustrations is the message that if you do not achieve faultless beauty, you have only yourself to blame. As Zsa Zsa Gabor once quipped, "There are no ugly women, just lazy ones."[6] In the new millennium, no self-respecting American woman wants to be considered lazy or ugly! So she takes these examples seriously and uses her body, and its adornments, as a means to prove herself as a worthwhile human being.

What progress have we made toward giving women control over their own bodies? We have come a long way since the Chinese tradition of foot-binding, yet full liberation entails women's bodies and psyches as well as their feet. In fact, although women's feet are no longer bound,

"Everyone asks me, 'Have you lost weight?' Little do they know its your Stretch Side-zip Twills."
—letter from "satisfied" customer to Land's End clothing catalogue, August 1999

they are still affected by our Body Wars. High heels, like most fashion dictates, may increase a woman's sexual power, but at the same time they diminish her physical strength, and can—and often do—lead to serious health problems, such as bunions, hammer toes, neuromas, and orthopedic problems in legs, hips and spine.7

Women are forced to contend with fashion conflicts almost every day of their lives at home, at work, and on the street. Decisions about short versus long skirts, tight-and-revealing versus loose-and-camouflaging tops have meaning. Sexy clothes might increase power, but they can also undermine respectability in a culture where sexual double standards abound.

"The model they are preparing . . . is twelve years old. What emerges is a preadolescent girl, with slender arms and shoulders, underdeveloped breasts and hips and thighs, whose body has been covered in sexy clothes, whose face has been painted with a false allure and whose eyes imitate a sexuality she has, by her own confession, never experienced. And this, says fashion, is what a mature woman should attempt to look like."
—Kim Chernin, author,
The Obsession

Stereotypes equate business suits with intelligence and power, and sweat suits with stupidity, for instance. Court decisions about serious issues, such as sexual harassment and rape, may even revolve around clothing.8 All this staying "hip" with fashion keeps women off balance and in doubt, while taking time and energy away from other pursuits that might be more gratifying, creative, or empowering.

The Size of Fashion

The most harmful stereotype of all is that large women do not belong in fashionable clothes. When creating a season's line, most designers ignore the important fact that the *average* American woman is 5'4", 143 pounds, and wears a size 10 or 12. She has a belly and thighs and breasts. Plus, more than one-third of American women wear size 16 or larger.[9] Yet most styles are created for thin, boyish bodies. Both average-sized women with curves and large-sized women have traditionally faced limited choices and pressures to lose weight to fit fashion. Again, the message is that women's bodies are not okay as they are and that looking like a clothes hanger is a measure of a woman's success.

Designers are beginning to create more plus size clothing lines, if only because they realize that there is a profitable market of plus-size women. Ironically, many of these companies still use relatively thin models for their ads. Bathing suits, lingerie and shoes are difficult to find in plus sizes; and rarely do stores put their plus sizes on sale, knowing that with few options, many women will pay full price.

It is time for the Body Wars caused by fashion to end. As Naomi Wolf said, "In a world where women have real choice, the choices we make about our appearance will be taken at last for what they really are: No Big Deal."[10]

STRATEGIES FOR CHANGE

Examine your own adherence to fashion. Answer the following questions:

Do you agonize about how others will evaluate you?

Do you feel enslaved by your wardrobe?

Do you buy the latest fashions whether you like them or not?
Do you wear colors you do not like because they are "in"?
Do you wear styles to cover up your body "flaws?"
Do you choose clothes to make you look thin?
Are you concerned that others will judge your clothing?
Is style more important to women than it is to men?

If you answer "yes" to all or most of these questions, you have succumbed to an oppressive line of fashion. Your self-esteem needs a boost. Set a goal for yourself to minimize the importance of fashion. Risk wearing whatever clothes feel best on you.

10 IDEAS TO FIGHT FASHISM

1. Be a positive role model for other women, especially young girls, by challenging fashion dictates and being true to yourself. Talk about your feelings and choices, so others may also take these risks.

2. Encourage others to free themselves from fashism; also, be supportive of friends, associates, and young people who express their own sense of style despite the latest trends.

3. Challenge others when they criticize people who are not following current fashion fads. We should never judge a book by its cover!

4. Fashions give you a negative, demeaning message, or just does not fit, tell companies, designers, manufacturers and stores what you do not like. Begin to assume control over your body by controlling what you wear.

5. If you belong to a nationally-organized group—i.e. sorority, Junior League, or the American Association of University Women—pick a fashion trend that contributes to Body Wars and ask your organization to boycott it. Examples: the Miracle Wonder Bra, girdles disguised as slips, clothing that only looks good on a hanger. Then draw media attention to your efforts and see what happens!

6. Organize a community or school campaign to publicize the negative effects of fashion on women. Start with a consciousness-raising session with others who share your concerns (call it a "focus group" if you want it to sound more current). Get women and men of all ages talking about how the fashion industry has affected and oppressed them. Publicize your group's sentiments in the newspaper or on local radio. Use your creativity to design flyers, buttons, or signs, to distribute at school or community events, such as sporting events, rallies or parades.

7. Research resources for alternative styles, such as specialty shops, mail order catalogues or the internet.

8. Get your clothes made for you or learn to sew your own! Define your own fashion style and flaunt it!

9. Write the fashion houses or designers directly to request styles for your particular lifestyle. For instance, if you are a woman who works at home, you may not want suits or shoes with heels. Make the greatest impact by sending a copy of your letter to your local media or women's groups: the more attention the better.

10. In other words, just say no to allowing the fashion industry to take our money and our self-esteem away from us so easily. Let's rid the world of fashism.

RESOURCES

For the addresses of individual companies, visit or call the reference desk of your local library which has the AT&T directory of toll-free numbers and other resources such as: *Standard & Poor's Register of Corporations, Directories, and Executives,* the *Standard Directory of Advertisers,* or the *Trade Names Directory.*

Suggested Reading

The Fashion Conspiracy: A Remarkable Journey Through the Empires of Fashion
Coleridge, N., New York, HarperCollins, 1988.

Let There Be Clothes
Schnurnberger, L., New York, Workman, 1991.

9

Models and Beauty Pageants
UGLY BUSINESS

"The whole thing about models, and I hate using this term, but we are genetic freaks."
—Linda Evangelista, model

Modeling and pageantry are ugly businesses that hold women back by promising them opportunity, recognition, and power, while failing to deliver on their promises. These institutions keep women preoccupied with their bodies, insecure about their abilities, and unable to pursue more fulfilling activities. Power based on looks is illusive, arbitrary, and temporary.

In general, women value connection, relationships, and caring over traditional male values, such as competition and rivalry. Due to this gender socialization, females are easy targets for conformity, cooperation, and collusion with beauty requirements. Our culture, plagued by ambivalence about women's roles, encourages all of us to consider models and beauty queens as idols to emulate. Yet, self-esteem gained by a successful modeling career or winning a beauty pageant is based on a shallow value system; there is no power in adhering to external standards.

Ironically, the businesses of pageantry and modeling picked up momentum as women gained basic rights. The Miss America pageant emerged within one year after American women won the right to vote. The suffragette movement had finally accomplished a goal that validated a woman's voice, beliefs, intellect, and contributions to society. Defining women in narrow, physical terms of beauty, the Miss America pageant questioned both this progress and women's competence overall.

Later in the 20th century, when the women's movement again took hold, skeletal models appeared who wore clothes that look best on coat hangers. Next to the strength of feminism, the weakness portrayed by emaciated bodies stood in stark contrast.

Twiggy and the Shrinking of Ideal

The entrance requirements for the runway grow more absurd with each decade. The first fashion models, weighing 155 pounds and more, were not the sylphs of today.[1] Nor would Mary Campbell, who was Miss America in 1922-23 and a "flapper," thin for that era at 5'7" and 140 pounds,[2] dare to appear on the runway today. In 1967, coinciding with a burgeoning women's movement, London's Twiggy came to the U.S. and our images of beauty began to change. Described by *Newsweek* as "4 straight limbs in search of a woman's body,"[3] Twiggy presented a prophetic shape. At 5'6" and 91 pounds, measuring

31-22-32, Twiggy was the original international model and the first fashion star with a child's body.[4] The modeling business expanded as the models drastically shrank, illustrated by the popular 60's waif model, Penelope Tree, who had anorexia throughout her career.[5]

In both the U.S. and England between 1967 and 1987, as models became more tubular, average women were actually gaining weight.[6] The dieting industry exploded, leading to an epidemic of yo-yo dieting as women went on and off diets. Conforming to outrageous size standards required relentless deprivation, which triggered bingeing. In four short years, from 1968 to 1972, the number of diet articles in magazines increased by 70%.[7] The number has continued to grow, feeding our Body Wars and starving our bodies. Women of all shapes and sizes began hating their normal, healthy bodies and engaged in damaging practices hoping to look like Twiggy and her colleagues.

In the 1970's, the average fashion model weighed 8% less than the average American woman, but in the 1990's, the difference was 23%![6] Similarly, the weights of Miss America contestants and winners have steadily declined since the 1950's. Now 60% of the contestants weigh 85% or less of their ideal body weight, meeting one of the diagnostic criteria for anorexia nervosa.[7] Contemporary Miss America winners are taller, but 15 pounds lighter than their 1950's counterparts.[8]

Models pay a dear price for the business of their bodies. Entrenched in diet mania, they typically exist on infrequent, small meals, black coffee, diet soda and cigarettes. Drugs like speed, cocaine, diet pills, appetite suppressants, caffeine pills and diuretics, and illnesses like anorexia and bulimia are commonplace in the model world. Supermodels Carol Alt, Beverly Johnson, and Kim Alexis have all discussed their chronic, severe dieting and the relentless pressure to lose more weight. In fact, Alt did not menstruate for two years, as amenorrhea affects countless underweight women.[8]

> *"When you have a certain number of pictures taken of you, you feel robbed. . . Drugs made it a lot easier to sit there and look dumb in front of the camera."*
> —Lisa Taylor, model

From time to time, a model with fuller breasts is featured, but she usually has had implants, as it is unusual to be so thin and have much breast tissue since breasts are composed of fat. And although full-sized models are gaining popularity and prestige, the non-curvaceous bodies of the waif models like Kate Moss have remained the prevailing standard. In a fashion preview in the *New York Times*, one observer summed it up by saying, "The ideal body is now a boy's body with breasts."[9]

The Real Business of Pageants and Modeling

When the Miss America contest first began, many saw it as a way for women to gain influence, scholarships and other perks. Modeling also promises to be a glamorous and lucrative profession, yet only a few hundred of the countless young women aspiring to be models will ever be able to support themselves financially. In 1995, the top American model, Claudia Schiffer, made $12 million.[10] However, a book about the "ugly business of beautiful women" describes a more common story: "Wannabe models…are junk food for modeling's predators and bottom feeders."[11] Abuse is rampant, with agents sleeping with minors who are hoping for a break. Rape, prostitution, alcohol and drug abuse, starvation, anxiety, depression, and suicide are not rare events in the world of modeling.

Even as the women's movement grew in the 1960's, more beauty pageants were born, even some for young children. Miss Hemisphere, for three-year-olds and up, began with a few hundred participants and grew to be the largest pageant in the world. There, toddlers are evaluated for their "beauty, charm, poise and personality."[12]

"In 1969, I competed at the Miss Universe pageant. I was 18, had done nothing special, but was treated like I had accomplished great things. I now understand that the only area that expressed the power of the feminine in my culture was the beauty industry."
—Anita Johnson, author, *Eating in the Light of the Moon*

Parents involve their children in beauty pageants by rationalizing that they want to offer new experiences and opportunities to their little ones. In reality, pageantry exploits, sexualizes, and adultifies children. At critically young ages, kids learn to dress up, look cute and coy, please and perform, and use their bodies to win attention and affection. In many cases, the children may be competing instead of sleeping, for pageants often run into the night.

As with adult pageants, beauty contests for children have become big business. Privately owned, entry fees can be steep, with extra charges frequently added. The Southern Charm national contest costs $175, with additional fees of $50 to $100 for special categories. Clothing, makeup, travel expenses, as well as coaches, instructors, and agents increase the cost. Sometimes coaches recommend plastic surgery to give a youngster a "special" look. Some pageants have proven to be scams, issuing bad checks, promising award money only if the competition continues, or going bankrupt before prizes are awarded.[13]

Beauty contests have caused many other tragedies. Contestants frequently battle their bodies, starving, purging, and beating themselves into an

> *"Through modeling, I've also learned another truth I could have suspected: Plus-sized women aren't the only ones who are prisoners of poor body image. Plenty of "straight" models—models size six to eight—are as insecure about their bodies as I'd long been."*
> **—Emme, model, author, True Beauty**

ideal of beauty in order to compete. Contenders for the Miss America crown work out an average of 14 hours per week, with some reporting as many as 35 hours.[14] The 1996 Miss Universe, Alicia Machado, from Venezuela, was told to lose weight or lose her crown. She won the pageant weighing 116, slim for 5'7". But when the pressure was off, she gained 19 pounds, a weight considered ideal for that height. Like many contestants, she had starved herself for months before the pageant. Describing that time in her life, she says, "I was anorexic and bulimic, but almost all of us are…When I was preparing for Miss Universe, it was an obsession for me to not gain weight…[T]he year leading to it I didn't eat at all. And whatever I ate, I threw up. . . . I was skeletal."[15]

Some pageants claim to be based on attributes other than beauty. Miss Teen-Age America, founded in 1962, no longer has the appearance competition and reportedly focuses on grades, community and extracurricular involvement, emphasizing "role models" not "cover models."[16] Still most of the girls attracted to this competition are tall and slim.

Both the modeling and pageant industries are big business, with millions of dollars riding on them, so changes will come slowly. However, "all women are hurt by such contests in a culture that substitutes the worship of female beauty for the recognition of female equality."[17] As long as women's dreams and aspirations are focused on external appearance, their real accomplishments will be elusive. Models are not "models," and "beauty" pageants are ugly.

STRATEGIES FOR CHANGE

Once more, it is time for consciousness-raising and soul-searching. Be honest about how these ugly businesses have affected you and your view of women. Ask yourself these questions and commit to freeing yourself from the influence of beauty queens, models, and the businesses they represent.

1. What are your childhood memories of Miss America and other pageants? Were they important to you?

2. Did you ever aspire to be a beauty queen or a model?

3. Have you tried to lose weight, dress a certain way, or do other things to emulate a fashion model?

4. Have you ever bought a book, magazine, tape, or other product promoted by a model? If so, why?

5. How important is beauty, weight, shape, and appearance in your judgment of women?

Consider your influence over the young people in your life. The more girls know about powerful, creative, strong, interesting women, the less they will imitate cover models and beauty queens. Talk about the great women you know—the aunts, grandmothers, neighbors, friends—describing what you value in them. Discuss women in politics and in the workplace who have power and influence. Read about the extensive, but often unrecognized, accomplishments of women. There are many books chronicling women's history. Share the excitement you feel as you learn and discover this world, especially with the younger women in your life.

Be sure the textbooks in your school system are routinely examined for gender bias, and that the teachers actively acknowledge the accomplishments of women in all areas, from art to science. Boys must also learn about women's contributions to our culture so their attitudes toward girls can reflect a broader base of knowledge.

Do not encourage any child to enter beauty pageants or modeling contests. Instead, encourage competition in healthy areas. Help children, especially girls, to focus on ability, competence, dedication, enthusiasm, cooperation, and the joy of taking risks by trying new things and mastering the old. Examine the systems around your children; be sure girls and boys are given equal opportunities in sports, computer time, all academics, and exposure to nontraditional roles, for instance boys to home economics, and girls to hard science and industrial arts.

The next time a national pageant is televised, arrange an alternative empowering ritual for the girls and women in your life. Have a party, enjoy food and your bodies, or get together to talk about the impact the modeling and pageant industries have had on you. Write, draw, sing, listen to music, write poetry and celebrate your real beauty!

Protest beauty pageants, just as feminists did at the Miss America Contest in Atlantic City in 1969, by stuffing a trash can with curlers, wigs, false eyelashes, bras and girdles. They crowned a sheep to protest women being treated like animals. A former model, Ann Simonton, creates Myth California outside the Miss California contest each year. She once made a swimsuit of steak, and another time an evening gown of bologna, both to illustrate how pageants treat women like meat.[18]

Write letters to editors of gender biased materials, distribute flyers about your criticisms of pageants, and hold an open forum at a school or community organization. Throw away any pictures of models or beauty queens that you have idealized or emulated.

"It's a scary world when all you are is a face."
—Nancy Berg, model

Decide who your real models should be.

Refuse to buy products advertised by unhealthy models and return catalogs and magazines that use undernourished women to sell products. Make noise!

RESOURCES

National Association to Advance Fat Acceptance (NAAFA)
This advocacy group has made great strides toward celebrating size diversity in the media, and in the modelling, fashion, and beauty industries. The increased exposure and influence of plus-size models is one example. NAAFA has regional chapters, an annual convention, a newsletter, and print materials.
PO Box 188620
Sacramento, CA 95818
916-558-6880
www.naafa.org

To protest pageants, find out when and where they are:
Miss America
609-345-7571
Miss Teen USA and Miss Universe
310-553-2555.

Ann Simonton, Myth California
c/o Media Watch
PO Box 618
Santa Cruz, CA 95061
408-423-6355
mwatch@cruzio.com

Books

The Information Please: Girls' Almanac
McLoone, M., Siegel, A., New York, Houghton Mifflin Co., 1995.

From Pocahontas to Power Suits: Everything You Need to Know About Women's History in America
Mills, K., New York, Plume, 1995.

Model: The Ugly Business of Beautiful Women
M. Gross., New York, William Morrow, 1995.

10

Plastic Surgery
SELF-IMPROVEMENT OR SELF-HARM?

"We know more about the life span of automobile tires than we do about breast implants."
—Jennifer Washburn
Ms, March/April 1996

For people who enjoy gambling, the big business of cosmetic plastic surgery promises to provide a risky thrill. With procedures that can complement any cultural beauty standard, cosmetic surgery could be renamed "fashion surgery."[1] Ideals for appearance constantly change; medical techniques now follow to promote the latest trend. The promise of a more positive self-image and increased confidence makes cosmetic surgery almost like "psychiatry with a knife"[2]—a dangerous practice at best.

How can anyone make peace with their bodies when cosmetic surgery is equated with self-improvement? These drastic measures reflect a sincere desire for beauty and power, but potential feelings of disempowerment and disconnection from one's body are rarely anticipated. Plastic surgery wastes our money, our resources, and our health, and creates endless new opportunities for Body Wars.

A Bit of History

Cosmetic surgery has been considered part of health care for almost a century, with the first practice opening in Chicago in 1903. In the 1920's, plastic surgeons used their talent and training to remove healthy breasts from women aspiring for the flat-chested look of the flapper.[3] In the early 1980's, however, the American Society of Plastic and Reconstructive Surgeons saw a lucrative market in the formerly-admired flat-chested women, declaring that small breasts are a treatable "problem." The diagnosis of "micromastia" emerged, based on the premise "that these deformities are really a disease."[4]

During the 1980's and 1990's, the marketing of plastic surgery became sophisticated and seductive. By emphasizing the importance of a youthful look as a competitive advantage in the workplace, surgeons promised to help potential clients—both male and female—meet their career goals, as well as to acquire the "look" of the moment.

What Kind of Investment?

The marketing of plastic surgery, guided by brilliant advertising consultants, creates and then exploits the insecurities of consumers. Women are encouraged to "invest" in breast augmentation, liposuction, facelifts, tummy tucks, nose jobs, collagen injections, and other surgical interventions to prove their worth for both social and economic gain. Many women now see these procedures as survival techniques. A campaign by the American Society of Plastic and Reconstructive Surgeons has promoted body sculpting not only as safe, effective, and affordable, but also as essential to women's mental health.[5]

> "This recent phenomenal growth in plastic surgery is the byproduct of a change in the role of appearance...the face and the body are being increasingly pressed into service as essential business accessories, as a mobile billboard for their owner's brilliance, energy and savvy."
> —Judith Rodin, author, *Body Traps*

Marketing to men initially promoted plastic surgery for their wives, but now targets them as well, especially the anxious executive who feels the need to fight age discrimination. Men most often opt for liposuction, nose jobs, hair transplants, hair removal, eyelid surgeries—all to attain the youthful appearance that will make them seem more valuable. As an article in the *New York Times* recently stated, "fearing the ax, men choose the scalpel."[6] In the 1990's, some have reported that men comprise as many as 25% of the plastic surgeries in the US,[7] while others report 10%.[8]

The promotion of plastic surgery has clearly paid off. An estimated 2.8 million plastic surgery procedures took place in the United States in 1998, up 4% in one year.[9] Adding to their appeal, procedures have become more affordable in the past ten years, as less-experienced physicians, many not even trained in plastic surgery, are providing this service to augment their income and to avoid the hassles of insurance, HMO's, and managed care. Cosmetic plastic surgery is primarily a cash business and very profitable.

Normal Practice?

Previously, women who elected to go under the knife were seen as unstable, narcissistic, or neurotic. Today, they are often viewed as motivated and achievement-oriented. In fact, cosmetic plastic surgery is becoming so popular that the children of many baby-boomers may not recognize their parents' early photos, nor will they have a sense of what their bodies should naturally resemble as they age. Because of plastic surgery's mass cultural acceptance, it now seems "normal" to have body-altering procedures performed, reminiscent of the "Twilight Zone" episode in which humans regularly choose to emulate a model in hopes of attaining everlasting happiness.

Cosmetic surgery assumes that the body has "flaws" which can, and should, be "fixed." Could deciding not to have plastic surgery someday be interpreted as a failure to care for oneself? These are the subtle messages women absorb in this era of medically-endorsed slaughtering. Unlike 20 years ago when facelifts were reserved for women in their late 50's and 60's, today, many are having these procedures done before menopause. Some even undergo facelifts in their 20's or 30's so that they will never look middle-aged.[10] Teenagers are opting for nose jobs and other kinds of body sculpting before their bodies are even developed. Girls as young as 14, barely into puberty, are seeking breast reductions to reduce their overall presence![11]

Take a minute to look at the table which breaks down the different procedures for each age range. Over 3% of cosmetic surgery is performed on kids, but body hatred persists and becomes more frequent as people age, with most procedures done on those 35-50 years old. Unfortunately, Body Wars do not retire. In 1998, nearly 150,000 senior citizens underwent cosmetic surgery.

AGE AND THE KNIFE

Percentage by age group of specific plastic surgery procedures.

Procedure Age (years):	<18	19-34	35-50	51-64	>65
Tummy tuck	.4	19.5	58	19.9	2.3
Eyelids	.1	5.3	38.6	43.2	12.7
Breast augmentation	1.3	61.3	33.3	3.8	.3
Breast reduction (women)	4.6	42.4	39.1	12.2	1.8
Breast reduction (men)	22.9	47.9	20.2	7.8	.9
Chin augmentation	7.1	44.8	34.1	10.4	3.5
Hair transplants	.3	30	49.4	15.1	5.2
Liposuction	1.3	35.6	45.7	14	2.5
Nose reshaping	17.2	52.3	24.3	4.9	1.2
Total	3.1	26	42.2	23.3	5.3

Statistics from The American Society for Aesthetic Plastic Surgery, Communications Office, 36 W. 44th St. Suite 630, New York, NY, 10036.[12]

What Price Beauty?

In more ways than one, the Body War of plastic surgery comes with a hefty price. Frequently, our quest for beauty ends up costing us our health, as plastic surgery can result in both temporary and permanent medical problems. The aftermath of many procedures entails pain, bruises, damage to surrounding tissue and subsequent absence from work. The recovery process is often compared to recuperation after a car accident. Why do people choose this discomfort and sacrifice? Only in a culture that promotes beauty at any cost will otherwise-sane people be brainwashed into choosing to inflict violence on their bodies.

Further, most insurance policies do not cover plastic surgery; patients must pay out of pocket. One survey found that 50% of plastic surgery patients earned less than $25,000 per year and financed their treatment through loans and mortgages.[13]

Small lenders looking for new markets have begun to develop credit programs specifically for elective surgeries. In its first four months, one company lent more than $1.6 million for plastic surgery. Due to the risks involved in this business, finance charges are routinely as high as state regulations allow, up to 22.5% annually.[14] The American Society of Plastic Reconstructive Surgery also offers a finance program for their members' benefit, collecting interest on loans to their patients.

Take a look at the following prices for perfection to appreciate how much money is wasted on this Body War.

PRICES FOR PERFECTION

	Cost	# Performed (1998)
Facelift	$4,895	100,208
Breast augmentation	$3,001	126,913
Liposuction	$2,562	218,064
Tummy tuck	$4,058	42,249
Eyelid surgery	$2,187	182,456
Collagen injection	$347/per cc	367,170
Hair transplants	$3,123	35,237
Nose jobs	$3,304	133,058

Average fees for popular procedures in 1998, excluding anesthesia, operating room, and other expenses, as reported by the American Society for Aesthetic Plastic Surgery. Note: these statistics are based on ASAPS members primarily and do not necessarily reflect the number of procedures done by non-plastic surgeons. Thus, these estimates may be quite low, particularly of procedures such as hair transplants.[15]

The Breast Business

Between 1997 and 1998, nearly a quarter million American women risked general anesthesia, routine surgical complications, and known long-term side-effects to increase their bust size. In that time period alone, the number of procedures increased by 25%. Although some were reconstructive surgeries following a mastectomy, the majority were cosmetic. In the same time frame, over 116,000 women had breast reductions, an increase of 43% from 1997 to 1998.[16]

The public has long been fascinated with altering female breasts. Beginning in the 1940's, right after World War II, transformer coolant fluid, based on silicone, was used to increase breast size of Asian prostitutes to enhance their appeal to American soldiers. Exotic dancers in California, Nevada, and Texas were next. Soon, the risks became apparent. Accidental injections into the bloodstream resulted in blindness and sometimes death. Many developed gangrene, pneumonia, infections, lumps, or collapsed lungs. Some implants could be removed, but many women had to have mastectomies. Later, Nevada and California made silicone breast injections illegal.[17]

In the 1960's, despite knowledge that silicone is potentially damaging to both the central nervous system and the immune system (and is an effective insecticide), Dow Chemical developed and marketed silicone breast implants, failing to disclose the information of the risks involved.[18] Within two to four years of receiving silicone implants, 70% of the recipients suffer hardening of the scar tissue that squeezes the implant into a dense disc. Over time, 71.3% experience a rupture or leak, causing a cellular immune reaction. Since our bodies cannot metabolize silicone, the final result may be an autoimmune disease.[19] No governmental approval was required, however, when Dow began to market silicone, and no safety standards were developed. The FDA did not require premarket approval and did not regulate medical devices until 1976, after the Dalkon Shield product

"During the 80's, mannequins set the beauty trends—and real women were expected to follow. The dummies were 'coming to life' while the ladies were breathing anesthesia and going under the knife."
—Susan Faludi, author, *Backlash*

liability issues became a legal and medical concern.[20]

Between the 1960's and 1990's, Dow Corning (part of Dow Chemical) and other companies released a variety of implants, whose safety did not improve. In fact, Dow Corning's 1975 implant model caused more bleeding than earlier versions and often ruptured, even in surgical demonstrations. An FDA report in 1982 stated that breast implants have a "potentially unreasonable risk of injury," but made no recommendations for research or restrictions.[21] Until 1992, these dangerous devices were routinely placed in women's bodies. Now, after the largest class action settlement ever, they are restricted for use only in reconstructive surgery research trials.[22] Ironically, it allows women who already have battled cancer the opportunity to risk silicone transplants.

The safety of breast implants continues to be contested in the courts. In 1999, a court-appointed panel of experts concluded that there was no link between silicone implants and connective tissue and autoimmune conditions. However, the National Cancer Institute is still pursuing answers. Some medical experts and consumer advocates maintain that the panel finding is inconclusive because it examined only a few of the ailments associated with implants.[23] As it can take years for these problems to be identified, current knowledge remains limited.

Today, most implants are saline, a relatively safe substance, although contained in a silicone envelope. The long-term risks for this type of implant are still unknown, but some obvious problems follow:

• Implants last 10 years. Each replacement surgery involves

all the risks involved with general surgery and anesthesia.

- Implants may rupture, deflate, harden, move, cause pain, or develop fungal or bacterial infections.

- Implants may impede mammography and detection of breast cancer.

- Implants may contaminate breast milk.

- Implants may decrease sensation or cause wrinkling.

- Implants may cause serious autoimmune disorders, like lupus.

- Implants are expensive. Surgery for implants costs $2,000-$3,000; $2,500-$8,000 for removal. Anesthesia, hospital stays, medications, and aftercare costs are additional.[24]

Liposuction—Vacuum Cleaning the Body

Introduced in 1982, liposuction is now the most commonly performed plastic surgery procedure.[25] The instrument used is similar to a vacuum cleaner. It breaks up and removes fat from various body parts, especially from the abdomen, chin, thighs, ankles, and knees. Over 200,000 procedures are performed each year at $2,500 or more per site.[26] Although actors and models, in attempts to maintain marketable contours, are frequent customers, liposuction also appeals to the masses. Regardless of intent, however, many suffer post surgical weeks of soreness and girdles, only to find that fat accumulates in other places.[27]

No follow-up studies on liposuction have been conducted.

Both formal and informal documents tell us that, like other forms of plastic surgery, liposuction carries risk. A 1988 congressional investigation reported 20 deaths from liposuction due to the release of embolisms to the heart, lungs, and brain. Clots, infections, and hematomas add up to a surgical complication rate of 9%.[28] A more recent study of New York City death records between 1993 and 1998 discovered five fatalities due to liposuction. The medical report concluded that this procedure can "kill otherwise healthy persons."[29]

The Medical Board of California is investigating three recent deaths related to liposuction. One California anesthesiologist reported that for every death, 15 to 20 severe injuries occur. With no formal tracking of the complications resulting from liposuction, these numbers may be just the tip of the iceberg. This investigation points out that physicians with very little training are doing these procedures. Adding to the risk, many operate in private outpatient offices or surgical suites with little scrutiny or attention to safety.[30]

> "If women suddenly stopped feeling ugly, the fastest growing medical specialty would be the fastest dying."
> —Naomi Wolf, author, The Beauty Myth

Like other Body Wars, liposuction appears more satisfying than it often is. Many people regain the lost weight, particularly if they do not stick to a rigorous diet and exercise plan. Contours and depressions under the skin, as well as decreased muscle mass and changes in skin tone, are frequent complaints.[31] Some plastic surgeons remove more than two or three pounds at a time, possibly affecting the metabolism of body fat. Subcutaneous body fat on hips or thighs may be replaced by visceral fat, the "bad body fat" associated with health problems, which may, in turn, promote the acquisition of more fat.[32]

Each year, "fashion surgery" advocates promote new, unproven, but "promising" procedures. Soft-tissue shaving, for example, mimics liposuction, but reports less damage to surrounding tissue.[33] Unfortunately, the risk of damage to nerve and blood vessels is higher. The question remains: How far will society go to avoid making peace with women's bodies?

Put on a Happy Face?

If you have a problem, plastic surgery promises a solution. Currently, there are at least 40 plastic surgery procedures to alter the face alone.

For those who are scared of "the knife," laugh lines can be erased by collagen injections that last up to six months. Chin implants can recontour the face. Eyes can be reshaped or lifted. A "yuppie lift" is a cheaper alternative to a face-lift, performed on younger adults to take five to ten years off the face. "Waifing" removes the fat under cheekbones for about $3,000, but may cause the face to prematurely age.[34]

The chemical peel is touted as one of the newer ways to avoid aging. This process burns layers of skin with acid to get to undamaged skin, resulting in swelling and blisters that peel off, usually within ten days. Pink skin lasts for another month. Sometimes permanent scars, changes in the pigment, fever blisters, or infections occur. Some lawsuits are pending due to burns.[35] Over 550,000 chemical peels were done in 1996, averaging $825 each.[36]

Laser surgery is another way to erase wrinkles. This procedure causes oozing, puffiness, scabs, and red skin, and patients must take pain medications and antibiotics as well as protect their skin afterwards. Healing takes three months, and the price ranges from $550 to $6,500.[37] Since this technique is so new, few data are available regarding long-term safety and outcome. The FDA suggests that people with autoimmune diseases should avoid collagen injections,[38] but as an alternative, Botox (botulinum toxin, best known for causing botulism) may be injected into facial muscles to paralyze them into a line-free, youthful look.[39]

Homogenizing Beauty

One ill effect of cosmetic plastic surgery is the homogenizing of beauty. Today, to gain acceptance in mainstream American culture, some women of color are choosing plastic surgery. In 1998, 14% of the patients in the United States were non-white.[40] Although the aesthetics and norms governing cosmetic plastic surgery are Caucasian, Asian women in the United States and abroad are also pursuing this Body War at alarming rates. They choose eyelid and nose reconstruction, changing their most distinct genetic features to become more Western in appearance. Africans, Asians, and Caucasians with dark or ruddy skin risk more scarring and keloid formation after surgery than do fair-skinned Caucasians.[41]

Multiculturalism has always been an asset in the evolution of American culture, but in this era of plastic surgery, our greatest strength—our individuality—is being lost. In its disrespect for differences, the scalpel in the surgeon's hands is threatening the diversity of the countless ethnicities, religions and races which have enriched our culture. Body Wars have become a standard ingredient in the melting pot.

STRATEGIES FOR CHANGE

Decide right now to love yourself exactly as you are. Counteract every negative statement you make about your body and appearance with a positive one. Enforce this commitment by fining yourself $10 for each criticism that slips out. Then, send the money to an organization that fights Body Wars. (See the Resources sections throughout this book.) If you are considering cosmetic surgery, use the money to do something good for your soul (instead of your vanity), like give it to charity.

Two professions—law and medicine—can greatly help in our efforts to fight the harmful popularity of plastic surgery. The most radical solution to the fashion surgery trend is to end the practice entirely, allowing reconstructive plastic surgery only for those with injuries or health conditions. The number of plastic surgery residencies would have to be decreased to reflect this policy. Medical schools must also take responsibility by examining the ethics of practices that have little to do with healing and much to do with profiting from dangerous or poorly researched procedures. Students, residents, interns, fellows, and physicians must discuss how performing cosmetic surgery fits with the physician's role as a healer.

The legal profession can also play a powerful role in our campaign against plastic surgery. Product liability, personal injury, and class action suits can be strategic weapons in our fight to regain control of our bodies and our well-being. However, under the guise of "tort reform," big business has been chipping away at the rights of ordinary citizens to sue medical personnel and product makers. Tort reform legislation would curtail the possibility of product liability suits, so companies like Dow Corning could continue to make dangerous products with little or no liability risk. Corporate America has convinced many legislators and voters that the courts are packed with unnecessary lawsuits, clogging the legal system and resulting in unwarranted settlements. In reality, a study by the National Center for State Courts found that only 9% of filings are torts and only 4% of those are product liability cases.[42] Exercising our legal rights is an effective weapon. Explore the tort reform efforts in your state. Lobby against any measures that prevent us from protecting ourselves and that absolve companies like Dow Corning of accountability.

PostScript: The class action suit against Dow Corning and the four other companies selling silicone implants resulted in a global settlement of $4.25 billion to pay off the 400,000 claims. After this was ordered by the court, Dow Corning declared bankruptcy, and the global settlement collapsed. Many women who have suffered severe autoimmune diseases for years still have not received financial compensation. On the other hand, Dow Corning still has money. They declared bankruptcy although their profits were up 33% that quarter, to $49.5 million on record sales of $612 million.[43] If big companies can declare bankruptcy when they're making millions, you and I must be able to file product liability suits!

RESOURCES

American Silicone Implant Survivors (ASIS)
For legal and medical information:
1288 Cork Elm Dr.
Kirkwood, MO 63122
fax: 314-821-0115
Breast implant settlement claims office: 800-600-0311
Breast implant settlement information line: 800-887-6828 or
fax: 713-570-7221

Children Afflicted by Toxic Substances (CATS)
For information on silicone-related diseases in children of mothers with implants.
413 Fort Salonga Rd.
Northport, NY 11768
516-757-4829
Catstoxic@aol.com

Command Trust Network
Information for women with breast implants.
256 Linden Dr.
Beverly Hills, CA 90212
310-556-1738

FDA
5600 Fishers Lane
Parklawn Bldg.
Rockville, MD 20857
888-INFOFDA or 888-463-6332

National Alliance of Breast Cancer Organizations (NABCO)
9E 37th St., 10th Floor
New York, NY 10016
800-719-9154
nabcoinfo@aol.com

National Women's Health Network
Has a clearinghouse for information on women's health, including implant-related questions.
514 10th St. NW., #400
Washington, DC 20004
202-628-7814

11

Violence Against Women
THE DEADLIEST BODY WAR

"Rape will not stop until both men and women are allowed our full humanity. It is difficult, if not impossible, to harm another whom one perceives as equally human."

—Peggy Miller and Nancy Biele,
Twenty Years Later:
The Unfinished Revolution

Violence against women is the deadliest of Body Wars. In all of its ugly forms, on a continuum of subtle to severe, it conveys complete disregard for women and creates an atmosphere of fear and self-loathing. It also sets the stage for other societal disrespect and abuse.

Sadly, some women believe that changing their bodies or their appearance will protect them from harm. They may even believe that their "imperfect" bodies invite harassment or violence. Despite a woman's efforts to alter herself, in a culture of sexual violence and objectification, she is not safe. Her dieting, bingeing, purging, exercising until it hurts, being a slave to external standards of beauty and fashion provide only a false sense of security. In reality, her desperate attempts to ward off danger do not protect her; they are merely hiding places. And by taking refuge in other Body Wars, she punishes herself for being a victim by revictimizing herself.

Women under Attack

To be in a woman's body means to live under attack. Verbal or sexual abuse can be a daily event that occurs even while walking down the street or getting a cup of coffee at work. Women feel less safe today than they did 20 years ago. In a country with a rich and impressive heritage of civil liberties, American women still feel threatened, which is no wonder. Rape is one of the most frequent crimes in the United States, with over 683,000 women raped annually, 60% under 18 years old. Over 12 million American women will experience rape in their lifetime.[1] In the 1980's, the number of women seeking help at shelters for domestic violence doubled.[2] The Center for Disease Control calls domestic violence the number one public health problem for women of childbearing age.[3]

In America—"Land of the free, home of the brave"—young girls are warned that their bodies are not safe. At risk for harassment, violence, unwanted sexual contact, pregnancy, STD's (Sexually Transmitted Diseases), HIV (Human Immunodeficiency Virus), and AIDS (Acquired Immunodeficiency Syndrome), they are cautioned against contracting life-threatening conditions before they even know what they are. Their bodies represent sources of stress, rather than joy, as their childhood feelings of pride turn into adolescent feelings of shame. Natural female desires are virtually off limits. It's no mystery why young girls so readily succumb to Body Wars: their bodies have become the enemy.

Pornography and Media Misogynism

Pornography and the sexual objectification of women are ubiquitous. Although most of us are aware of hard core porn, less obvious is the soft porn that permeates most homes in magazines and music lyrics on the radio and TV, all promoting violence against women.

Defenders of pornography claim that the objectification of women is merely an outlet for sexual impulses and is protected by the First Amendment: the right to free speech. But a double standard exists when it comes to naked bodies. For example, New York City subway police removed posters showing an erect penis with instructions on condom use, but left the Penthouse ads with naked "pinup girls."[4] Further, one court case ruled that men are entitled to display pornography in the workplace, even when it offends female coworkers.[5] It is time we demand respect for the sexual interests and civil liberties of all human beings.

The impact of pornography warrants serious consideration by anyone who believes in women's rights. Soft porn objectifies the female body, making rape and abuse victims appear less believable. Hard core porn does not stop at objectification; it implicitly condones violation of women's bodies. Consequently, men trivialize such treatment and often find it erotic, rather than dangerous.

The norms for mainstream films have changed, as our culture has grown desensitized to sexual violence. In the 1950's and 1960's, women were seduced and kissed; now they are raped and murdered. In fact, in 1989, the Screen Actor's Guild reported that only 14% of roles went to women, and that increasing numbers were posed as rape victims or prostitutes.[6] While a 1998 update of this study showed an increase of roles for women, men still outnumbered them by two to one. Further, the male actors studied were cast in more powerful and credible roles.[7] Since the average American home plays television eight hours a day, the images depicted, for both men and women, have a tremendous impact on us all.

"...pornography is not about sex. It's about an imbalance of power that allows and even requires sex to be used as a form of aggression."
—Gloria Steinem, founder of Ms. Magazine, author, *Revolution from Within*

Just as toxic as blatant objectification of women is "beauty porn" which conveys the message that women must be underweight, perfectly sculpted, or powerless, to be attractive. A surgically-altered silicone breast, with little or no sensation, is now considered sexier than a real one. A skeletal body, appearing as if it has little zest for life, is preferred over a natural one with muscles or flesh. For women, the impact has been an increase in self-mutilation, a decrease in self-esteem, and a distorted link between sexuality and appearance—fertile ground for Body Wars.

Sexual Harassment—Subtle but Violent

In 1991, the Civil Rights Act expanded to include two forms of sexual harassment. "Quid pro quo" occurs when an employee's status suffers if she does not acquiesce to sexual advances. A "hostile work environment" is an atmosphere of sexual tension or intimidation that makes work unmanageable. Physical touching, lewd jokes or comments, and pornography are examples of conditions that may lead to charges of sexual harassment. Since the passage of this Act, some court cases have overruled the "free speech" defense previously used to justify pornography in the workplace.[8] Enforcing this civil right is absolutely essential to women's ability to survive and succeed in their jobs.

> "One astounded male college athlete demanded, 'Do you mean that if I grab a woman's crotch, that could be rape? That's unfair.'"
> —Joseph Weinberg & Michael Biernbaum, activists for men stopping rape in Madison, WI

Despite how often we doubt the reports, sexual harassment is a real problem. Between 1991 and 1997, the number of federal cases more than doubled to nearly 16,000 per year. Companies now insure themselves against sexual harassment and some states mandate training for employers.[9] In fact, 64% of human resource executives in Fortune 500 companies believe that most complaints are valid. In the early 1990's, sexual harassment complaints cost the average Fortune 500 company $6.7 million per year because of absenteeism, decreased productivity, and employee turnover .[10] In such circumstances, women are nine times more likely than men to quit, five times more likely to transfer, and three times more likely to be terminated.[11]

The more traditionally male-oriented the work environment, the worse the problem. Two of every three women in the military admit to having been victims.[12] In 1997, six women who had not known each other, filed charges with similar details against a former Sergeant Major of the Army. Once the highest ranking enlisted man, his "character" and record as a soldier overrode 18 of the 19 charges. The only charge on which he was convicted was obstruction of justice. He was found guilty of trying to influence the testimony of one of his accusors, even though he denies having done anything wrong.[13]

> "As a man, I accrue privilege by remaining silent, accepting this legacy, and saying nothing about its cost in terms of women's lives."
> —Terrence Crowley, instructor for men stopping violence, Atlanta, GA

Even though a handful of cases have received notoriety, sexual harassment is rarely reported. Many women consider it to be a "normal" part of life, and do not discuss it. Ninety-five percent of adult victims tell no one, but more than one-half of working women report feeling uncomfortable at their jobs due to sexual jokes and demeaning comments.[14] Eighty-eight percent of respondents to a *RedBook* survey had endured such experiences.[15]

Blaming the Body

More often than not, women respond to sexual harassment by blaming themselves for provoking it, whether because of their clothing, appearance, or style. What's more, the legal system often supports personal feelings of culpability. In a case of sexual harassment that included rape, one court stated that the victim's "provocative dress" indicated that "she welcomed rape from her employer."[16] Another upheld a corporation's denial of a partnership to a woman because she didn't walk, talk, or dress in a feminine manner. Finally, when an employer explained that a woman's physical characteristics prompted sexual harassment, the court ruled that Title VII of the Civil Rights Act protects gender, but not appearance.[17]

Such legal decisions suggest that women do not have the same rights as men, that their bodies are public property, and that their appearance is paramount and subject to arbitrary judgments. Women can be fired for not looking attractive, but they can be harassed with no legal retribution if they look "too good." Some spend hard-earned dollars on a wardrobe consultant just to acquire that attractive-but-not-provocative look. Most resort to some form of Body Wars as they wrestle with the paradox and risk of beauty in the workplace.

Unfortunately, sexual harassment also affects young people. Eighty-nine percent of girls aged 9 to 19, surveyed by *Seventeen* magazine, had already encountered abuse in school. All reported inappropriate sexual comments, gestures, and looks both from students and staff. In addition, 83% had been touched, pinched, or grabbed, and for 40%, this contact had been daily.[18] The following is one 16 year old girl's description of this traumatic experience:

> It was very painful for me. I dreaded school...I started to wear clothes that wouldn't flatter my figure, and I kept to myself...I'd cry every night...I thought I was a total loser...Sometimes the teachers were right there when it was going on. They did nothing...they took away my self-esteem, my social life, and kept me from getting a good education.[19]

Most girls do not report sexual harassment to their parents or school, having already incorporated the message that it is part of the landscape for contemporary females. Still, they feel guilty, powerless, responsible (but not sure how), and they gradually grow silent, avoiding situations where these incidents occur. Such withdrawal costs them socially, academically and emotionally.

The shame that girls feel about their bodies as a result of sexual harassment is often translated into the "language of fat,"[20] which is readily witnessed when girls turn their difficult feelings against themselves, rather than expressing them directly. The statement, "I feel fat" is an indicator of far more complex emotions, but becomes the focus of their energy.[21] It is easier for girls to battle with their bodies than to confront a problem like sexual harassment.

Intimacy Violence

Violence against women does not just occur in the workplace or at school. Sadly, women are more at risk in their homes and with the men they love than they are with strangers. Domestic, or relationship, violence occurs in the lives of more than four million American women every year, with over one million reporting physical injury. According to the FBI, a woman is beaten every nine seconds.[22] Women are reluctant to report violence to the police or to tell their friends or family, so these dismal statistics may even be low.

SAD FACTS ABOUT VIOLENCE AGAINST WOMEN

- Women are the victims of one quarter of the violent crime in the United States.[23]

- Domestic violence is the leading cause of injury to women. As a result, at least one-half of homeless women choose the safety of the street rather than their own houses.[24]

- Half of the female murder victims each year are killed by a male partner.[25]

- 8% of pregnant women are battered, risking miscarriage, low birth weight, and increased infant mortality.[26]

- Domestic violence precedes one quarter of women's suicide attempts, and abused women are five times more likely to attempt suicide and need psychiatric care.[27]

- In only 22% of reported rapes, the assailant is a stranger; 78% of the victims know their rapist.[28]

- Of the over 1.4 million hospital emergency department admissions in 1994, about 1/4 were treatments for injuries sustained in an assault by an intimate partner or family member.[29]

• On average, between 1992 and 1996, about one million women and girls over 12 years of age each year experienced violent victimizations, including rape, sexual assault, robbery, aggravated and simple assault, by a current or former intimate partner.[30]

Sex or Rape?

For too many women, sex and violence are partners. Date rape has become a common phenomenon. In only 22% of reported cases, the assailant is a stranger. Seventy eight percent of the victims know their rapist![31]

This pattern starts early, with 26% of high school girls reporting having been sexually or physically assaulted, and nearly 10% having been date raped. Yet most remain silent, with 27% telling no one. Data on the emotional health of these same women reveals that 25% feel depressed and suffer feelings of inferiority and inadequacy.[32]

Living in a culture that fails to respect women's bodies has a profound effect on our beliefs about rape and similar violations. In one study, over half of high school boys, and nearly half of the girls stated that rape was acceptable if the male was sexually aroused! Eight percent of college men have either attempted or successfully raped. Thirty percent say they would rape if they could get away with it. When the wording was changed to "force a woman to have sex," the number jumped to 58%. Worse still, 83.5% argue that "some women look like they are just asking to be raped."[33]

Unfortunately, we are primarily socialized in a super-masculine environment, wherein men are encouraged to be aggressive, persistent, and oblivious to pain—theirs or others'. Ignoring feelings, fearing vulnerability, and pushed to compete, men learn that to "score" will bring them admiration. Members of collegiate athletic teams and fraternities are notorious offenders. A National Institute of Health study found athletes responsible for over one third of the sexual assaults on the college campus.[34] Another reports that 55% of the acquaintance rapes involved male athletes.[35] Actually, some male heroes and role models set a standard of disregard, disrespect, and violence towards women which reaches young and old alike.

> *Of the nearly 700,000 rapes which occur in the United States each year, only 16% are reported to police; only 17% of those raped have a medical exam, and of those who do, 55% receive no counseling about pregnancy or its prevention, 33% no information on STD's, and 50% no information on HIV or AIDS.*[36]
>
> *As many as 60% of women in treatment for serious eating disorders have a history of physical abuse.*[37]

STRATEGIES FOR CHANGE

Consider how you have been affected by the sexualization, objectification, and constant violations of the female body. Answer the following questions; write and/or share your answers with a person from the opposite sex.

HOW DOES VIOLENCE AGAINST WOMEN AFFECT YOU?

WOMEN

• How has pornography affected your feelings about your body, sex, relationships and your safety?

• How has beauty porn affected your body image? How about your feelings about other women's bodies?

• Has any male ever made a comment about your body that made you uncomfortable or angry?

• What have you said or done in response?

• How comfortable are you walking down a city street or in other public settings?

• Has a man ever touched you, grabbed you, or fondled

MEN

• How has pornography affected your views of women and your desires in relationships?

• How has beauty porn affected your beliefs about women's bodies and your comments to women in your life? To other men?

• What do you say to women about their bodies?

• Have you ever told a friend that his comments about women are offensive to you?

• Do you whistle, call out, honk, or comment on a woman's appearance?

• Do you ever ask permission before you touch a woman?

you when you did not want
him to? What did you do?
What do you wish you had
done?

• Do you worry about your
physical safety on a daily
basis?

• Do you worry about your
physical safety on a daily
basis?

• Do you worry about the
physical safety of men that
you love in the same way?

• Do you worry about the
physical safety of women that
you love in the same way?

• How has violence against
women and the fear of it
affected your life?

• What have you done to
assure the safety of the
women in your life?

In order to protect yourself, take a class in self-defense,
martial arts, or model-mugging. These methods are great for
building strength, self-confidence, and competence. Children
can take these courses as well.

Stop watching TV shows or paying for movies that glamorize and normalize violence against women's bodies. Ask for a
refund when you leave the theater and tell the manager why.

If you have been a victim of violence, remind yourself that
you do not deserve to be threatened, hit, or intimidated. Seek
help. In a violent situation, if you can, call 911 for police assistance. Most communities provide shelters for women and their
children, as well as crisis hotlines. If you cannot find a shelter or
hotline, call your YWCA or local hospital, as many offer services for battered women. Also, there is a national information

line: 800-799-SAFE or 800-787-3224 (TDD) for the hearing impaired.

If you know someone who has been a victim of violence, research and share information about available resources. Remember that it can take a while before a woman actually feels ready to confront the situation. In the meantime, help her to be safe and feel worthy of better treatment.

Community

Look at how your community approaches issues of violence against women. Consider forming a task force if there are not clearly identified advocates for women's safety.

Make sure your police are appropriately trained to handle domestic violence, and locate shelters and other resources available for women in danger.

Learn about your state and local laws. Are police mandated to arrest the perpetrator in domestic violence so the victim does not have to press charges? What legislation has been passed regarding stalking, handguns, and classification of crimes?

Investigate courses on domestic violence and rape that might be provided through your local Women's Resource Center. Take one and become a volunteer at a shelter or hotline.

> *"The goal of our speaking must be to develop a new understanding that violence is the resort of the resourceless; that poverty, sexism, and racism provide the seedbed for its development; and that all prevention must be grounded in this perspective."*
> —**Sandra Campbell, educator and consultant on violence in children's lives**

Schools

Make sure that your schools are educating students about these issues. Do they provide escort services or other security when needed? Is there a program that will educate staff to help young women identify and talk about experiences of sexual harassment or abuse? Do they explore these issues with boys to help them avoid becoming perpetrators, or do they put the responsibility solely on girls to protect themselves? Even in the elementary schools, teasing and name-calling—especially attracting negative attention to girls' bodies—are examples that can easily escalate into more serious problems.

RESOURCES

Men Overcoming Violence (MOVE)
1385 Mission St., Suite 300
San Francisco, CA 94103
415-626-6683 (626-MOVE)

National Partnership for Women and Families
(formerly Women's Legal Defense Fund)
Workplace and fairness issues.
1875 Connecticut Ave., NW, Suite 710
Washington, DC 20009
202-986-2600

National Organization for Women
NOW Legal Defense and Education Fund
395 Hudson Street, 5th Floor

New York, NY 10014
212-925-6635
www.nowldef.org

Violence Against Women
This office sponsors the hotline listed and provides information about
the Violence Against Women Act signed into law in 1994, as well as
about resources, activities, and organizations to reduce violence.
810 7th St. NW
Washington, DC 20531
202-616-8894
www.usdoj.gov/vawo

YWCA
Week Without Violence
Launched in 1995, this public education campaign challenges people
to live for one week without participating in, promoting, or observ-
ing violence. Held annually the third week of October, YWCAs in
more than 30 countries organize coalitions of community groups
to hold activities that highlight alternatives to violence.
800-YWCA-US1

WEEA (Women's Educational Equity Act Resource Center)
Located in Newton, MA, also has school curriculum and parent education material about sexual harassment, dating violence, and related
issues. Provides a catalogue for purchasing the curriculum. A techni-
cal assistance line offers assistance on a range of topics to teachers,
community organizations, parents, and girls.
800-225-3088
www.edc.org/WomensEquity

American Association of University Women
Educational Foundation
(1993) *Hostile Hallways: The AAUW Survey on Sexual Harassment in*

America's Schools. Washington, DC
PO Box 251
Annapolis Junction, MD 20701-0251
800-225-9998, ext. 249
www.aauw.org

Campus Violence Prevention Center
An excellent model of prevention:
Student Services
Towson State University
Towson, MD 21204
410-830-2178

Books

How to Stop Sexual Harassment in Our Schools
Shoop, R., Edwards, D., New York, Prentice Hall, 1994.

Sexual Harassment and Teens: A Program for Positive Change
Susan Straus, Minneapolis, MN, Free Spirit Publishing, 1988.

Flirting or Hurting: A Teacher's Guide on Student-to-Student Sexual Harassment in Schools (grades 6-12)
Stein, N., Sjostrom, L., 1994.
Secrets in Public: Sexual Harassment in Our Schools
Stein, N., Marshall, N. L., Tropp, L.R., Wellesley, MA, Center for Research on Women, Wellesley College and the NOW Legal Defense and Education Fund, 1993.
Both available through:
Wellesley Centers for Women
Publication Office/Wellesley College
106 Central St.
Wellesley, MA 02181-8259
781-283-2510 or 781-283-2532
www.wellesley.edu/wcw/index.html

Videos

The Date Rape Backlash: Media and the Denial of Rape

A 60-minute discussion by journalists and researchers about the political issues related to date rape.

Sexual Harassment: Building Awareness On Campus

A 23-minute exploration of this issue, providing constructive solutions.
Media Education Foundation
26 Center Street
Northampton, MA 01060
800-897-0089; 413-584-8500
www.igc.org/mef

Stickers

"This Insults Women" stickers, and other ideas for activists. Put them on ads, "adult" book stores, and other places/things that trivialize, objectify and endanger women.
Donnelly/Colt Progressive Resources Catalogue
PO Box 188
Hampton, CT 06247
800-553-0006, 860-455-9621, fax: 800-553-0006

12

Ageism
WHEN BEAUTY, WISDOM, AND EXPERIENCE GET OLD

"Fair-skinned blacks invented 'passing' as a term, Jews escaping anti-Semitism perfected the art, and the sexual closet continues the punishment, but pretending to be a younger age is probably the most encouraged form of 'passing,' with the least organized support for coming out as one's true generational self."

—Gloria Steinem
Moving Beyond Words

Body Wars do not retire at the age of 65. In fact, for many people, they worsen. Dieting, plastic surgery, cosmetic use, hair coloring and replacement, and other appearance-altering techniques often escalate in the later years in attempts to defy the natural process of aging. This is in large part because, in a culture obsessed with youth, "old age" has negative implications, such as the loss of power, sexuality, and health, laziness, and mental decline. These stereotypes result in a devaluing of elderly people and their contributions—a phenomenon called ageism.

The Origins of Ageism

The notion that the American worker is automatically obsolete by age 65 has had a powerful impact on our beliefs about age and aging. Having systematically removed older Americans from positions of power and respect in the workplace, western culture has instilled a tremendous fear of wrinkles, gray hair, and birthdays despite demographic trends showing a steady increase in this population. For many, even passing age 30 is a sensitive issue.

In order to better understand why this is so, it helps to know the origins of this prejudice. In the 19th century, the German social security system established 65 as the age for retirement. At the time, average life expectancy was 37 years. A century later, although life expectancy doubled, people in their 60's were still considered obsolete; and, in 1935, the U.S. established a mandatory retirement age of 65. This was not due to concerns about the abilities or well-being of the elderly, but was rather an attempt to create jobs for younger people.[1] The link between obsolescence and age 65 soon became a simple legal way to winnow out more experienced and costly employees. In the current era of corporate downsizing to increase profit margin, ageism has become stronger than ever.

Today, legal protections exist for older workers, and retirement is no longer forced at 65, but age discrimination still thrives. Between the 1980's and 1990's, age-related legal complaints doubled.[2] But these days, the age at which this discrimination occurs begins earlier. By the time both male and female workers are in their 40's, they become easy targets for downsizing, despite laws that require equal training and opportunities for all ages. In fact, age-sizing more aptly describes the process, as seasoned workers who command more compensation are most apt to be eliminated. The message is clear: we best not look our age as we get older!

Anti-Aging Medicine

With one American turning 50 every 7.6 seconds,[3] products which promise the fountain of youth have enormous potential sales. One of the latest is human Growth Hormone injections (hGH), promising glowing skin, the metabolism of a teenager, and improved mood, sex drive, muscle mass, and mental abilities. Developed to treat dwarfism, hGH has been approved only for adult use, and specifically to treat rare hormone deficiencies or AIDS related wasting syndrome.[4] But among the worried wealthy, this hormonal supplement is the latest answer to the "problems" of aging, despite extremely limited research on safety or effectiveness.

The National Institute of Aging warns that hGH may contribute to diabetes, heart failure, elevated blood pressure, and the pooling of fluid in skin and tissues. Because it stimulates growth, it may lead to cancer cell formation, enlarged heart and bones, and joint problems, including carpal tunnel syndrome. Weekly injections cost $200-$400 each, driving annual costs as high as $20,000.[5]

The current market for hGH and other age-defying products illustrates our society's emphasis on staying young. In fact, a whole new branch of medicine is developing—the American Academy of Anti-Aging Medicine—which began with 12 members in 1993, and in five years boasted more than 4,300.[6] The tools of the trade include plastic surgery, hormones, and expensive nutritional supplements. The concept of "growing old gracefully" is meeting stiff opposition.

Ageism and Sexism

While ageism targets both sexes, women are hit hardest. For instance, when women enter mid-life, their social value rapidly diminishes compared to men. Without a youthful appearance, females are rarely considered beautiful by social standards and are taken even less seriously as they age.[7] This loss of status occurs earlier and faster for women than for men. Only those who appear

> *"That old women are repulsive is one of the most profound esthetic and erotic feelings in our culture. Women share it as much as men do...Like men, they find old age in women 'uglier' than old age in men."*
> **—Susan Sontag, feminist**

considerably younger than their age, either naturally or due to some body-altering technique, are considered attractive.

Also, as women age, their economic stability weakens, evidenced by the fact that females over 65 are poorer than males of the same age. Older women have usually earned less, and have a smaller pension or retirement plan, if any. If widowed, they receive only two-thirds of their husband's social security. Furthermore, more than 25% of white and 50% of black and Hispanic older women living alone are poor.[8]

Finally, society continues to place more emphasis on women's appearance than men's well into their later years. Hair coloring is far more common for women than for men, as are products that claim to erase wrinkles and age spots. Women represent 90% of the plastic surgery market, and outnumber men at every age when it comes to "going under the knife" to reverse aging.[9] Older women are also under continual pressure to be thin. A longitudinal study of people older than 62 found that concerns about weight were second only to concerns about memory loss for women, but were rarely mentioned by men.[10]

The Media's Role

Once again, the media is a major influence on our beliefs, in this case about growing older. When most of the sympathetic characters we see on the screen and in print are young, and ad after ad promotes products to keep us looking young, a youthful appearance becomes desirable. In the same way that waif-like models and diet ads create the idea that

> *"The only sanctioned image of a woman in the beauty culture is one who does not show her age. Older women are played by wrinkle-free younger women. Grown women are portrayed by adolescent girls."*
> —Linda McBryde, M.D., author, *The Mass Market Woman*

thin is "better" than fat, youth as commodity creates the belief that being young is more "valuable" than being old.

Advertising consistently uses teens and young adults to promote products that are designed for the older population. Anti-aging creams, hair dyes, even pain relief for arthritis are just some of the products that are promoted by actors who are usually younger than the target market. Lauren Hutton has revealed that as she began to age, she felt so invisible that she returned to modeling to force the industry to incorporate older women.[11]

SOME FACTS ABOUT AGEISM

Print Media

- Of 290 faces identified in one issue of *Vogue*, only one woman appeared over 50, while four older men were shown.

- Of 116 faces identified in one issue of *Vanity Fair*, only two females who appeared over age 60 were shown, while ten older males, all of whom were powerful or famous, were shown.

- Less than 10% of the men in an issue of *Esquire* appeared to be over age 60.[12]

Visual Media

- A survey of the characters on prime time TV over one week revealed that seven of 464 characters (1.5%) look to be in their 60s or older.

- In TV ads surveyed, roughly 2% of the actors look 60 or older.[13]

- Men of any age are more likely to be cast in movies, securing twice the number of roles as women. After 40, they receive three times as many roles as women.[14]

- In 1996, 18 films featured male leads over the age of 65, but only one had a female star that age.[15]

- In mid-life, women's earnings for films fall, while men's peak.[16]

- The characters on TV are younger now than they were five years ago, and there are more younger women/older men pairings.[17]

- Television women age faster, and older women are portrayed more negatively, even as evil, than are men.[18]

- On TV, women's career opportunities peak at the age of 30, then rapidly decline. Thirty-eight percent of male performers, compared to 25% of females, are at least 40 years old.[19]

Aging Does Not Equal Alzheimer's

In our culture, age is associated with sickness, dependence, and helplessness. Research focuses on the infirm, resulting in statistics that support this notion. Although we seldom hear about the active, healthy elderly who are enjoying their aging process, they do exist!

In fact, older Americans are a dynamic and powerful segment of the population. Over 323,000 participated in elder hostel camps and trips in 1996.[20] Seniors are taking computer classes, joining exercise programs, and returning to college in impressive numbers. They also represent a strong electoral force, well organized by the American Association of Retired Persons. In 1994, 45% of American voters over age 60 voted, while only 36% of those under 60 went to the polls.[21]

Why, then, isn't the voice of the elderly better heard? Perhaps because bad news sells, as illustrated by the way the media consistently emphasizes deterioration rather than vitality. Based on these negative messages, who would know that less than 5% of older Americans have Alzheimer's, or that less than 10% will ever be in a nursing home, with just 5% currently living in one.[22]

Today, Americans enjoy longer lives than ever before. Each year, life expectancy increases, demonstrating that our ideas about aging and human potential have not caught up with changing life expectations and demographics. Aging does not equal Alzheimer's. We have been misinformed by the propaganda that distorts a beautiful and natural process.

> *"We who are older have enormous freedom to speak out, and equally great responsibility to take the risks that are needed to heal and humanize our sick society...we can try new things and take on entirely new roles—dangerous roles."*
> —**Maggie Kuhn, Founder of the Gray Panthers**

Other cultures honor their elderly, awarding them special status for their wisdom, experience, and contributions to the community. If this were the case in the U.S., we might not have as many negative stereotypes associated with aging. We might welcome, or at least accept, the process of maturation, instead of waging war against it.

STRATEGIES FOR CHANGE

The following list provides some questions and ideas to help you understand your feelings about aging. Take time to reflect honestly.

- How do you feel about yourself at your current age?

- Do you lie about your age?

- What feelings come up as you consider getting older?

- Do you attempt to defy your natural aging process by purchasing products that promise to hide the signs?

- Make a list of anguished, resentful older people. Describe how their attitude might impact their quality of life.

- Make a list of peaceful, creative older people. Describe how their attitude might impact what they get out of life.

- Visualize yourself as an old person. Do you feel excited by the opportunities or distressed by the limitations?

Decide now what kind of an older person you want to be, and if you choose to commit to aging with acceptance, grace and dignity, feel the power behind that choice. Know that in handling your own aging process well, you show respect to others.

AGING BEAUTIFULLY

1. Develop a flexible beauty ideal. Remember that a negative body image is not a necessary side effect of getting older. Age can give you the confidence to create your own unique style.

2. Identify with realistic role models. Find older, unglamorous role models who are truly magnificent and hold them up as images with whom to identify. Counteract your own ageism and looksism by trying to see older women as total women.

3. Own up to your age. Age acceptance doesn't mean resigning yourself to the stereotype of ageism, but redefining those myths as time redesigns your body. If you learn to see yourself in terms of your total assets, not merely in terms of appearance, the loss of youthful beauty can be balanced by the accomplishments of age.

4. Hang on to your sensuality. Indulge your body in all the physical pleasures that you've earned by virtue of having lived this long. Keep enjoying the sensual side of movement and keep challenging your body with physical activity.

5. Use the wisdom you've acquired over the years. With maturity comes an understanding of what works well for you cosmetically, sexually, athletically, dietetically. This knowledge can help you nurture your aging body with attention and respect.

Reprinted with permission from *BodyLove* by R. Freedman New York, HarperCollins, 1988, p.186[23]

Ideas for action:

Pay attention to how your employer, community groups and other institutions treat older people; consider how they could fight the inherent ageism that leaks into our culture. Encourage corporations, institutions, legislators and other policy makers to make it easy and attractive for companies to hire older people to work part-time or as consultants or mentors, rather than eliminating them. Older people may enjoy working flexible hours part-time, or on special projects that reflect their interests and experiences. Job-sharing, temporary work pools or assignments, and phase-in retirement programs are great options. Companies that have experimented with such practices have reported positive results, including better

"Coming of age with dignity means looking as mature as we really are and still seeing ourselves as sensuous human beings."
—**Rita Freedman, author,** BodyLove

productivity, improved morale, decreased pension costs, a greater return on their investment in training employees, and lower turnover.[24] Explore employee reaction to these ideas by conducting a focus group and by providing companies or policy makers with alternative approaches to older workers.

Create a foster grandparent program in your community, linking senior citizens with children. Call your local senior citizen center or department of social services to see if any similar programs exist. If not, enlist their help with getting one started.

To assist elderly men and women to live as comfortably as possible, make sure that your local agencies and healthcare systems provide the services they need, i.e. Meals on Wheels, and programs for "shut-ins." Again, your local senior citizens center or department of social services should know what services are already provided, what is needed, and how to obtain funding and support for new programs. If your community has existing programs, become a volunteer. Through your church, community organizations, or social contacts, share your enthusiasm about getting to know and respect the elderly citizens in your community. Learn from the wisdom acquired over years by welcoming elderly people to share their oral histories.

RESOURCES

AARP (The American Association for Retired Persons)
Provides education, advocacy, and many services for people at or approaching retirement. They publish vital information regarding economic issues for older women through their Women's Initiative Publications List.
601 E. St., NW
Washington, DC 20049
202-434-227 or 800-424-3410
www.aarp.org

Equal Employment Opportunity Commission
To register complaints about age discrimination.
1801 L. St., NW
Washington, DC 20507
800-669-4000
You can also consult your local commission on Human Rights and Opportunities. If you work for a large corporation, the company will

have an equal opportunity agent on site. The federal law protects people over the age of 40 from being denied training, advancement, or other employment activities based on age.

National Institute on Aging
Educational information resources on a broad variety of topics.
9000 Rockville Pike
Bethesda, MD 20892
800-222-2225

The Gray Panthers
Founded by Maggie Kuhn in 1970 after she was forced to retire, promotes peace, justice, and social change by bringing the generations together rather than segregating the old.
PO Box 21477
Washington, DC 20009
202-737-6637
www.graypanthers.org

OWL (the Older Women's League)
Dedicated to promoting equity for women at mid-life and beyond. With over 70 local chapters, they have educational materials, publications, and a members newsletter.
666 11th St. NW, Suite 700
Washington, DC 20001
202-783-6686
www.owl-national.org

13

Women's Health Care

AN OXYMORON?

"The state of a woman's health is indeed completely tied up with the culture in which she lives and her position in it."
—Dr. Christiane Northrup,
Women's Bodies, Women's Wisdom

Traditional American medicine continues to disempower women. Reflecting the gender biases in the culture at large, the medical model views women's bodies as intrinsically flawed, and in need of control and intervention. Even the natural events of women's lives such as menstruation, pregnancy and menopause are considered problems to be solved rather than processes to be honored.

Despite all the achievements of modern medicine, our knowledge of women's bodies is extremely limited. Showing impressive disregard for other physiological systems or for the woman as a whole person, doctors historically have ignored anything other than reproductive functioning when studying or treating women, in effect, "operating in the dark." As one male physician said in the 1880's, "Almighty, in creating the female sex, (has) taken the uterus and built a woman around it."[1]

A century ago, the dominant culture viewed women as reproductive subjects. Today, they are sex objects. Not much has changed. In the world of medicine, respect for women's bodies has been, and remains, elusive—one more reason to engage in Body Wars.

The Right to be More Than a Uterus

In the 19th century, American medical practitioners developed rigid beliefs and practices regarding women's health care. Reproduction was thought to overshadow other interests of women, who were then considered "collections of reproductive organs."[2] Physicians discouraged athletic, educational, or intellectual activities during childbearing years, believing they would compromise ovarian functioning. Women were advised to stay in bed, avoid strenuous activity, and to rest much of the time, especially when menstruating. The Journal of the American Medical Association published an article in 1892 cautioning

> *"No woman can call herself free who does not own and control her own body."*
> **—Margaret Sanger, founder, Planned Parenthood**

that even singing during menses could impede the healthy functioning of the uterus.[3]

These sexist beliefs were reflected in a set of regulations called the Comstock laws, which banned any material mentioning contraception, abortion, or other "moral" issues, under the guise of controlling obscenity.[4] Although the real intent was to keep women barefoot, pregnant, and in the kitchen (or bedroom), the Comstock laws ironically inspired the women's rights movement of the early 20th century, leading to the battle for the right to vote, finally won in 1920.[5] Margaret Sanger, an early champion of reproductive rights and founder of Planned Parenthood, was an obstetrical nurse in New York City at the time. Sanger witnessed women barely survive poverty and poor health due to pregnancies, sexually transmitted diseases, and failed abortions. Like other feminists, she recognized the connection between health and political power—without one, women were denied the other.

The Uterus Business

Even today, women experience a host of medical, psychological, economic, and legal issues just because they have a uterus. Faced with increasingly complicated reproductive decisions during their childbearing years, women often feel intimidated by health care providers when they should feel supported.

Incredibly, more than a third of American women lose their uterus before the age of 50! Hysterectomy is the third most frequent surgical procedure of all, commonly recommended when women have (non-cancerous) fibroid tumors. Fibroids, which usually shrink at menopause, are a normal condition found in approximately 33% of premenopausal women. Less than 15% of hysterectomies are performed because of cancer or other life threatening conditions, but half result in surgical complications.[6] Fortunately, women with serious health challenges do have surgery as an option, yet many normal uteruses are removed every year. This shows what little respect medicine has for women's bodies.

Our legal system also contributes to women feeling a lack of control of their bodies when facing medical issues. The court can mandate procedures without a woman's consent, such as a Caesarean section for a pregnant woman who is ill. A newborn can be removed from a chemically dependent or otherwise "unfit" mother. Under the rubric of "fetal rights," physicians and judges can make decisions about a mother's medical care based on their own beliefs regarding the rights of the unborn.

> *"If you are an adult and are treated like one—whether you are buying insurance or organizing a business—you get the facts. In negotiating for their own health and safety, women deserve no less."*
> **—Naomi Wolf, author, in Minding the Body**

Finally, the one legal right critical to women's autonomy— the right to choose—has been increasingly challenged in the past decade. In 83% of counties and 70 of 305 metropolitan areas in the United States, a legal abortion is not available and federal funding does not allow abortions for poor women.[7] Even when it is legal and available, an abortion is not guaranteed to be safe, as protesters threaten women's lives before they even enter abortion clinics.

This pattern of ignoring or defying women's wishes regarding their medical care extends to many other issues, including decisions regarding termination of life supports. A review of 14 years of appellate court cases found that male requests to be removed from life supports were more frequently honored than similar wishes of women. Courts describe women as "immature" or non-reflective, whereas men are perceived as rational and decisive.[8] A vicious circle indeed, for until our system gives women back her right to choose what is best for her body, she has no option to be reflective. Without real choice, women cannot demonstrate the ability to make mature, thoughtful decisions.

WOMEN'S HEALTH CARE FACTS

• Women comprise the majority of health care consumers, and are most likely to make health care decisions in the family, as they influence 70% of all family health care and 80% of pediatric decisions.[9]

• Women make 90% of the calls to physicians or health information services.[10]

• Women represent over 65% of office visits and prescriptions.[11]

• Women represent 75% of nursing home residents and 66% of home health care recipients.[12]

• Women are more likely to spend their own money on health care.[13]

"It's All in Your Head"

In spite of the fact that women comprise the majority of health care consumers, when they do speak about what they know and feel, their health concerns are often trivialized. Physicians are twice as likely to discount female concerns by stating, "It's all in your head."[14] The results of such a cavalier approach can be fatal. In the past decade, cardiac related deaths for women have outnumbered men's, possibly because women are not taken seriously at the hospital. When they present with symptoms, such as general malaise and difficulty breathing—rather than severe chest pain typical of males with cardiac problems—women's concerns are often dismissed as anxiety. Similarly, abnormal treadmill results are twice as likely to be seen as "psychological" in women, while men's self report and test results are routinely believed by their primary care doctor.[15]

This gender gap is also evident in professional advertising. Women are the latest "niche market," exemplified by Wyeth Ayerst spending $9.2 million marketing Premarin—a hormone replacement used to "treat" menopause, making this natural process a defect to be attacked. It instantly became the best selling drug in America.[16] In medical journals, ads showing male physicians interacting with patients abound, but rarely is a female doctor highlighted. This skewed portrait reflects the dearth of women and particularly women of color in the higher ranks of medical and academic institutions. When women are portrayed in medical advertising, they appear like most other female models—rail thin. In illustrations, older women look depressed and anxious, and younger ones sexy and voluptuous.

Women are more likely to be naked, with full body exposure; men who are unclothed show only their torsos. Ads for psychotropic medicines in these journals feature women 80% of the time and, in turn, women receive 80% of the mood- or mind-altering medications prescribed by primary care doctors.[17]

The Gender Gap

Until recently, few American women knew that the medical treatment they receive today is largely based on knowledge about the male, and not the female, body. Much research has excluded women from clinical and pharmaceutical trials. This focus on men is rationalized by the increased costs of recruiting both sexes and analyzing more data, as well as women's fluctuating hormones, and liability concerns about pregnancy during clinical trials. Furthermore, women report more drug-related side-effects, possibly confabulating the data. Women weigh less than men on average and metabolize medications differently, but research on men determine the standard dosages and put women's bodies in constant peril.

"This is the part of health history that is most distasteful: the use of the medical, biological, and anatomical sciences to keep women in their place."
—**Leslie Laurence and Beth Weinhouse, authors,**
Outrageous Practices

In practice, male subjects are the universal standard used to generalize findings to all other groups, despite obvious differences. Bias is glaring in the lopsided ratio of males in research on heart and lung disease, despite that these are among the leading causes of death in American women. Investigation on the following common practices have never included women: taking one aspirin a day to avoid heart attacks; the effects of cholesterol-lowering drugs or oat bran on cardiac health; benefits of cardiac surgery; behavioral changes to reduce cardiac risk.[18] In the 1980's, the National Institutes of Health (NIH) elected to deny funding on a study examining the link between dietary fat and breast cancer, based on inconclusive findings on males who were unable to make necessary dietary changes for the purposes of the trial. Although preliminary findings in females yielded far different results, studying this at-risk population was not deemed a priority.[19]

Gender Gap Damage

The repercussions of the gender gap in medical research are serious and potentially deadly. Women suffer twice the number of fatal drug responses since their bodies metabolize cardiovascular, anti-inflammatory, and central nervous system medications differently.[20] Differences in physiology, such as variations in brain structure, body weight and composition, and cerebral blood flow also impact treatment response; for example, fat-soluble medications stay in women's systems longer due to their higher percentage of body fat.

In many cases, limited information guides major medical decisions. The new fertility drugs and in-vitro fertilization techniques are the latest medical practices with significant risk, particularly for ovarian cancer. Unaware of the paucity of long-term research, women take these drugs and undergo these invasive procedures daily. Ovarian cancer is the deadliest reproductive cancer, which kills nearly 15,000 American women each year. Yet today, no effective screening exists.[21] Take note that most well-known, medical product liability cases involve feminine concerns, such as the Dalkon Shield, super-absorbent tampons and toxic shock syndrome, silicone breast implants, thalidomide, and DES, a synthetic estrogen used to prevent miscarriage between the late 1940's and early 1970's.[22]

Once medications or medical procedures are approved, they are administered freely, regardless of their unknown effects on women. One example is the widespread use of DES. Although the drug trials never included females, between three and six million pregnant women took DES under doctor's orders. Their daughters have experienced a high incidence of gynecological cancers, fertility and other health problems.[23] The effects may even be multi-generational, as some DES granddaughters are now suffering increased incidence of tubal pregnancies, miscarriage, premature births, and immune system disorders.[24]

MORE FACTS ABOUT WOMEN'S HEALTH CARE

- Some heart medications are less effective and more dangerous for women.[25]

- Women are less likely to receive cardiac catheterization, angioplasty, and bypass surgery and more likely to die on the operating table. Most of these procedures and technologies were developed on men who have larger blood vessels.[26]

• Lung cancer is the deadliest cancer for both sexes, but men are more likely to be screened.[27]

• Women with kidney disease are less likely to receive dialysis or transplants.[28]

• Gastrointestinal disease and arthritis are three times more frequent in women; lupus is nine times more frequent. Little research has been done to explain these discrepancies. 27% of women aged 65-85 have two chronic diseases and 24% have three.[29]

• A woman having unprotected sex contracts STD's (sexually transmitted diseases) twice as frequently as a man. The younger the woman, the higher the risk due to immature cervical tissue. Most federal money for screening and detection has gone to men.[30]

• STDs cause more illness for women than AIDS causes for men, women, and children combined.[31]

Diversity and the Gender Gap

Minority women and women in poverty are at an even greater disadvantage when it comes to being the focus or the beneficiaries of research. Poor women have actually been over-represented in invasive clinical research, but under-represented in more routine trials. In 1973 the Southern Poverty Law Center filed a suit on behalf of women sterilized against their will. These subjects are recruited through inner-city hospitals staffed by physicians affiliated with medical schools, yet they are not systematically included in clinical studies for the purpose of representative sampling. For instance, women of color and low income women have only minimally participated in research on Cardiovascular Disease (CVD), and thus the impact of race and low socioeconomic status on CVD has been understudied.

In 1975, the National Women's Health Network was founded "to develop a strong women's voice in the national political arena and to provide women a source of balanced information on health issues."[32] The Network's goals were consistent with those of the women's health movement: to unite women around shared health concerns. However, diversity in women's health was not formally recognized until 1981, when African American health activist Byllye Avery founded the National Black Women's Health Project (NBWHP), an international self-help and health advocacy organization, to address the specific needs of black women. The National Latina Health Organization was founded in 1986, followed by the National Native American Women's Health and Education Resource Center in 1988. These initiatives focused on the social construction of health; however, they were isolated attempts to shed light on differences in biomedical research.

Research has been largely dedicated to white, upper-middle class values and priorities and has eschewed testing of hypotheses about the relationships among several variables. Lifestyle factors, such as diet, smoking, and exercise, have a greater impact on risk for disease in women than in men. Meanwhile, the ostensibly objective science of medicine systematically ignores race, class, and gender as conditions influencing the health of women. The shift in consciousness away from the medical model, which views "health" as the absence of disease and illness, and towards a more holistic view which encompasses relationships, institutions, lifestyle choices, violence, and culture, as well as genetic and biological determinants of health, has only occurred in the last decade, since women have begun to play a more pivotal role. Today, although women represent 70% of the workforce in health care and 40% of medical students, less than 10% are full professors, and less than 3% are medical school deans.[33] However, according to the AMA, in the year 2010, one-third of all physicians will be women.[34] Now policy and action must fill in the gaps in gender biased research so that research will guide education, intervention, prevention and treatments as well as support political power on behalf of women.

Throughout the 20th century, women have continued to make headway in the fight for equal rights. Following suffrage came Title VII of the Civil Rights Act of 1964, which outlawed sex discrimination in employment. In 1972, Title IX of the Education Amendments prohibited sex discrimination in public and private schools that receive federal dollars. The inclusion of sexual harassment in the Civil Rights Act of 1991

"It is very little to me to have the right to vote, to own property, etcetera, if I may not keep my body and its uses, in my absolute right."
—Lucy Stone, suffragette

also promoted gender equality. More recently, women's entry in the political arena, universities, and in the medical profession as practitioners and research scientists has created champions of women's health policy. In the early 1990's, after considerable effort from women's health advocates, the National Institute of Health began to address the critical issue of gender bias. Now the NIH bans funding for any exclusionary studies. It also has established the Office of Women's Health and has dedicated $625 million to the Women's Health Initiative, a 15-year study of 150,000 women.[35] However, even though the medical community is beginning to show some respect for the uniqueness of women's bodies, it is past time for women to be respected and treated with compassion by the health care industry—in every situation, at all times. Only then will the medical Body Wars cease.

STRATEGIES FOR CHANGE

Today's health care system, lacking in many areas, does not always provide its patients with adequate information. Relying on medical experts to inform your decisions may not be wise, since their knowledge base does not always include a good understanding of women's health. You, therefore, must be an active participant in your own health care.

- Become a critical consumer and your own advocate. Take time to recognize your risk factors for disease based on your family history, and explore the roles of lifestyle and nutrition in keeping you well. When dealing with a health issue, ask (lots of) questions. Let your doctors get tired of answering! If they refuse to discuss certain issues, treat you with disrespect, or act as if they know more than you sense they do, find a new doctor.

- Learn about your insurance policy, particularly the coverage of services and the schedule for preventive and early detection procedures, such as mammograms. If you have medical needs that are not covered, request them and explain why you need the service. Ask your doctor to advocate for you. Appeal any rejected claims through the company, but do not hesitate to write a letter to the state insurance commissioner, with copies to your legislator, legislative committees (both insurance and public health) and the local media; insurance companies and health maintenance organizations do not like negative press.

- Fight for good medical care for all women. Today, more than 12 million American women have no medical coverage and millions more have inadequate benefits.[37] Advocate for health care reform that ensures universal access, affordability, and a range of services from prevention to long-term care.

- Become a community activist by seeing that women and their interests are included on any health care planning boards or committees.

- Support Planned Parenthood and other organizations that serve women.

- Encourage your local hospital to develop a high quality women's center so care can be integrated rather than fragmented.

- Form an *ad-hoc* committee to identify the health needs of women in your community.

- Work with health care organizations to develop and disseminate information for women that will help keep them and their families healthy.
- Partner with local high schools, colleges, or organizations like the YWCA on projects to educate young women about behavior and lifestyle issues (such as exercise, nutrition, birth control and smoking) that can improve their health.

RESOURCES

American Association of University Women
Dedicated to gender equity, including health care.
1111 16th St., NW.
Washington, DC. 20036
202-785-7712
www.aauw.org

Boston Women's Health Book Collective
Advocacy organization to promote women's role in health care policy decision making. Publishes periodic updates of seminal work, *Our Bodies, Ourselves.*
240 A Elm St.
Somerville, MA 02144
617-628-3030/Info. Center 617-625-0271

Harvard Medical School Health Publications
Publishes a monthly newsletter for women:
Harvard Women's Health Watch
164 Longwood Ave.
Boston, MA 02115-5818
617-432-1485
www.harvard.edu./publications/Health_Publications

National Abortion Rights Action League
Supporting reproductive freedom.
1156 15th St. NW., #700
Washington, DC. 20005
202-973-3000

National Black Women's Health Project (NBWHP)
Dedicated to improving the health of black women. Publishes quarterly newsletter, *Vital Signs.*
1237 Ralph David Abernathy Blvd., SW
Atlanta, GA 30310
800-ASK-BWHP or 407-758-9590

National Institute of Health
Office of Research on Women's Health
Bldg. 1, Room 201
9000 Rockville Pike
Bethesda, MD 20892-0161
301-402-1770

National Institute of Health
Women's Health Initiative
Federal Building, Room 6A09
9000 Rockville Pike
Bethesda, MD 20892
301-402-2900

Native American Women's Health Education Resource Center
Dedicated to the health needs of Native American Women.
PO Box 572
Lake Andes, SD 57356
605-487-7072

Planned Parenthood
Reproductive, educational and health service reaching 5 million women each year.
810 Seventh Ave.
New York, NY 10019
800-829-7732 - general info.
800-230-7526 - to locate your local office
www.plannedparenthood.org

Women's Health Network
514 10th St NW, Ste. 400
Washington, DC 20004
202-347-1140
202-628-7814 (information line)
www.womenshealthnetwork.org

Health Wisdom for Women Newsletter
Dr. Christiane Northrup
Discusses alternative healing remedies and the impact emotions have on women's health.
Phillips Publishing Inc.
7811 Montrose Rd.
PO Box 60110
Potomac, MD 20897-5924
800-804-0935

To find the name of your state insurance commissioner, look in the government section of your phone book and call the insurance commissioner's office. To identify the chairpersons and members of the insurance and public health committees, contact your state representative or state senator. They should be listed in your phone book in the government section. Remember, your representatives work for you and they depend on your vote. Let them know your concerns about women's health and about Body Wars.

14

Kids on Diets
AN EARLY START FOR BODY WARS

*"I really wanted, needed, my dad to be proud of
me. I wasn't sure how to get that, but I know he
thought being thin was good, so I started to diet.
It showed self-control and all the things he
valued. I nearly ruined my body."*
—recovered anorexic in *Father Hunger*
by Margo Maine

According to the book of Genesis, Eve's conflict centered
around whether or not to eat an apple. Amazingly, millions of
today's children still agonize over a choice this simple. Plagued
by body insecurity in a culture of "ideals," they are dieting,
overexercising, getting plastic surgery, and abusing food, steroids, laxatives and diet pills—just like the adults. Body Wars
don't discriminate: they target all ages.

CHILDREN, WEIGHT & APPEARANCE

- In a study of nine to eleven-year-olds, 46% said they were sometimes, or very often, on diets; 82% reported that their families were sometimes, or very often, on diets.[1]

- Few female adolescents like their shape. The norm now is for girls to feel unhappy about their bodies and to feel fat even when they are average or low in weight.[2]

- Typically, girls see themselves as less attractive than their peers, while boys see themselves as more attractive. Twice as many girls as boys want to change their appearance, and girls are dissatisfied with more body parts.[3]

- The number one wish for females 11 to 17 is to lose weight.[4]

- A recent study of fourth grade girls revealed that 80% had already dieted.[5] Another study found that weight and body image concerns were present in girls as young as seven.[6]

Not suprisingly, parents often feel powerless and doomed when it comes to Body Wars. They perceive the influence of the world outside the home, especially the images in the media, as more influential than anything they can do or say. Stressors such as drugs and alcohol, unsafe sex, and college tuition overwhelm parents who are uncertain about where to devote their parenting energy. Many simply don't know what to say.

However, families can be safe environments and parents must not underestimate the power of communication, in both what they do and say. By talking to children about weight and health issues, parents can buffer society's harmful messages. First, in order to avoid inadvertently contributing to a child's body shame, parents must examine their own feelings and prejudices. Then, they should share what they have learned with their kids and incorporate that into their lives as a group. Parents who model size acceptance and healthy attitudes about food and eating are the front line of the battle against Body Wars. Prevention begins at home.

Dieting in Utero

Dieting and weight concerns are so pervasive in American culture that some infants are born having already experienced a diet! Although we now know the dangers of inadequate weight gain to fetal development, many pregnant women restrict their eating during pregnancy to avoid "getting fat." Minimal weight gain can result in low-weight infants who have a mortality rate six times that of normal-weight infants, as well as poor mental, physical and motor performance.[7]

An expectant parent who is weight-preoccupied jeopardizes a baby's health right from the start. Later, he or she might feed the baby inconsistently, sometimes overfeeding, other times underfeeding, often in a hurried, tense manner.[8] Food easily becomes an emotional issue rather than fuel for growth, setting the stage for eating problems.

In a study of 1400 new parents, many were unaware that infants need fat to grow, or that babies' nutritional needs are greater than adults.[9] Healthy infants triple their weight and double their height in their first year. Fat and cholesterol are essential to the development of the brain and nervous system. In this regard, breast milk is ideal because half of its calories come from fat.

Many young mothers are proud of their baby's chubby cheeks, but have to argue with family members and pediatricians who question that a round baby can be a healthy baby. One mother told me that her pediatrician had not been concerned about the weight of her first child, a big boy, but suggested her second child—a girl—be put on a diet at the age of four months! This mother was wise enough to ignore that advice, and to consider changing pediatricians.

When Parents Encourage Dieting

Some parents who want the best for their children encourage dieting, because they truly believe it will help them succeed. Realizing that fat people face the threat of discrimination, teasing, and stigma, they want to protect their loved ones from that pain. They also know that thin kids are considered more attractive and have a competitive edge both academically and socially. In magazines and newspapers they see questions like, "Is weight holding your daughter back?"[10] While such an ad might not cause parents to enroll their child in a weight loss camp, it may create the belief that they should "control" his or her weight.

Parents may project their own body dissatisfaction onto their children. A mother who dislikes her body will help foster in her daughter the same inclination. A weight- or image-preoccupied father will engender the belief in his child that appearance, weight, and shape are critical to earning dad's love. Parents who criticize each other's bodies or compare them to thinner counterparts are drafting their children into future Body Wars.

Adults who live in the war zone of body dissatisfaction do not trust their own body's urges for food. They do not appreciate the self-regulatory function of the human body. Babies instinctively stop eating when they have had enough and signal to the feeder by turning away from the spoon and closing their mouth. Over time, children naturally eat an appropriate amount and variety of foods if given the opportunity to respond to body cues.[11]

"We cannot expect individual fat kids to rise up courageously and silence their tormentors any more than we expect children of color to defend against racist comments all by themselves. I know it may seem scary to speak up. If it scares us, think how fat children must feel."
—Marilyn Wann, author, *Fat!So?*

Parents who distrust their own appetites distrust their children's appetites, too. They often become overinvolved in their children's eating patterns, making them consume certain foods, at specific times, in particular quantities. Imposing set ways of eating is not a good idea because it suggests that parents know children's feelings better than they do. This ignores children's individual preferences and disrespects their desire for autonomy and self-control. It also alienates children from their bodies by preventing them from recognizing their natural hunger and fullness cues.

Children acutely experience the dilemma of how much to satisfy the self and how much to please other people. When it comes to food, this can be trouble. Eating or not eating for others can lead to disordered eating because it interferes with self-awareness and self-regulation. Instead of children being the experts about their bodies and feelings, someone else is. This can generalize to other areas of life and, soon, a youngster can feel confused, insecure, and overly dependent on what others think. The "clean-plate club" can be dangerous! For youngsters, being in charge of one's own food intake is a building block to feeling capable, competent, and confident. Learning to trust one's body and appetite is an important step in healthy development.

Dieting—A Misguided Solution

The number of overweight children in this country is on the rise. Currently, almost 25% of children in the United States are obese, an increase of 50% in the past 20 years.[12] Many factors contribute to this inflation, but dieting is not a solution. Dieting actually contributes to the problem by lowering basic metabolic rates, leading to weight gain.[13] Furthermore, childhood fat is not necessarily an indicator of obesity or of poor health in adulthood.

Our sedentary lifestyles, characterized by hours in front of the computer and television screens, are a prime contributor to excess weight in childhood. In fact, the degree of fatness in children is directly related to the number of hours of television watched.[14] Not only are kids inactive, but they often snack due to boredom or in response to tempting food commercials. Most studies indicate that heavier children may not necessarily eat more, but they are less active than their peers.[15]

Problems with weight also reflect emotional issues. Like adults, some children overeat or undereat in response to depression or stress. They may overeat to soothe themselves when they are upset, frightened, anxious, or sad, or undereat to feel a sense of control or direction. When kids gain or lose a considerable amount of weight, though, parents should step in and talk about what is going on in their lives and how they are feeling. A diet is rarely the answer. Therapy may be.

In some cases, family interactions and conflicts can contribute to eating issues. Several studies of plus-size adolescents point to a lack of connection and communication in the family as major problems. As the family becomes more distant, less talkative, and less supportive, and the adolescent withdraws, the risk for obesity increases.[16] In these cases, interventions to improve emotional expression and relationships in the family are more useful than prescriptions for diet and exercise.

Further, if emotional or familial problems are present, the deprivation, the withholding, and the judgment involved in the dieting process

> "Kids need to know that dieting is like having just a couple of cigarettes. You might get hooked."
> —Marcia Herrin, Nutritionist, Dartmouth College

can interfere with a positive parent-child relationship. A child who is not allowed candy or chips may crave them and then overeat to get back at parents who are controlling. Secretive eating can lead to dishonesty and guilt.

While childhood dieting might appear to be a straightforward solution to a simple problem, food, fat, and feelings are a tangled web. Putting a child on a diet will never be the solution for the lifestyle trends that contribute to obesity, nor will it resolve the emotional issues that trigger unhealthy eating habits.

When Kids Want to Diet

In a culture of Body Wars, many children learn to dislike their bodies at an early age. Kids in preschool, kindergarten, and early elementary grades are already criticizing their bodies, striving to lose weight, and fearing fat and its symbolic meaning. By the age of eight or nine, many have developed serious eating disorders. What a challenge for parents! Children who talk about hating their bodies need a tremendous amount of encouragement, support, redirection, and guidance in building self-awareness and self-esteem independent of body size and shape.

Girls typically succumb to pressures to diet earlier than boys. When girls enter seventh grade, they are often ahead of their male peers physically, academically, and emotionally. They are outspoken in their beliefs and confident in themselves. Shortly therafter, however, as girls' sexual characteristics take shape, much of their strength and zest are lost. Adults seem less available for close connections; boys are growing even more rambunctious and demanding, and the world suddenly feels unsafe. New demands for competition, aggression, and independence often do not feel right. Many girls report feeling depressed and inadequate. They may blame their changing figures, and strive to control their shape to compensate for a lack of control in other areas.

Most girls do not realize that, during puberty, their bodies need to gain, on average, 10 inches and 40 to 50 pounds, including more body fat.[17] Females need 17% body fat in order to menstruate for the first time and 22% to have regular cycles.[18] Their hips and breasts blossom, changing their body shape. Girls who mature earlier are prone to diet in the attempt to arrest daunting, however natural, development. Much of the identity confusion and feelings of powerlessness and insecurity that accompany adolescence get transferred to the body. Encouraged by Body Wars, girls translate a variety of complicated emotions into the simple language of fat.[19]

> *"Study after study shows that girls know, in spite of the overt messages of success and achievement proffered them, that their body is their most valuable commodity; indeed they believe it defines them."*
> —**Peggy Ornstein, author,** *Schoolgirls*

Regardless of sex, physical development is an uneven, bumpy progression. Parents need to accept pubescence as tumultuous, learn about it, discuss it, and normalize it. Some kids gain weight before puberty and then slim down, others gain weight later. Boys may also struggle with developmental changes. If they are fat, peers may challenge their masculinity, particularly when it comes to sports. If they are of slight build, however, boys may be teased. Although they enter puberty later, usually adding 12 inches and 50 to 60 pounds, boys primarily add muscle and lean tissue as opposed to fat.[20] This does not mean that boys are immune to the pressure to achieve a certain "look." Many males exercise obsessively and engage in binge eating followed by restrictive eating. Others substitute protein powders and other supplements for meals. Over one-quarter million male high school seniors report abusing steroids![21] Eating disorders are on the rise among all males, who have their own Body Wars to fight!

Still, girls report more negative feelings about themselves than do boys. Certainly, media images and irresponsible advertising compound the challenges of growing up female in America. Young girls, in the delicate process of forging an identity, are the targets of endless marketing. Shopping for a self amidst Body Wars is a treacherous undertaking. Only those with blinders on could expect girls to go through adolescence without some feelings of vulnerability about appearance and weight.

Dieting Danger Zone

Our culture fails to protect children when it treats them like adults. It is bad enough that adults are subjected to endless imperatives to change their bodies; it is unconscionable that children are scrutinized and reprimanded for growing into their bodies. Not only do we overwhelm kids with ads that suggest that they should be suspicious and critical of their natural bodies, we also promote the idea that their bodies are biological miniatures of adults. In fact, children's food and nutrient needs far exceed those of adults, and the dangers of dieting are more serious.

When youngsters restrict their intake, they may delay puberty and arrest their growth permanently. Some childhood dieters develop eating disorders that will consume years of their lives. In the short run, kids who do not eat enough can have poor concentration, irritability, mood swings, weakness, dizziness, fainting, nausea, constipation, or diarrhea. In the long run, they can permanently retard growth, sexual maturation, and miss the joys and challenges of normal development. [22] Dieting for control, self-improvement, and happiness is misguided and counterproductive, leaving dieters of all ages feeling worse.

"It used to be women, teenage girls, who were ashamed, but now you see the shame down to very young girls—10, 11 years old. Society's standard of beauty is an image that is literally just short of starvation for most women."
—Mary Pipher, author,
Reviving Ophelia

Whether fat or thin, whether the diet is self-imposed or imposed by others, children who undereat are plagued by self-doubt and dissociation. What a price to pay!

STRATEGIES FOR CHANGE

Assess your attitude toward children's bodies. Do you treat a thin child more favorably than a fat one? Does the child's gender make a difference? If you are an educator, childcare worker, or involved directly with children, consider how your feelings about their bodies affect your interactions with them.

Remember that people come in all shapes and sizes. A large child who has grown in a smooth, predictable way, is probably biologically programmed to be big. A sudden increase in weight can be transient, or it can be a sign of external stress or depression. Never, ever suggest or impose a diet. If a child is gaining weight rapidly, observe his or her eating habits, particularly in response to feelings and access to high fat foods. Provide alternatives, without entirely excluding favorite foods. Limit time in front of the TV or computer and help the child find other activities for entertainment. Most importantly, pay attention to the child's emotional state. Could the eating be a sign of anxiety or depression? Nurture your child with attention and a willingness to listen, rather than with diet suggestions.

If you are concerned your child has an eating problem, discuss this privately with your pediatrician. If the doctor wants to place the child on a diet or suggests medications such as diet pills, get a second opinion from a behavioral pediatrician who is more likely to understand the connections between emotions, behaviors, and health.

Also, children need education and preparation for the changes their bodies will experience as they mature. They need to know (and to be reminded often) that their weight is going to increase and that they must consume fat. Both boys and girls need education about the dangers of dieting so they will understand their body's needs for adequate nutritional intake and balance and will trust their appetites. Be sure to give them this information.

Finally, keep the lines of communication open! Talking to children about these important issues is a way of immunizing them against future Body Wars.

Good Intentions Turned Bad

Family and friends, coaches and teachers sometimes say damaging things with the best intentions—and the message can be powerful: someone who loves you a lot thinks there is something wrong with your body. Now, be honest, have you heard yourself saying things like this?

Don't eat that—it'll go right to your hips.
You could stand to lose some weight.
Pull in your stomach—you'll look better.
You're getting a little chunky. Might want to go on a diet!
That makes you look fat. Wear this—it hides more.
You're not going to make the team if you keep eating.
I only want you to be happy—are you sure you need that snack?
You're going to have to watch your weight—we all have to.
You body is just like (mine, your father's, your grandmother's), so you'd better *be careful.*
It's a shame—you have such nice features.
You know you're going to have to work hard to stay thin.

The next time you are tempted to warn a child to watch their weight, remember how important it is for them to trust their bodies and their appetites, to feel good enough. Give them a loving message of concern and affection that has nothing to do with weight, shape, and appearance. Let them know you love them as they are. If you feed your child's soul, the body will take care of itself. Don't let your good intentions backfire and cause a Body War.

The following "Ten Tactics for Healthy Eating" offers some ideas on how to keep Body Wars out of your home.

TEN TACTICS FOR HEALTHY EATING

1. Always provide and encourage children to taste a wide variety of foods.

2. Avoid dichotomizing food into "good" or "bad," "healthy" or "unhealthy." Any food in moderation is acceptable.

3. Introduce new foods slowly, in small portions.

4. Never insist that children eat foods or amounts that they refuse.

5. Serve meals and snacks at predictable, regular intervals. If your child is hungry at other times, be sure to honor this natural hunger.

6. Trust your child's appetite. It often surges right before a growth spurt, and wanes at other times.

7. Make mealtimes pleasant. Do not use them as a time to discuss conflicts or to administer punishments. We attend best to internal cues when we are relaxed.

8. Keep food a neutral part of your life. Do not use it to reward or punish other behaviors. If you do, food will take on a symbolic meaning that might contribute to overeating or undereating.

9. Avoid focusing on weight, dieting, and body hatred in your conversations.

10. Cultivate a healthy relationship with food yourself, without fearing or abusing it.

Twelve Strategies to Make Your Home a Refuge from Body Wars

1. Stop obsessing about your own weight and appearance. Discover other, more important things about yourself. Seek out a therapist if you feel you need professional support.

2. Become aware of the negative comments or teasing about body weight and shape that take place in your home. Talk about them.

3. Create rules about teasing. Make teasing or insulting others based on weight and looks off-limits.

4. Show respect for others no matter what their size or shape. Make a list of people you admire and why. Share this with your children so they will learn that in this era of glamor, models, and Body Wars, it is what is on the inside that counts.

5. Be careful of how you judge people's bodies. Don't place more emphasis on appearance than on achievements.

6. Become aware of what your school system is teaching kids about health and weight. Be sure it is a comprehensive health promotion approach rather than the thin-is-good, fat-is-bad model. Posting weights, body fat analyses, and Body Mass Indexes only increases the shame and ambivalence kids feel about their bodies.

7. Turn off the television or watch with your children. Discuss what you see that relates to weight prejudice, dieting, etc.

8. Become critical consumers; do not buy products that contribute to Body Wars.

9. Write letters to companies and editors when you see images or ads that could hurt your children.

10. Have books on women's history and biographies of positive female role models around the house. Stow or get rid of magazines with advertisements or copy that might be damaging.

11. Recognize the contributions women make to your community, your personal life, and our culture; once we show respect for them as human beings, their bodies will be less important to all of us.

12. Learn as much as you can about adolescent development so you can support your kids through the time in which they are most at risk for Body Wars.

RESOURCES

Girls, Incorporated
Has many local chapters where girls gather.
30 East 33rd St.
New York, NY 10016
(212) 689-3700

Girl Scouts of the USA
420 Fifth Ave.
New York, NY 10018-2702
212-223-0624
www.gsusa.org

Feeding with Love and Good Sense
A series of four 15 minute videos about feeding children from infnacy to preschool.

Ellen Satter Associates
4226 Mandan Crescent
Madison, WI 53711
800-808-7976
www.ellynsatter.com

Books for Kids:

Girl Power in the Mirror
Cordes, H., Minneapolis, MN, Lerner Publishing, 2000.

Perfectionism: What's Bad about Being Too Good
Adderholdt-Elliott, M., Minneapolis, MN, Free Spirit Publishing, 1987.

Real Gorgeous: The Truth about Body and Beauty
Cooke, K., New York, W.W. Norton, 1996.

What's Happening to My Body: A Book for Girls
Madares, L., Madares, A., New York, Newmarket Press, 1998.

What's Happening to My Body: A Book for Boys
Madares, L., Saavedra, D., New York, Newmarket Press, 1998.
The companion workbooks are called, *My Body, My Self for Girls* and *My Body, My Self for Boys*. New York, Newmarket Press, 1993.

Books for Parents:

Preventing Childhood Eating Problems
Hirschmann, J., Zaphiropoulos, L., Carlsbad, CA, Gürze Books, 1993.

When Girls Feel Fat
Friedman, S., Toronto, HarperCollins, 1997.

Am I Fat? Helping Young Kids Accept Differences in Body Size
Ikeda, J., Naworski, P., Santa Cruz, CA: ETR Associates, 1992.

Father Hunger
Maine, M., Carlsbad, CA, Gürze Books, 1991.

How to Get Your Kid to Eat but Not Too Much
Satter, E., Palo Alto, CA, Bull Publishing, 1987.

Like Mother, Like Daughter: How Women are Influenced by Their Mother's Relationship with Food and How to Break the Pattern.
Waterhouse, D., New York, Hyperion, 1997.

Working as a Team to Enhance Eating Habits and Self-Esteem
Waterhouse, B., Portland, ME, Waterhouse Publications, 1997.

Afraid to Eat: Children and Teens in Weight Crisis
Berg, F., Hettinger, ND, Healthy Weight Journal, 1997.

Reviving Ophelia: Saving the Selves of Adolescent Girls
Pipher, M., New York, Putnam, 1994.

If My Child is Too Fat, What Should I Do? (a booklet)
by Joann Ikeda. Order: 501-642-2790.

Children and Weight and Family Choices for Good Health
(easy reading booklets)
by Joann Ikeda and Rita Mitchell
ANR Publications
University of California
6701 San Pablo Ave.
Oakland, CA 94608
510-642-2431

15

Barbie Dolls & Body Image
TOYS ARE US

"For women under 40…Barbie is a direct reflection of the cultural impulses that formed us. Barbie is our reality…Barbie is us."
—M.G. Lord from *Forever Barbie: The Unauthorized Biography of a Real Doll*

As symbols of a particular era, toys reveal deeply embedded cultural values which are handed down from one generation to the next. Psychologists consider toys to be transitional objects that both stimulate and comfort children as they progress from one developmental phase to the next, particularly as they move away from their parents into the world. What does Barbie™ symbolize in the minds of children?

™ Barbie is a registered trademark of Mattel Toys.

Barbie is not just a toy that girls outgrow and throw away. Rather, this pencil-thin doll looms as a standard of perfection, preventing girls from being content in their own bodies and, thereby, keeping "women in their place."

Who is Barbie?

Barbie, introduced by Mattel in 1959, has been a prominent force in the fantasy life of girls raised in western nations since mid-century. In 1993, $1.2 billion dollars worth of dolls and her accessories were sold.[1] Mattel estimates that two dolls are sold every second. Annual sales surveys indicate that Barbie is always in the Top 10 of toy sales, frequently first or second.[2]

The average American girl has at least one Barbie by the time she is three years old,[3] and collects seven Barbies during her childhood,[4] when body image and gender roles are rapidly forming. As growing girls adjust to their changing bodies, attempt to accept their maturing shape, and figure out what is important about being female, Barbie accompanies them every step of the way.

How does Barbie Measure Up?

Exceptionally tall, but with a child's size three foot permanently molded in a high-heeled position, Barbie's measurements read 39-18-33. Barbie calls this a "full figure," adding that "at 5'9," my happiest weight is 110 pounds."[5] A minimum expected weight for that height is 145 pounds; 110 pounds poses medical risk. Contoured with no body fat or belly, a human Barbie could not menstruate. Her indented ribcage could only be achieved through plastic surgery and the removal of ribs. In fact, Barbie has lost weight since she was created in 1959.[6]

Barbie's accessories, replete with sexy, form-fitting outfits, accessories, and games, reinforce her messages about women's bodies. Slumber Party Barbie (1965) came with a bathroom scale permanently set at 110 pounds, and a book, "How to Lose Weight," with the direction inside, "Don't Eat." In contrast, the Ken doll's outfit came with a sweet roll and milk. A later version came with an exercise video to assist Barbie in maintaining her shape. Since body image is strongly correlated with social expectations, these messages about body size, dieting, and appearance lay the groundwork for a girl's negative body image.

> *"You never hear little girls saying, 'When I grow up I want to be Madeleine Albright (the first female Secretary of State).' Instead, they are all fixated on Barbie."*
> **—Adrienne Ressler, body image therapist**

Barbie was introduced at about the same time as Body Wars, when beauty standards for women were shrinking. A year after her creation, Overeaters Anonymous was born, and in 1961 Weight Watchers emerged. Barbie reinforces cultural messages in ever younger children who are stuck in a diet mentality and body dissatisfaction.

Is Barbie Changing?

In the fall of 1997, Mattel announced that Barbie is due a makeover! A company spokesman denied that this response is connected with consumer complaints, but organizations like Women Insisting on Natural Shapes (WINS) have been campaigning for years for an end to Barbie's absurd body proportions. Changes will include smaller breasts and hips, a larger waist, less make-up, and closed lips to replace the "kiss-me-now" look. Mattel, however, has not announced the specifics, and assures us that the current model will still be the prototype for their special dolls, such as "the princess."

"Barbie's literal plastic surgery is just a commercial confirmation of what we already know: that history, politics and economics continue to influence the 'preferred' female body size and shape. The fact that a doll's 'makeover' is being treated as a news event only further underscores this. If you ask me, Barbie's "new" bod is really just the same old thing"
—**Lisa Jervis in *Hues Magazine***

How much will Barbie have to change to approach normal dimensions? Here she is compared to the L.L. Bean measurements for a size 10 woman.[7]

	Barbie	Size 10	Difference
Bust	39"	36 1/2"	+2 1/2"
Waist	18"	28 1/2"	-9 1/2"
Hips	33"	38 1/2"	-5 1/2"

Beyond the Body: Barbie's Other Messages

Barbie is only a doll, of course, and alone cannot cause the body image or eating problems that plague females of all ages in Western society. She does, however, convey powerful messages about what we expect from women.

Barbie is presented as infallible in the comics and storybooks. She is marketed as the ultimate consumer, teaching impressionable girls the "importance" of clothes, material goods, and appearance. Bloomingdale's recently carried an exclusive Calvin Klein Barbie in CK logos for $70. Shopper Barbie has her own charge card, and in the Barbie Dream Date Game, the player who gets Ken to spend the most money on her wins! The first edition of Talking Barbie included her saying, "Math class is tough!" Although Mattel introduced a black Barbie in 1968, and other races and cultures later,

> "Birkenstock Barbie: Finally, a doll made with horizontal feet and comfortable sandals. Made from recycled materials."
> —Susan Jane Gilman on Barbies she'd like to see, from *Adios Barbie*

the dolls have only the most superficial skin color variations. It is the blonde Barbie that dominates girls' fantasies and undermines pride about appearance, ethnicity, or competence.

Positively Political

Some people have already demonstrated their feelings about Barbie's influence on our culture. A number of artists, such as Maggie Robbins, Susan Evans Grove, and Julie Mandle have featured Barbie in their political art. Mandle, a performance artist, transformed herself into a Barbie image, filled a shopping cart with Barbies and diet literature, and gave out statistics about eating disorders.

One group, the Barbie Liberation Organization, formed

by a graduate student from the University of California at San Diego, went so far as to swap the speech mechanisms of the Talking Barbies with those of G.I. Joes, causing havoc for the toy stores that received the tampered merchandise. The Talking Barbies were saying things like, "Vengeance is mine," while the G.I. Joes were saying, "Let's go shopping."[8] This political art expresses the distress many feel about the status of women in our society and the symbols that threaten the self-esteem of females.

Many parents will not let their children own toy guns but fail to see the potential damage of fashion dolls. Nevertheless, her influence cannot be separated from the many other negative forces on girl's self-esteem and body image today.

STRATEGIES FOR CHANGE

Take time to reflect on how Barbie and her entourage affected your transition from girlhood to womanhood. If you played with one, what did you think about her body and appearance? How did Barbie contribute to your feelings about your appearance? Talk to your mother, sister or friends about Barbie's role in your lives.

A step in raising happy, healthy children is recognizing the influence of toys. If the children you love already have Barbies, observe their play. Attempt to understand what the doll represents and how your children feel about Barbie's body in relation to their own. Sponsor an event where people gather to give up their Barbies. Become aware of other influences that might contribute to girls' body despair. Be aware of your gender bias regarding how girls should play. Be sure to offer other dolls, games, and play experiences to girls. Form a group to raise money to buy healthy toys for local child care centers or for Christmas toy drives. Write an article for your newspaper or local parent-teacher organization to heighten people's awareness of the influence of fashion dolls.

"Today's more conscious parent will gladly buy their children a Barbie Doll porportionately correct to normal, healthy woman... Mothers would be tickled to death to find a Barbie Doll with a bit of cellulite on her thighs, a bustline small than her hips, and even a little roundness to the belly. The real winners...would be the little girls who, upon growing up... would in no way feel that they needed to alter their natural body shape to have a "dream life."
—Letter to Mattel from WINS

RESOURCES

Cathy Meredig, aware of the impact of fashion dolls on body image and self-confidence, created a new doll! The **Happy To Be Me Doll** is normal height, with an average (though certainly on the thin side of average), well-proportioned body (36-27-38) and a size 8 foot. The company currently produces two different dolls with different shapes and features. The dolls are accompanied by storybooks showing them as competent, creative, resourceful girls and important members of their families. The company is developing dolls to reflect different

ethnicities and cultures.
Happy To Be Me Dolls
Esteem International, Inc.
6563 City West Parkway
Eden Prairie, MN 55344
800-477-9235

Another healthy alternative to Barbie is the collection of **American Girl Dolls**—Felicity, Kirsten, Addy, Samantha, and Molly—who represent girls that grew up in different eras in the U.S., from the 1770's to the 1940's. Accompanied by books that tell their stories, struggles, accomplishments and emotions, the American Girls educate kids about history as well as the importance of families, friendships, and feelings. The company has a new doll that can be created by choosing hair, skin, eye color and name. This "Girl of Today" comes with six blank books to enable her owner to develop her own doll.
American Girl Dolls
Pleasant Company (owned by Mattel)
8400 Fairway Pl.
P.O. Box 620190
Middleton, WI 53562-0190
800-845-0005

Mattel
333 Continental Blvd.
El Segundo, CA 90245
310-252-2000

Women Insisting on Natural Shapes (WINS)
PO Box 19938

Sacramento, CA 95199
800-600-WINS
winsnews@aol.com

The Body Shop
Features Ruby as their centerfold in a publication called *Full Voice*.
Ruby is a full-bodied Barbie look-alike whose accompanying message
is, "There are 3 billion women who do not look like supermodels and
only eight who do." She may upset the executives at Mattel, but women
love her.
The Body Shop
www.thebodyshop.com
full_voice@bodyshop.co.uk

The Distorted Barbie@
www.users.interport.net/^napier/barbie/barbie.html
This and other websites have reportedly been scrutinized by Mattel,
with demands by the company attorneys that they shut down.

16

Schools

A PROBLEM OR SOLUTION?

"Calling a child 'fat,' saying 'oink' in a cafeteria line, or... 'You can't play, you're too fat,' are all too frequent events in school...Fat jokes are so popular...their meanness is often ignored."
— Catherine Steiner-Adair and Amy Purcell Vorenburg, advocates for media literacy

Schools have a tremendous influence on children's lives, but most have limited their efforts at combating Body Wars to teaching about the dangers of eating disorders and obesity. Unfortunately, these interventions can backfire by glamorizing anorexia and bulimia and increasing negative attitudes about weight and fat. In response to lectures about signs and symptoms, for instance, some students might experiment with purging or severely restrict food intake for fear of getting fat.

Also, the traditional "Just say no" approach, featuring occasional educational programs on issues such as eating disorders and steroid abuse, is ineffective as long as students are rewarded or punished for their appearance. In fact, schools may inadvertently contribute to Body Wars by allowing negative behaviors and attitudes to exist on campus. Choosing or excluding kids based on looks or size for teams, special activities, or even informal assignments, and condoning teasing are destructive norms in many schools. These practices remain unchanged when only symptoms or consequences of Body Wars are addressed. Prevention requires transformation, not just education.[1]

Below are some well-researched but frightening statistics, with significant implications for the well-being of all students from first grade through college. When asked why they do these things, students simply reply, "I just want to be thin."

FACTS ABOUT KIDS AND DIETING

- 42% of first, second and third grade girls want to lose weight.[2]
- 45% of boys and girls in grades three through six want to be thinner; 37% have already dieted; 6.9% score in the eating disorder range on a test of children's eating habits.[3]
- 51% of 9- and 10-year-old girls feel better about themselves when dieting; 9% of 9-year-olds have vomited to lose weight; 81% of 10-year-olds are afraid of being fat.[4]
- 4% of middle school girls turned to vomiting to lose weight in 1984; in 1992 more than 11% did; less than 1% abused diet pills in 1984, and more than 6% did in 1992.[5]
- 70% of normal weight high school girls feel fat and are on a diet.[6]

- 13% of 15-year-old girls diet at least ten times a year.[7]
- 90% of high school junior and senior girls diet regularly, although only 10-15% are "overweight."[8]
- 50-60% of college women are currently dieting.[9]

Some people argue that schools and colleges should attend only to the academic aspects of education, and not to social and personal issues. In reality, though, how students feel about and take care of themselves affects how well they do in school. An undernourished anorexic student, a dehydrated wrestler, or an exhausted and depressed bulimic are surely working below full capacity. Dieting alone will diminish school performance by decreasing concentration, attention, and memory, and increasing obsessive thoughts about food—an inevitable result of starvation. Body Wars are a public health issue and schools need to intervene.

The educational system is well positioned to attack Body Wars throughout its hallways, gyms, and classrooms. However, anything less than a total assault is just a Band-aid on a gaping wound of negative body image, low self-esteem, and preoccupation with appearance. Schools that make systemic efforts to prevent Body Wars create healthier environments, as reflected in a philosophy that de-emphasizes the importance of weight, shape, and other external symbols of self-worth. Students, parents, teachers, coaches, administrators, and ancillary staff must all be involved by questioning societal norms and discussing the personal prejudices that maintain the status quo, as well as establishing a variety of school-wide anti-Body Wars policies.

Gender-Based Education

Sometimes, schools contribute to Body Wars by perpetuating the gender-based messages inherent in the culture at large. Neatness, conformity, and the appearance of assignments dominate teachers' comments to girls, while boys are frequently encouraged to take risks and to think independently. The subliminal message conveyed is that looking good is important for girls, while living fully is what counts for boys. Both ends of this spectrum can contribute to poor body esteem and dangerous practices: girls may begin restrictive eating to conform to the beauty ideal, and boys may take risks with their bodies beyond what is healthy.

"Girls today deserve better. Their gender journey must end in self-affirmation and full participation in the educational, economic, and social life of this nation. True educational reform will happen when girls, as well as boys, become all they can be."
—Jackie DeFazio, President, American Association of University Women

From elementary school on, gender impacts the educational process. At all levels, boys receive more active instruction. In the early grades, they speak out eight times more often than girls, who are quickly punished for not following the rules.[10] Teachers are more likely to call on boys—in science this occurs 79% of the time. Many girls give up when they see the opposite sex actively encouraged while being ignored themselves. This has unfortunate repercussions—the highest salaries for women are in science, math, and computers,[11] the areas in which girls get the least encouragement in school.

This problem continues after high school. In college, professors offer males more eye contact, wait longer for them to answer, and are more likely to remember their names. In response to this "chilly classroom climate,"[12] many young women turn to their bodies for attention and proof of their self-worth. Frequently, their negative feelings about their bodies are strongly associated with the desire to die, and they attempt suicide four to five times more frequently than males.[13] Again, schools could help to change this.

The Social Scene

Friends and classmates are another important influence on body satisfaction; and, once puberty hits, sexual tension is pervasive, especially on school campuses. Sexual harassment affects both sexes: 81% of girls and 76% of boys in middle and high schools report experiencing unwanted sexual behavior; 65% of girls and 42% of boys said they had been grabbed, touched, or pinched. Girls, however, experience this earlier and more repeatedly.[14]

In middle school, sexual objectification and intimidation intensifies. While boys are grow bigger and stronger, in a sense *into* the cultural ideal, adolescent girls are gaining weight, in *contrast* to the cultural ideal. At a time when their bodies are beginning to attract attention, they often feel embarrassed, scared, and ashamed of their sexual development. Self-confidence decreases and anxiety, avoidance, and withdrawal increase. This is especially true for girls who are teased about their weight, shape, and appearance. They may focus on losing weight or somehow changing the way they look as the solution to a demanding or abusive social scene.

Rather than disappearing, this harassment often becomes more insidious in college. Frat parties with scales on the

"I think you should talk back to anyone who makes a mean comment about your body. You should say 'I want to stay how I am and be healthy.' Then walk away. "
**—Jenna Sol, 8 yr. old,
in New Moon, Nov/Dec. 1997**

front porch, allowing only women who are under a certain weight to enter, are an example. Some schools have rituals, such as face parties, where guys study the student directory and invite only the most attractive women. These same young men will not only be critical of women who are struggling with eating disorders, but will fail to see a connection.

A discussion of the social scene would be incomplete without examining the competition girls feel about their appearance. They can be harsh with themselves and each other, and many have rivalries over dieting and clothing fads, which is a more socially-sanctioned arena for competition among females than academics, for example. Success is measured by superficial judgments about their own and others' bodies, without acknowledgment or respect for natural beauty—unless it's skinny.

Schools can either be part of the problem by reflecting societal norms or part of the solution by challenging them. If prevention works, someday students at every school and college will be unimpeded by obsessions about weight and appearance.

STRATEGIES FOR CHANGE

From pre-school to grad school, all personnel must examine their beliefs about the importance of weight, shape, and appearance. Be honest about how often students with more "ideal" figures are rewarded for their looks. Think about how these preferences encourage Body Wars. Weightism is a serious form of prejudice. Assess your own attitudes toward weight and body image by completing the two-part "Weight and Shape Attitudes Test for Teachers" which follows. Discuss what you learn about yourself with friends or colleagues and examine how these attitudes may affect your interactions with students.

WEIGHT AND SHAPE ATTITUDES TEST FOR TEACHERS

Part 1

Answer each question in Part 1 with the following scale:
Never=0 Rarely=1 Sometimes=2 Often=3 Usually=4

1. When I exercise, my principal motive is compensating for food eaten, or otherwise managing my weight.

2. I weigh myself

3. I think negative things about overweight people when I see

them or talk with them.

4. I have admired slender people and think about how much better my life would be if I were slender.

5. I look at myself in a mirror.

6. I wear clothes I do not particularly like because they divert attention from my weight.

7. I avoid activities that I enjoy because they might call attention to my weight or body shape.

8. I think about my body shape.

9. My weight or my eating influences how I think about (judge) myself as a person.

10. I use the adjective "fat" when I want to make an insulting or disparaging remark about a person.

Part 2

Answer "True" or "False" for the following questions:

1. If I could take 15-25 pounds off my body from wherever I choose, and I would be guaranteed that I would not regain it, I would sacrifice five years of my lifespan.

2. As I read the word "slob," the first word that comes into my mind is "fat."

3. Schools should maintain weight-for-height standards for participation in dance or cheerleading or drama.

4. Regardless of my weight and shape, I like myself. It would not matter if I gained or lost weight; I would still be me, a worthwhile person.

Scoring

Part 1: Add the numbers for your answers.
Part 2: Give yourself 1 point each for the following answers:
1=T; 2=T; 3=T; and 4=F.

Evaluation

If your score on the first nine items is greater than 26, and your score on the second section is greater than 2, you may be promoting negative attitudes that are part of the cultural foundation of eating disorders.

From: A 5 Day Lesson Plan Book on Eating Disorders
M.P. Levine and L. Hill. (1991) The National Eating Disorder Organization.[15] Reprinted with permission.

Parents, students, teachers, and administrators should join together in the fight against Body Wars on campuses of all levels. Here are numerous action items to use:

• *Discourage dieting.* Adopt the EDAP slogan, "Don't Weigh Your Self-Esteem—It's What's Inside That Counts" (posters and buttons are available from EDAP).

• *Practice what you preach.* Create a safe environment by eating well-balanced meals, not diet bars or drinks. When you hear teachers talking about "being fat" or going on diets, challenge them. The same goes for kids. Whenever students begin talking negatively about their bodies or about restricting their food intake to lose weight, respond immediately and stress that their bodies need fuel several times daily to be able to think, study, grow, and be healthy. Remember, internal—not external—beauty is important.

- *Find out what the kids are eating.* Encourage the school food service to provide a broad range meal options: nutritious, tasty, balanced, including vegetarian and lactose-free choices. Help students learn to trust their bodies, their hunger, and their ability to self-regulate.

- *Encourage healthy exercise.* Help your school develop physical education programs for all students to enjoy. (One-sixth of school aged children in the U.S. are so weak and uncoordinated that they are considered "physically underdeveloped" by the President's Council on Physical Fitness and Sports.[16])

- *Teach respect!* Establish a zero tolerance stance on teasing, taunting, and negative talk about children's bodies in schools. Treat derogatory behavior the same way you would racial or sexual harassment.

- *Teach Media Literacy!* Media literate students are more critical consumers because they know that every image, commercial, and television show has a message, constructed by an individual or a group with a particular agenda or point of view.[17] Create experiential lessons, such as photo shoots and ensuing touch-ups, visiting ad agencies or developing a news show.

- *Write letters and make phone calls!* Survey your school for weightism and do something about it. For example, if P.E. teachers practice routine body fat testing, tell them why that is unacceptable. You might need to take your issue to the administration, in which case you would want to forward copies to local newspapers, radio stations. Here's a sample letter:

Dear Superintendent of Schools,

We are writing to express our dismay over the use of body fat testing with elementary school children. Our daughter's teacher has done this with her students, and we have expressed our concerns to her. We encourage you to cease this practice, as the consequences are serious and far-reaching.

Body fat testing of young, growing children reinforces the harmful messages we send to our children about the need to be overly concerned with bodies and appearance. Eating disorders experts report that group weigh-ins and body fat analyses, as part of school or athletic activities, directly contributes to poor self-image, weight preoccupation, body loathing and restricted eating—all precursors of serious eating disorders. For vulnerable youngsters, this type of activity or intervention can be devastating.

We want our children to be confident, content, and self-assured. Giving them numbers about their body fat will lead them to equate their self-worth to their body weight, shape, and size. We believe that the School District could find much better, more meaningful ways to teach about health and nutrition. Alternatively, teach them about the importance of respecting their bodies and natural human variations in shape and size.

Not only is the body fat testing of school children unwarranted, it is harmful. We look forward to your action on this matter.

Sincerely,

Mary and John Activist

Consider the following "Tips to Build Gender-Fair Schools" from the American Association of University Women.[18]

Tips to Build Gender-Fair Schools

- Learn about the impact and incidence of gender-bias, the subtle ways that teachers, text books, and testing deplete a girl's self-esteem and undermine her potential. Bring parents and teachers together to discuss the challenge of gender bias.

- Review textbooks and curriculum. Watch for messages that stereotype girls and women.

- Talk to children about their school experiences. Help girls develop positive views of themselves and their futures.

- Contact and work with the Title IX coordinator for your school district to assess compliance. Title IX of the Civil Rights Act is a law that forbids discrimination based on gender in any federally funded program or institution. School districts are responsible for assuring that both academic and athletic programs are equally available to boys and girls; most have a designated Title IX coordinator.

- Encourage and support girls studying science and mathematics by showcasing women role models in scientific and technological careers, and by offering hands-on experience and providing mentors.

- Conduct workshops on sexual harassment.

- Encourage parents to fortify their daughters' self-confidence through means outside appearance by supporting them in personal risk-taking ventures.

- Work with the business community to expand your students' awareness of careers for women.

How Schools Can Combat Body Wars

Schools can be mobilized to fight against Body Wars, be their students four years old or 40. Read this list, a progressive set of tactics, and find things you can do to make your school a safer place. These strategies build on each other, so read the whole list and pick out what will work in your system.

Preschool

- Give boys and girls the same opportunities and encouragement in learning and in play. Don't label some activities for girls and others for boys.

- Provide a broad range of food, and respect children's appetites and needs. Don't insist on a clean plate.

- Keep food in its place: it is fuel for the body and for our health. It is also enjoyable. We celebrate special occasions with food. Don't use food to punish or reward other behaviors—that gives it power and meaning that can be dangerous later.

- Educate parents about children's nutritional needs and how to handle conflicts in the family about food.

- Encourage physical activity and the natural joy of movement.

- Respond to any teasing of children's bodies with positive corrective messages.

Elementary

- Do not talk about eating disorders signs or symptoms, because this approach is developmentally inappropriate. Instead, do everything you can to encourage body pride, self-confidence, self-esteem, and expression of emotions.

- Convey that food is neither good nor bad—any food is acceptable in moderation. Don't try to eliminate the snacks, desserts, and other higher fat foods that kids crave.

- Become aware of any subtle weightism and looksism in your school. Be sure children are never favored because of their appearance.

- Listen to the children's conversations. Teasing and negative comments about those who are large or fat should be treated as prejudice. Discuss these comments so kids understand the power of such bias.

- Develop media literacy skills. Be sure your students have the skills to be critical consumers and to understand media images, not just to be passive recipients.

- Let parents know what your school is doing to develop media literacy, positive body image, and healthy attitudes toward weight, food, and appearance.

- Show respect for diversity. Help children to find the beauty in differences. Help them to feel proud of their bodies, no matter what their size, shape, or skin color.

- Avoid lining kids up or choosing them for activities based on size. Tall kids often become self-conscious and ashamed of their bodies, when they are singled out. Short children sometimes think they can't do things because of their size.

• School nurses, physical educators, teachers, and coaches should not discuss children's weights. Group weigh-ins or body fat analyses only make children consider weight an important marker of self-worth.

Middle School

• Teach kids about how bodies change as they grow and that gaining some weight and fat is healthy for teenagers.

• Be sure that your sex-education programs don't talk only about techniques of safe sex. Girls also need to hear that they have control; their body belongs to them, not to others.

• Encourage both boys and girls to be active physically. Provide opportunities beyond competitive team sports. Hiking, biking, dancing, and other, individual activities are often more appealing.

• Talk about body image. Provide safe places, such as groups led by a nurse or counselor, where girls can talk about how they feel about their bodies. Help them to accept their bodies as they are and to believe that " It's what's inside that counts."

• Health education should focus on enhancing the qualities that will help to resisit eating disorders, such as positive body image, media literacy, the importance of adequate nutrition, and the ability to assert oneself and communicate feelings. Do not focus on eating disorder behaviors and symptoms.

- Discuss the dangers of dieting, particularly the cycle of undereating and overeating that can develop. (What Really Happens When We Diet in Chapter 4 is a good resource for this discussion).

- Provide educational opportunities to parents so they understand the strong connections between body image and self-esteem.

High School

- Develop peer counseling groups, gender-issues study groups, and other opportunities for students who want to discuss the issues of gender, body image, and Body Wars. Provide faculty support and educational opportunities to these students.

- Provide some education to students about eating disorders—not just the signs and symptoms, but why people hurt themselves this way, prevention, and intervention.

- Investigate resources. Students, faculty, and parents need to know whom to contact if they're worried about an individual with an eating disorder, about a team that is being encouraged to diet, or about a teacher who is making weightist or other negative statements about a student.

- Become sensitive to the different Body Wars. Be aware that men may exercise excessively rather than diet. Be sure your athletic trainers, coaches, and staff are aware and can recognize when someone is having a problem.

- Develop a team approach to this problem. Educate all staff about eating disorders and the other Body Wars faced by your student body.

- Require that all coaches learn about the risks of eating disorders, poor nutrition, and Body Wars in athletes.

- Help students and parents to prepare for college by discussing separation issues and the powerful emotions kids and families experience during this transition.

College

- Teach stress management, coping skills, and relaxation techniques so that students won't abuse eating and exercise to cope during stressful periods.

- Examine your sexual harassment and sexual violence policies on campus. How safe are girls' bodies?

- Develop policies and personnel to help students who are struggling with Body Wars. Colleges need therapists, dietitians, nurses, and physicians who are knowledgeable about the range of assaults to body image and health on their campus.

- Since Body Wars affect more women than men, any support given to the status of women in your school or college (tenure decisions, gender representation in the administration, women's studies center, celebration of Women's History Month) will help both sexes to realize that women are more than fashion dolls.

RESOURCES

BODYWISE

A nationwide campaign from the U.S. Public Health Service's Office on Women's Health to emphasize the link between healthy eating, positive body image and favorable learning outcomes for middle school students. Educators can request a packet by calling:

800-628-8442
fax 202-628-3812
bodywise@esilsg.org
www.4woman.gov

The Ms. Foundation

provides research findings and publications, and sponsors events like "Take-A-Daughter-To-Work Day."

The Ms. Foundation
120 Wall Street
33rd Floor
New York, NY 10005
800-676-7780
www.ms.foundation.org

EDAP Puppet Program

Used with elementary school children to promote healthy eating and body image and to boost self-esteem no matter one's shape or size. They also have extensive educational materials for parents and others to prevent eating disorders. Produced by EDAP.

EDAP
603 Stewart St., Ste. 803
Seattle, WA 98101
206-382-3587
www.edap.org

No Weigh
A non-dieting program for use with teenagers to promote health by taking responsibility for one's self, and viewing health as energy, confidence, and well-being, not just a number on the scale.
HUGS International
Box 102A, RR3
Portage La Prairie, Manitoba Canada R1N 3A3
1-800-565-4847

The American Association of University Women (AAUW)
They have many resources for educational programs, including a video, Girls Can! They also have produced reports on gender equity called *Shortchanging Girls, Shortchanging America* and *How Schools Shortchange Girls: The AAUW Report.*
AAUW
Sales Office, Dept. 234
PO Box 151
Annapolis Junction, MD 20701-0251
800-225-9998 x 234
www.aauw.org

Vitality Program
A Canadian program for children which teaches about weightism and builds positive body image and self-esteem.
Health Services and Promotion
Health and Welfare Canada
Jeanne Mance Bldg. - 4th Floor
Ottawa, Ontario
Canada K1A 1B4
613-957-8331

The Women's History Catalogue
Books, video, posters, gifts, and classroom activities to promote awareness of the accomplishments and lives of women. Incorporating an

appreciation of women's history into the curriculum at all ages will also help girls to feel better about themselves and avoid Body Wars. The National Women's History Project
7738 Bell Rd.
Windsor, CA 95492-8518
707-838-6000

Books/Curricula

Am I Fat?
Helping Young Children Accept Differences in Body Size
Ikea, J., Naworski, P., Santa Cruz, CA, ETR Associates, 1992. Suggestions for teachers, parents and other care providers of children to age ten.

Healthy Body Image: Teaching Kids to Eat and Love Their Bodies
Kater, K., Seattle, WA, EDAP, 1998.
A comprehensive curriculum including eleven carefully scripted lessons for grades 4-6.

Just for Girls
Friedman, S., Vancouver, BC, Salal Books, 1999.
A guidebook for facilitating self-esteem/body acceptance groups with adolescence girls. A great resource for teachers, counselors, and others who work with groups of girls.

A 5-Day Lesson Plan on Eating Disorders
Levine, M., Hill, L., Seattle, WA, EDAP, 1991.
Includes helpful teacher preparation, overheads, and thoroughly prepared lessons to use with students in middle or high school.

Building Esteem
A booklet designed to mobilize college administrators and students to take systemic action against eating problems on campus. It de-

scribes a model peer health education program developed by students at Duke University which utilizes student activism, peer counseling, and consciousness-raising techniques.

Fed-Up

A 30-page guide for eating disorders information and prevention on college campuses. It features profiles of men and women who struggle with eating, body image, and exercise problems, and their return to wellness. Both published by:

Bold Print
PO Box 230360
New York, NY 10023
212-580-0015
www.boldprint.net

GO GIRLS

(Giving Our Girls Inspiration and Resources for Lasting Self-Esteem)
This is a prevention curriculum for high schools based on media literacy, activism, and advocacy. Produced by EDAP.

The Center for Media Literacy

Has curriculum units on various media themes for various ages.
4727 Wilshire Blvd. #403
Los Angeles, CA 90010
800-226-9494 or 213-931-4177
Fax 213-931-4474
www.medialit.org

"Resisting Weightism: Media Literacy for Elementary School Children" Steiner-Adair, C., Vorenberg, A. In:
Preventing Eating Disorders: A Handbook of Interventions and Special Challenges.
Piran, N., Levine, M., and Steiner-Adair, C., New York, Brunner Mazel, 1999.

Media Literacy: Keys to Interpreting Media Messages
Silverblatt, A., Westport, CT, Praeger, 1995.

Visual Messages: Integrating Imagery into Instruction
Revised in 1999 and gives background information and educational
activities for all ages to enhance media literacy.
Libraries Unlimited
PO Box 3988
Englewood, CO 80155
800-237-6124

Videos

Happy Healthy Shapes: It's Not How You Look, It's How You Feel
A 34-minute video with a curriculum for middle and high school
aged students. It explores cultural attitudes toward our bodies, self-
esteem, health, nutrition, psychological reasons for food and weight
issues, and has information about eating disorders.
WINS (We Insist on Natural Shapes)
PO. Box 19938
Sacramento, CA 95819
800-600-WINS
winsnews@aol.com

BodyTalk: Teens Talk about Bodies, Eating Disorders and Activism
A 28-minute video on body acceptance issues for 9- to 18-year-old
girls and boys. Kids from diverse ethnic backgrounds and a range of
socio-economic status and body sizes discuss the messages they receive from media, family, and friends about their bodies and eating
patterns. Produced by:
The Body Positive
2417 Prospect Street, Ste. A
Berkeley, CA, 94704
510-841-9389

Consumer's Union
They have three videos promoting media literacy in children. *Buy Me That* and *Buy Me That, Too* teach about the editing, special effects, and powerful influence of television advertising. *Buy Me That 3* is a kid's guide to food advertising.
Buy Me That and *Buy Me That 3* are distributed by:
Public Media Inc.
1-800-826-3456
Buy Me That, Too is distributed by:
Ambrose Video
1-800-526-4663

17

Sports

JUST ANOTHER WAR ZONE?

*"My coach's desire to win seemed stronger than
mine at times…I was yelled at, screamed at, and
had things thrown at me…Somehow, my coach
had convinced himself, and constantly reminded
me, that I was a fat imbecile, a bloody idiot, no
good, and worthless."*

—Danielle Herbst,
from *Little Girls in Pretty Boxes*

Today, more women are playing competitive sports than
ever before. Opportunities have broadened tremendously for
both the professional female athlete and the amateur. In 1973,
only 800,000 high school girls participated in team sports, as
opposed to 2.5 million in 1997, while the number of male high
school athletes held steady during this time period at 3.8 million. With the passage of Title IX of the Civil Rights Act, the
Federal Government has required that educational institutions

expand women's athletic scholarships to reflect more closely the number of women athletes. Girls now represent 40% of high school athletes and 39% of NCAA athletes.[1] Not a single full scholarship was given in 1972 as compared to 20,000 in 1997.[2]

Recognition of female athletes is a positive sign in terms of gender equality. However, it also means that female athletes are now susceptible to the same competitive pressures as their male counterparts. As a result, many are caught in deadly Body Wars in order to win at any cost.

FACTS ABOUT SPORTS & BODY WARS

- A 1992 study of 182 female college athletes found that 32% engage in one or more eating disordered behavior (vomiting, laxatives, diuretics, diet pills). Among gymnasts, the number jumped to 62%.[3]

- As many as 66% of female college athletes have amenorrhea or irregular periods.[4]

- Of 1,445 athletes (883 males, 562 females) in a National College Athletic Association Division I-A school study, more than 10% of female athletes report significant eating disorders (anorexia or bulimia); 58% suffer some disordered eating symptoms, significantly increasing their risk for eating disorders and medical problems.[5]

- Males in the above study demonstrated more eating disorders than expected. One percent met diagnostic criteria, and another 38% appeared at high risk. These Body Wars occur in a variety of sports, including gymnastics, track, basketball, swimming, cross country, crew, tennis, volleyball, and skiing. Pressure to lose weight is no longer associated with just a few sports that emphasize low weight and body fat composition.

The following table illustrates the percentage of NCAA Division I-A athletes reporting disordered eating behaviors.

College Athletes & Disordered Eating

	Males	Females
Diet Pills		
Lifetime	2.16%	14.30%
Monthly (last 3 mos)	.57%	1.42%
Weekly (last 3 mos)	.23%	1.25%
Daily(last 3 mos)	.23%	1.25%
Sauna/Steam		
Lifetime	24.26%	6.59%
In last year	14.63%	2.50%
Age started	16.8 yrs	17.1 yrs
Steroids		
In last year	2.0%	3.26%
Vomiting		
Lifetime	5.93%	23.90%
Monthly(last 3 mos)	2.04%	6.41%
Weekly(last 3 mos)	1.13%	3.20%
Daily(last 3 mos)	.34%	1.42%

Laxatives		
Lifetime	5.06%	11.72%
Monthly(last 3 mos)	1.02%	1.78%
Weekly(last 3 mos)	.34%	.36%
Daily(last 3 mos)	.23%	.18%
Diuretics		
Lifetime	3.65%	3.89%
Monthly(last 3 mos)	.23%	.53%
Weekly(last 3 mos)	.00	.36%
Daily(last 3 mos)	.00	.00

Johnson, Powers & Dick, NCAA Report[6]

The Shrinking of the American Athlete

While certain sports have traditionally emphasized low body weight, some standards are now dangerous. Figure skating and gymnastics, for example, emphasize small bodies since subjective scoring depends on acrobatic jumps, twists, and aesthetic forms that only very diminutive bodies can achieve. Research shows that judged sports, such as diving, figure skating, and gymnastics present more risk to body image and health than refereed sports.[7] With the focus on form rather than objective measures of athletic ability, the preferred aesthetic for these competitors now mirrors the cultural norms for beauty, distorted as they are.

The decline in the size of the average body of Olympic gymnasts underscores the trend toward smaller female athletes. In 1976, the females on the U.S Olympic Gymnastics Team were on average 17.5 years old, 5'3 1/2" tall, and 106 pounds. In 1992, the average team member was 16 years old, 4'9" tall, and 83 pounds.[8] Our Olympic stars shrank dramatically, losing 6 1/2 inches of height and 23 pounds!

Physical risks accompany this shrinking. Training more than 16 hours per week increases the likelihood of stress fractures for young bodies, yet the norm for aspiring gymnasts is to work out 30-45 hours per week, often in pain. Many of these young athletes will not grow to full height due to premature closing of the growth plate caused by pounding and stress on bones. Since 48% to 70% of bone mass and 15% of height is achieved in adolescence, nutritional intake is critical during those years. Additionally, many young female gymnasts do not menstruate. And rather than building bone density, they actually may be losing up to 5% of it a year.[9]

> "My coach used to weigh me in front of the whole team each week and then swear at me for not losing weight. Now I know how that affected me—I would throw up trying to make weight and ended up here."
> —college student in treatment for bulimia and depression.

Although some might argue that such training only occurs in the arenas of gymnastics and figure skating, other sports are developing similar negative attitudes toward weight by overemphasizing the drawbacks of a larger body, even for competitive athletes. The NCAA study clearly demonstrates that a high percentage of women participating in all sports show clinical or subclinical eating disorders.

Despite the larger female bodies seen these days in sports

like basketball, many women athletes still pursue extreme slimness, once more living by rules that may be okay for men, but are not healthy for women. Men are naturally leaner, with a lower body fat composition and a higher metabolic rate. Young women require 17% body fat to begin menses and 22% for normal ovulation cycles.[10] Still, most fall prey to the erroneous belief that thinness is a guarantee of health and better performance. But low body fat can be risky. Even if an athlete does not struggle with an eating disorder, a woman who trains with an ultra lean body may still be at risk for osteoporosis, amenorrhea, infertility, and other health-threatening conditions.

Sporty But Sexy: The New Glamor Quotient

Female athletes face conflicting pressures, not the least of which is how to "present" themselves. While they are expected to strive like their male counterparts for an athletic physique, they have the added societal expectation to look sexy and feminine. Achieving self acceptance in this type of atmosphere can be as challenging as mastering the sport itself.

> *"Why can't her body simply stand as a body—"a work of art" as bodybuilders put it—without having to insist that it is still "sexy," still "feminine," and thereby still desirable?"*
> —**Leslie Heywood, author,** *Dedication to Hunger*

Athletic wear and uniforms are more revealing than ever before. The governing board for women's beach volleyball has mandated that all players wear bikinis. Intending to attract more sponsors and spectators, organizations like the Women's Tennis Association (WTA) have actively promoted the importance of glamor in their stars. They arrange appearances on late night talk shows, spreads in fashion magazines, and clothing contracts to cultivate the connection between sports and sex. As the head of marketing for the WTA said, "This is what Madison Avenue wants."[11]

This sporty-but-sexy standard is both subliminal and powerful. A girl watching tennis may believe that she needs to be thin and glamorous to excel at her sport. Or, one who excels at and enjoys volleyball may not pursue it for the fear of the body exposure expected of players. Sports reporters frequently trivialize women by discussing their weight, criticizing changes in their shape (even when it is simply a matter of evolution from a teenaged to an adult body), and calling them "girls."[12] Although the American public has been concerned about male athletes as role models regarding values and behaviors, especially related to alcohol, drugs, and violence, we should be equally concerned about the impact of the sexualized and objectified female athlete on impressionable girls.

What Really Happens in the Locker Room

In many colleges, high schools, and even elementary schools across the country, group weigh-ins and the posting of body fat analyses are standard practices. Often, athletes are instructed to shed pounds. No guidance is given, nor any respect for the stress that dieting puts on a young athlete's active body. Weight requirements, rarely written or discussed in advance, are used to eliminate team members who fall out of favor for one reason or another. Some coaches recognize weekly "Fat Pig" awards, given to athletes who do not lose weight, who perform poorly, or who in some other way do not measure up.

As more girls participate in a wider range of sports, perhaps in the pursuit of gender-equity, what happens in our respective locker rooms becomes even more important. For males, the macho attitude that often results from taking competition to the extreme has led to casualties. For instance, in wrestling, where weight ranges are narrow and boys experience pressure to be lighter in order to compete with smaller opponents, weight loss techniques can be deadly. Within six weeks in 1997, three collegiate wrestlers died during workouts in the U.S. All three were restricting food and fluids, and dehydrating themselves by wearing vapor-impermeable suits and exercising in high temperatures. Their goal was rapid weight loss, but the result was hyperthermia, dehydration, and death.[13]

> "An athlete's personality is similar to that of someone at risk for an eating disorder—they're driven to be the best. And athletes, like anorexics, learn to ignore body signals like pain and hunger."
> —Marcia Herrin, Nutritionist, Dartmouth College

Since weight related tragedies have increased, the National Collegiate Athletic Association has revised many of its protocols. They now prohibit rapid weight-loss techniques and artificial rehydration before matches. Also, seven pounds have been added to each weight class, weigh-ins occur no more than two hours before a match, and wrestlers may not vacillate between weight classes.[14]

No athlete should have to risk their health to compete. Gender equity in sports does not mean repeating the past and having girls act like boys. Instead, it presents us with an opportunity to reexamine the goals and impact of sports, hopefully making the athletic arena safer for all.

Drugs and the Pursuit of an Athletic Body

Unfortunately, the world of athletics today brings with it a host of chemicals that promise to change the body and enhance performance. Even at highly-regulated events, such as the *Tour de France*, steroids are "as common as Gatorade."[15] In fact, performance-enhancing substances are so popular, many athletes assume they will have to use them to stay competitive.

Although we tend to associate these drugs with men, women are consumers too. A study conducted by Pennsylvania State University found that the number of adolescent girls taking steroids has doubled in the past seven years. As many as 175,000 high school girls may be using steroids now, and girls as young as ten are taking them as frequently as boys.[16] Adolescents rarely think about long-term consequences, but steroids can permanently damage the heart and liver, cause cancer, stunt growth, and impair fertility. In the short run, they decrease breast tissue and can result in a deeper voice, acne, increased body hair, and decreased scalp hair. Even worse, injuries frequently occur because the steroid-formed muscles outgrow their supporting tendons and ligaments. Unfortunately, many will choose to take these risks, knowing that steroids, combined with an extreme dietary regimen and rigorous workout schedule, will melt fat and change their body shape.

Steroids, however, are not the only performance-enhancing drugs taken by athletes. New variations of these and other so-called "nutritional" supplements regularly enter the market. Health food store shelves are stocked with a variety of them. Doctors even prescribe "anti-aging" agents such as synthetic human growth hormone for their clientele. While some of these drugs and supplements may be harmless, many have not been used long enough for us to know their effects.

SOME "PERFORMANCE-ENHANCING" FORMULAS:

- Cyproterone Acetate—the "brake drug"

Arrests sexual development; used by female gymnasts to prolong their career by avoiding the wider hips, breasts, and secondary sexual development that hinder agility.

- Creatine

Helps muscles to recover more quickly so athletes can work harder and bulk up faster, adding muscle definition. Results are temporary and, dizziness, diarrhea, and cramps are common side effects.

- EPO (erythpoietin)

A natural protein that increases red blood cells so more oxygen is available and endurance is enhanced. This also makes the blood thicker, so the heart has to work harder, increasing the risk for heart attack.[17]

Illegal substances are used by both professional and amateur athletes to sculpt the desired physique leaner and meaner. However, they are just one more price to pay in a sports culture dominated by winning at any cost, and a Body Wars culture convinced that a thinner body will assure ultimate success.

Calling a Truce

Despite the dangers involved, sports have much to offer women. The benefits of exercise last a lifetime. If a high school girl exercises at least two hours per week, she decreases her lifelong risk for breast cancer and osteoporosis. She is 92% less likely to become involved with drugs, 80% less likely to become pregnant, and three times more likely to graduate from high school. She is more inclined to do well in high school and college, to become involved in extracurricular activities, to be a leader, and to feel popular, self-confident, and proud of herself.[18]

"I try to build an atmosphere where women think of themselves as healthy, athletic women. We don't weigh our athletes and I never would prescribe a diet—it would create the potential for body paranoia and obsession."
**—Chris Wilson,
Yale University Rowing Coach**

Many coaches, athletic trainers, sports medicine staff, and student athletes are already making sports a safer place for young bodies and psyches. Although the potential problems are serious, so are the efforts to change them. For example, the International Olympic Committee (IOC) has created a task force to detect, treat, and prevent the "female athlete triad" (eating disorders, amenorrhea, and osteoporosis). With the recognition of these problems in all sports, they now require that medical histories, exams and screenings explore the risk for eating disorders.

The IOC and other organizations concede that the demand for peak performance at young ages is particularly risky. Younger psyches are more vulnerable to a coach's extremism, temper, and pressure, and are less able to set limits, defy authority and take care of their own bodies. Consequently, the Women's Tennis Council has raised the age for full international competition from 16 to 18. Similarly, the IOC and the United States Gymnastics Foundation have raised the minimum age for international competition to 16.

We need to attend to the girls and young women involved in sports, making certain that balance and health are as much a part of their training curriculum as the actual practices and events. We also need to routinely monitor and enforce gender-equity. For example, although girls' athletic opportunities are at an all-time high, the playing field is not exactly level. More often that not, their locker rooms are inadequate, practices and games are scheduled around the boys' teams, and they may not have access to school buses for transportation. Their games get less support and are predominated by male coaches, who are often unaware of key psychological differences between boys and girls. Consequently, girls are more likely to drop out or to feel disappointed and unrecognized. These negative feelings can lead to the pursuit of a perfect body to rebuild self-esteem and social status. By constantly examining gender equity issues we will ensure that the future of women's sports remains a safe and positive experience for all girls.

STRATEGIES FOR CHANGE

Sometimes participation in sports or exercise is in reaction to the Body Wars rather than in pursuit of health. Do the following descriptions apply to you? If so, you need to understand why exercise has become an obsession for you and what emotions or issues you may be avoiding by this. Excessive exercise can be associated with eating disorders and other psychological conditions such as body dysmorphic disorder and obsessive-compulsive disorder. It can become an addiction as serious as alcohol, drug abuse, or gambling and damage your physical health, because overtraining can result in chronic injuries, such as debilitating joint problems. Decide to put exercise in its place in your life rather than have it be the focus. If your own efforts are not enough, consider seeing a therapist, especially one with background in sports psychology.

WHEN EXERCISE IS EXCESS-ERSIZE

- You judge a day as "good" or "bad" based on how much you exercised.
- You base your self-worth on how much you exercise.

- You never take a break from exercise—no matter how you feel or how inconvenient it is.

- You exercise even though you are injured.

- You arrange work and social obligations around exercise.

- You cancel family or social engagements to exercise.

- You become angry, anxious, or agitated when something interferes with your exercise.

- You sometimes wish you could stop but are unable to.

- You know others are worried about how much you exercise, but don't listen to them.

- You always have to do more (laps, miles, weights) and rarely feel satisfied with what you have done.

- You count how many calories you burn while exercising.

- You exercise to compensate for overeating.

If you are a parent or have children in your care, take time to assess and understand how you feel about sports. Your experiences as, for instance, a star athlete or a "klutz," may affect your parenting. Inadvertently, you may be placing unhealthy pressure on your kids or giving them mixed messages. Talk to your children about how *they* feel about sports! Be sure their sense of self and identity is not just based on athletic prowess. The following questions may help you clarify your interactions with your children.

Mom and Pop Sports Attitudes Quiz

- What are the primary messages you hope children will learn by participating in athletics? Is it to win, or is it to have fun, to develop skills and to become a team player?

- How important do you think sports are to child development?

- If your child is not interested in sports, does that disappoint you?

- If your child likes sports but does not excel at them, how do you react?

- Were sports important in your family upbringing? Did you feel pressured to participate and to perform?

- Would you like your child's experience of sports to be similar to or different from yours?

- Do you think boys must excel at sports to be well-rounded?

- Is a female athlete less feminine?

- Are you encouraging your children to participate in sports primarily so they can control their weight?

- How much pressure are you putting on your children to win?

- How can sports help a child?

- How can sports hurt?

- Are you putting pressure on your children in sports so they will get scholarships to help offset educational expenses?

Learn what your local coaches are saying to your children about food, weight, nutrition, performance, and self-worth. Find out if their goals are to help produce well-adjusted human beings or simply champions. Remember, coaches often have little background in education or child development. Do not leave your child's psyche in someone else's hands—work together with the coach if concerns surface when you review the questions below.

If you see a coach treat your child or others unnecessarily harshly or focus excessively on weight and shape, make an appointment to discuss this privately and calmly. Give specific examples of what you have observed and why it could be harmful. If that does not result in a more positive, body-friendly atmosphere, approach the athletic director or principal of the school or league organization. Stress the importance of children feeling positive about their bodies, respected by others, and well-nourished physically and emotionally. What happens on the playing field can have a long-term consequences; you may need to withdraw your child from the activity.

QUESTIONS ABOUT COACHES AND TEAMS

- How does the coach treat children? Does s/he care about their feelings?

- Is she or he frequently irritated? How is this expressed? Is there sarcasm and name calling?

- How does the coach criticize? Constructively, clearly, and with encouragement, or is he or she vicious and demeaning?

- Do you interact well with the coach?

- Is favoritism occurring?

- Does the coach tell athletes they are fat and need to lose weight?

- Are food and adequate liquids available, particularly when traveling?

- How does your child feel after practice?

- What messages is your child getting about competition, cooperation, teamwork, success, failure, and friendship?

RESOURCES

The American College of Sports Medicine
Publishes a journal for professionals and applies the science of medicine to sports.
PO Box 1440
Indianapolis, IN 46206-1440
317-637-9200

Black Women in Sports Foundation
Sponsors activities to increase opportunities for African American females, with an annual conference and mentoring workshops.
PO Box 2610
Philadelphia, PA 19130
215-763-6609

Girls Incorporated
Has programs devoted to sports, including the "Sporting Chance" curriculum; "Stepping Stones" for 6 to 8 year olds; "Bridges" for 9 to 11 year olds; and "Sports Unlimited" for 12 to 14 year olds.

120 Wall Street
3rd Floor
New York, NY 10005
212-509-2000

Melpomene Institute
An advocacy and research organization promoting the connection between health and fitness and women; they provide a variety of educational materials on self-esteem and body image.
1010 University Avenue
St. Paul, MN 55104
651-642-1951

National Association for Girls & Women in Sports
Part of the American Alliance of Health, Physical Education, Recreation, and Dance (AAHERD). Sponsors an annual day celebrating women's involvement in sports, and works to achieve equity in sports.
1900 Association Drive
Reston, VA 22091
703-476-3400; 800-213-7193

National Women's Law Center
Addresses compliance with Title IX, as well as other legal issues for women.
11 Dupont Circle NW - Ste. 800
Washington, DC 20036
202-588-5180

Tucker Center for Research on Girls and Women in Sports
Conducts research and distributes the president's council report, "Physical Activities & Lives of Girls."
Tucker Center
University of Minnesota
203 Cooke Hall

1900 University Ave., SE
Minneapolis, MN 55455
612-625-7327

U.S. Olympic Committee
Provides information about children and competitive athletics.
One Olympia Plaza
Colorado Springs, CO 80909
719-578-4833

The Women's Sports Foundation
Founded in 1974 by Billie Jean King and other female athletes, is a clearinghouse for information about Title IX, and encourages healthy and equal participation in athletics.
WSF
Eisenhower Park
East Meadow, NY 11554
516-542-4700; 800-227-3988

Books

Eating Disorders: The Journal of Treatment and Prevention
Powers, P., Sherman, R., Special Issue: Athletes and Eating Disorders. Vol. 7, number 3. Bristol, PA, Taylor and Francis, 1999.

Helping Athletes With Eating Disorders
Thompson, R., Sherman, R., Champaign, IL, Human Kinetics Publishers, 1993.

How to Win at Sports Parenting
Sundberg, J. and Sundberg, J., Colorado Springs, CO, WaterBrook Press, 2000.

Little Girls in Pretty Boxes: The Making and Breaking of Elite Gymnasts and Figure Skaters
Ryan, J., New York, Doubleday, 1995.

Nancy Clark's Sports Nutrition Guidebook—Second Edition
Clark, N., Champaign, IL, Human Kinetics Publishers, 1997.

Our Athletic Daughters: How Sports Can Build Self-Esteem and Save Girls' Lives
Zimmerman, S., Reavill, G., New York, Doubleday, 1998.

The Exercise Fix
Benyo, R., Champaign, IL, Leisure Press, 1990.

The following position paper on *Athletics as a Risk Factor in the Development of Eating Disorders* was adopted by EDAP and The American Anorexia/Bulimia Association. It includes an Issue Statement, Background Information, Position to be Adopted, and Recommendations. Review this with your school's athletic director or with a committee of athletes, coaches, parents, and other school personnel.
EDAP
206-382-3587 or
AA/BA
at 212-575-6200

POSITION OF EATING DISORDERS AWARENESS AND PREVENTION, INC. AND THE AMERICAN ANOREXIA/BULIMIA ASSOCIATION:

Athletics as a Risk Factor in the Development of Eating Disorders
Issue Statement:
    Competitive athletic programs in elementary schools, middle schools, high schools, and colleges may place participants at increased risk to develop eating disorders. Anorexia nervosa, bulimia nervosa,

and related conditions conservatively affect between 1 and 4% of all high school and college-aged women. Recently, more young children, males, and women have been reported to have clinical eating disorders. These problems and milder or subclinical versions affect people of all classes, ethnicity, races, and cultures in the Unites States, They have potentially severe and adverse effects on the physical and psychological health of those who suffer from them.

Background Information

Athletes are at increased risk to develop eating disorders and other pathogenic weight control techniques. Often, sports place significant emphasis on weight and body fat composition. Athletes may be asked or encouraged to lose weight quickly. Most will do this through restrictive dieting, which can be a precursor to eating disorders. Like some people with eating disorders, athletes may be perfectionists, have a strong desire to please others, base their self-assessment on achievement and performance, and be willing to tolerate pain and to sacrifice themselves to meet their goals. Those sports which most emphasize weight control, thinness, and appearance, place athletes at significant risk to develop eating disorders. Gymnastics, cheerleading, dancing, figure skating, diving, swimming, crew, track, wrestling, and equestrian sports exert the most risk, due to the weight and appearance demands associated with them.

The recent death of competitive gymnast Christy Henrich illustrates the price an athlete may pay for compliance with the demands for a low body weight. Parents, education, health care personnel, coaches, and all schools and universities must work together to prevent similar future tragedies.

Position To Be Adopted

Eating disorders seriously endanger the health and well-being of student athletes. All personnel involved in the teaching, coaching, training, and support of sports, dance, and other physical activities should be aware of the risk factors and the pivotal role they can have in the prevention of eating disorders.

Recommendations

Coaches, trainers, physical educators, dance teachers, and related professionals have the unique opportunity to promote the physical and psychological development and well-being of young people. They should emphasize health at all times and recognize that student athletes are complex psychological beings who manage many stressors. To achieve this, the following recommendations are made:

• Coaches, trainers, and physical educators should receive education on the nutritional needs of athletes due to the stress of their training and competition.

• Coaches, trainers, and physical educators should be trained to recognize the signs and symptoms of eating disorders and to understand the potential effect sports may have on such problems.

• Coaches, trainers, and physical educators should identify and refer student athletes for assessment and treatment of eating disorders and should work cooperatively with student and clinical personnel to assure full recovery of eating-disordered athletes.

• Coaches, trainers, and physical educators should emphasize the physical risk of low weight, particularly when female athletes have menstrual irregularities or amenorrhea. Medical assessment should be obtained in such cases.

• Coaches, trainers, and physical educators should actively discourage dangerous weight control techniques, including restrictive dieting.

• Coaches, trainers, and physical educators should consider health, physical and emotional safety, and self-image of athletes when making decisions about inclusion and exclusion on teams.

• Coaches, trainers, and physical educators should provide information via guest speakers and educational activities and materials to inform athletes and their parents about the dangers of restrictive dieting and maintaining an artificially low body weight, the importance of appropriate nutrition, and the principles of set-point theory.

• Coaches, trainers, and physical educators should encourage a positive self-image and self-esteem in athletes and should understand the importance of their personal and professional role to communicate respect and validation to student athletes.

EDAP position adopted by the Board of Directors on November 13, 1994. AA/BA position adopted by the Board of Trustees on November 16, 1994. Drafted by Margo Maine, Ph.D. and approved with revisions by EDAP Board of Directors and AA/BA Board of Trustees.

18

Ballet
THE OLYMPICS OF BODY WARS

"If obsession with fat is a national pastime, then surely dancers are Olympic contenders."
—L.M. Vincent,
Competing with the Sylph

The ideal body type for today's ballet student is one that few people come by naturally. Consequently, although this type of dance can lend to strength, self-confidence and grace, it can also become a nightmare of self-denial. Even in small, local dance schools, young women internalize unrealistic standards and feel pressured to maintain a light, lean body by eating as little as possible. Alluring on the outside, dangerous on the inside, the world of ballet can be extremely damaging to the health and happiness of its eager participants.

Setting the Stage for Body Wars

Ballet is an exacting pursuit, attracting the most perfectionist, self-sacrificing and serious young people. A combination of art and athletics, ballet is ranked as second of 61 sports in terms of performance demands.[1] Unlike other sports, though, it is a year-round activity with no off-season.

In fact, nothing about ballet is easy, nor does it offer instant gratification. Discipline and the ability to deny physical and psychological pain are prerequisites. Dancers have to put up with distress, discomfort, and sometimes agony, while expecting few rewards and little recognition for their efforts. Disciplined dancers sacrifice by skipping meals, sleep, and social activities. Knowing that only a lucky few rise to the top, they push themselves and deny pain, hunger, and emotions. Further, dance companies and schools, especially the more competitive ones, are intense, self-involved settings with strict rules and customs. They are separate subcultures, without input and feedback from the outside, where the abnormal can appear normal.

Training, which often begins in pre-school, is intense for dancers. The time requirements—long sessions, three to seven times per week, more when preparing for a performance—prohibit other social activity. Although the isolation and pressure can be grueling, the dancer's self-image relies on a sense of control and structure. When primary feelings of accomplishment and adequacy come from dance, the risk of Body Wars is high.

"Must See the Bones"

George Balanchine, a Russian immigrant, is responsible for popularizing ballet's skeletal-thin body type in the U.S. In contrast, jazz, modern, and other forms of dance are not as dictatorial about weight and shape. Balanchine set the standard for taste, methods and aesthetics by selecting extremely lean female dancers with prominent collarbones and long necks. His signature was an unhealthy body type, called by one of his own dancers a "concentration camp aesthetic."[2] This ideal has incited generations of dancers to engage in destructive behaviors like extreme dieting, smoking, laxatives, vomiting, and abuse of diet pills and diuretics.

> *"For kids like me, the pleasure in eating was the taste of independence, but the aftertaste was one of shame. We got called 'fat face' in preschool and were told by our dance teachers at the age of five, that ballerinas never have such big tummies."*
> —Laura Fraser, author, *Losing It*

Gelsey Kirkland, Balanchine's student and premiere ballerina during the 1970s, exposed the dark side of dance in her book, *Dancing on My Grave*. To drive home the message that one can never be good or thin enough, Balanchine would tap her sternum and ribcage with his knuckles during rehearsals, saying, "Must see the bones…Eat nothing."[3] At the time, Kirkland was 5'4" and less than 100 pounds. In pursuit of the perfect body, she was both anorexic and bulimic, and had plastic surgery, including breast implants. She struggled for years with eating disorders and emotional chaos. As is the case for many, her survival required that she give up dance.

The Thinner the Better

In the ballet arena, everyone looks at the world "through fat-colored lenses."[4] Every ballerina and aspiring ballerina knows she must "watch her weight." She needs a long, lean, pleasing "line" and a body type that complements the others in the group. Differences in shape, weight or height are considered displeasing to the eye.

During class, she constantly sees these differences in the mirror. Such scrutiny makes her more sensitive to any potential flaw or imperfection, possibly resulting in disgust, despair, and self-destructive behavior. Slight shifts in water weight, a normal human occurrence, can disrupt her sense of control and prompt her to limit fluids or to take diuretics. Paradoxically, this may lead the body to increase sodium and to retain water as a defense against dehydration. The stage is set for a destructive cycle of laxatives, diuretics, and starvation.

To the dancers' surprise, denied hunger leads to increased appetite, so bingeing frequently accompanies efforts to avoid food. Purging, by vomiting and/or laxatives, follows. Occasionally, a group of dancers binge together, a ritual that can precede a group or solo purge. Few dancers are able to maintain an acceptable weight without implementing these unhealthy practices.

Severe food restriction causes dancers long-term as well as immediate problems. Poor nutrition, inadequate calcium intake, hormonal and menstrual irregularities, and constant stress on the musculo-skeletal system can all contribute to recurrent stress fractures and early-onset osteoporosis. One study of ballet students in prominent New York schools found only one-third over 16 years old had regular menstrual periods; one-third experienced irregular periods; one-third never menstruated at all.[5] Another study reported amenorrhea in half of adolescent dancers.[6] In fact, 50% of teen ballerinas do not consume enough calories for normal growth and healing, despite extreme physical demands on their bodies.[7] These abnormalities, however, are considered normal in the world of ballet.

Examining competitive dance companies in the U.S. and abroad, one study found 15% of American and 23% of European ballerinas to be anorexic. Nineteen percent of the Americans and 29% of the Europeans were bulimic.[8] Another study of 183 serious ballet students found that 38% scored in the eating disorder range on a standardized test. Although 6.5% met all the criteria for anorexia, their faculty had not identified any of them. The dancers in professional schools had a higher incidence of eating disorders than those in college dance departments,[9] which likely is due to the fact that college dance mostly features modern and jazz, not ballet.

It is no secret that the hierarchy of ballet is based on the "lower-archy" of weight. The thinnest dancers are in the most competitive dance schools or companies, and they receive the prominent roles. In such closed environments, eating disorders are not necessarily considered illnesses—they are a means to success.

The Benefits of Systemic Change

Typical interventions in dance include simple steps, such as lectures on nutrition, the effects of starvation, self-esteem, body image, and coping strategies. Usually a specialist visits the dance school and talks to students, parents, and teachers. Occasionally, follow-up occurs, with a dietitian or therapist available for individual consultation. More often than not, these programs are a one-time event, with minimal impact.

However, appropriate interventions can change the current state of dance if the entire system is willing to look at itself. One dedicated specialist in eating disorders has helped a prominent and competitive dance school to address this problem. Dr. Niva Piran, a psychologist in Toronto, has had considerable success consulting with a residential ballet school. Well aware of the limitations of the classical approach, Dr. Piran choreographed a program based on systemic changes.

> *"...to be a member of top classical ballet companies... a female dancer may need to be in the range of 75% to 80% of average body weight...the most pervasive norms of thinness in the ballet world are extreme ones...conveyed through ethereally thin idealized role models..."*
> **—Dr. Niva Piran**

First, Dr. Piran developed focus groups to include all 100 dancers at the school. The dialogue in these focus groups revealed which problems within the school were contributing to Body Wars, and guided the intervention plan.

The social context and relationships between students and teachers needed attention. The dancers discussed their feelings of fear, shame, vulnerability, powerlessness, and disconnection from the self and the body. More importantly, they revealed how the school environment contributed to feelings of constant pressure, unreasonable expectations, and disregard for the individual.

Putting an end to self-abuse in this kind of milieu requires changes in policies; dancers will feel differently if they are treated differently. So Piran recommended many innovations, and the school agreed. Now, teachers are penalized if they criticize a student's weight. Dancers are encouraged to confront teachers or peers if they experience criticism, degradation, or insults. Piran also asked that the school no longer allow actively eating-disordered dancers prominent roles in productions. Furthermore, anyone who appears preoccupied with weight receives immediate help.

These interventions have dramatically changed the school's atmosphere. Standardized scores of disordered eating have dropped. For example, binge-eating decreased from 35% to 13%. Of the seventh- and eighth-graders, 58% had reported dieting before the program, and only 28% after. Of the tenth- through twelfth-graders, 48% had scored in the eating disorder range initially, and only 16% did later. In the next eight years, only one student had been diagnosed with a fully developed eating disorder; before the program, the average was one to two cases per year.[10] Through Piran's work, we can see that the prevention of eating disorders is possible. Her work with the ballet school is an excellent example of the intricate, complex process of successful social change.

STRATEGIES FOR CHANGE

Dance can be a positive experience, depending on the practices and policies of the particular school. For parents, explore the relationship between your child's self-esteem and dance, and answer the questions below. Talk with your child, with other parents, and with teachers to learn if your school needs intervention.

Questions for parents of dancers:

How does the dancer feel after class? Is she usually happy, or does she feel defeated and inadequate?

Does she frequently criticize her body, especially her weight?

Is she developing friendships with other dancers or are her relationships primarily competitive?

Does she have friends outside of dance?

Does she have other interests, or is all her energy devoted to dance?

Do the teachers convey concern about the dancer as an individual, or is their focus on technique, skill, and performance?

Do the teachers criticize the students' weight or shape?

Are decisions about leads and performances based on the weight of the dancers?

If teachers know that a student is dieting or bingeing and

purging, what do they do?

Do the teachers encourage healthy (not fat-free or restricted) eating? Do they ever discuss nutrition and the need for both adequate food and fluid intake?

Are healthy snacks and fluids, not just diet sodas, available?

Does the school welcome your involvement? Are teachers responsive to your parental concerns?

Observe the atmosphere: do the students seem to feel positive, energetic, and confident? Or is the environment overly serious and negative?

Is your daughter dancing because she truly wants to, or is it to prove her self-worth, to please you, or to meet her teacher's expectations?

Many dance teachers are already creating a healthy environment for their students. To ensure your dance school is on the right track, make sure of the following:

"TEN SHOULDS" FOR DANCE TEACHERS:

1. At all times remember how fragile the self-esteem and egos of growing girls can be. Be sure to convey positive messages about your dancers' self-worth.

2. Learn how to criticize constructively. Be sure to give helpful hints and to avoid degrading a dancer for not meeting your expectations.

3. Convey to your students the importance of a healthy, well-balanced diet so they can be strong dancers. Organ development and bone density formation can be impaired when young bodies do not eat enough. Do not encourage or toler-

ate overly restrictive diets, as you may put your students' health in jeopardy.

4. Learn about eating disorders. Be sure that you know the signs and symptoms, as well as the potential risks for vulnerable dancers. Consider how to approach a student and family when you are concerned. Advise dancers to get help.

5. Understand how your perception of your students is based on weight, shape, and appearance. Commit to seeing them as whole people.

6. Promote a positive atmosphere in your class. Remember: most of your students are not going to be premiere dancers. Create an atmosphere of joy and celebration of the body to counteract the other messages your students receive.

7. Listen to yourself and change destructive habits. When you are criticizing a student or a class, how often do you degrade them by saying something negative about their weight or shape of a body part?

8. Come to terms with how you feel about your own body. If you are constantly degrading yourself, even slightly, this negative attitude will come across to students. Learn to love yourself and your body, no matter what it looks like.

9. Focus on the beauty and power of what our bodies can do. Think of the body as an instrument, not an ornament.

10. Decide to be part of the solution, not part of the problem. Dance can be a wonderful experience—affirming, joyful and long lasting. Also, talk to other teachers about their approach. Educate them about the "Ten Shoulds" and learn what they have done to create a peaceful environment.

As consumers of the arts, we have dollar-power. Do not support dance schools or companies that continue to idealize Balanchine's "concentration camp aesthetic." Convene with supporters of the arts in your area to discuss how dance, and specifically which schools and companies, have contributed to eating disorders. As an individual or group, bring your concerns to the directors of dance schools. Suggest to the arts community that contributions or funding be cut off if a school is not adequately addressing the Body Wars of its dancers. Use the media to publicize the problems if those in charge do not respond appropriately. If the school reacts favorably, contact a local reporter in the feature department of your newspaper. An article about positive steps taken by schools might raise consciousness.

RESOURCES

A number of associations concern themselves with the health of dancers and other performing artists, but none are solely devoted to the nutrition and body image issues raised here. They need to hear your concerns about the atmosphere of many dance schools or companies.

AAHPERD
American Alliance for Health, Physical Education, Recreation, and Dance includes six other organizations, including the National Dance Association. They provide resources, support, publications, and programs to help professionals involved in these fields promote health.
1900 Association Drive
Reston, VA 20191

800-213-7193 or 703-476-3400
webmaster@aahperd.org

Dancer Transition Resource Center
Helps dancers retrain for other fields by providing support and counseling.
66 Gerrard St. E. Suite 202
Toronto, Ontario
CANADA M5B1G3
416-595-5655

International Association for Dance Medicine Science
Promotes the care and prevention of dancer injuries by examining biomechanical and physiological as well as psychological aspects of dance. Members are health care providers, educators, administrators, and dancers. They have a journal and other resources.
2555 Andrew Dr.
Superior, CO 80027
phone/fax: 303-554-8040
IADMS@aol.com

The Performing Arts Medicine Association (PAMA)
Includes physicians and other professionals involved in the performing arts. They provide education, information, and research on the prevention of health problems, publish a journal, and host an annual conference.
PO Box 61228
Denver, CO 80206
301-751-2770
artsmed.org
Or, contact PAMA member, Elizabeth Snell, a nutrition consultant at the National Ballet School in Canada, who has written and lectured extensively about nutrition issues in dancers. Her article, "Some Nutrition Strategies for Health Weight Management in Adolescent

Ballet Dancers" can be found in *Medical Problems of Performing Artists*, Philadelphia, PA, Hanley & Belrus Inc., Sept., 1998.
Elizabeth Snell
Snell Associates Nutrition Consultants Inc.
1100 Sheppard Avenue E#412
Toronto, ON M2K 2WI Canada
416-733-3438

19

Men
TARGETS AND TEAMMATES

*"This cause is not altogether and exclusively a
women's cause. It is the cause of human brother-
hood as well as human sisterhood, and both must
rise and fall together. Woman cannot be elevated
without elevating man, and man cannot be
depressed without depressing woman also."*
—Frederick Douglas in 1848.

Today, the social and economic system that has attacked
and undermined women's body image is proving to be equally
capable of doing the same to men. Studies reported in the popular press, magazine headlines, fitness club memberships, and
even casual conversations all prove that body dissatisfaction is
increasingly the norm for *both* sexes. Men, whose bodies are
now at risk to become ornamental, rather than instrumental,
are internalizing the cultural gaze. Body Wars no longer discriminate.

Men have long tuned out words like body image, dieting, plastic surgery, or purging. Yet modern masculinity encourages them to fear fat, to battle their bodies, and to stare critically in the mirror while they lift weights or ride stationary bikes, often accelerating far beyond fitness or health. Before they can defend against women's Body Wars, men must recognize their own vulnerability.

Sad and Bad News About Men and Their Bodies

Once more, Americans are leading the way when it comes to Body Wars. Cross-cultural research shows that American college men are more dissatisfied than their peers in Europe.[1] Listed below are the body parts men dislike most. According to a recent survey, every category has worsened by at least 10% in the last decade:

Abdomen	63%
Weight	52%
Muscle Tone	45%
Overall Appearance	43%
Chest	38%[2]

Men are also taking drastic measures to feel better about their bodies. In the five-year period between 1992 and 1997, the number of men undergoing liposuction tripled and face lifts doubled. Eyelid surgery, nose reshaping, breast reduction, and pectoral and calf implants are other popular choices. In 1996, men spent $12 million on penile enlargements, a painful procedure sometimes complicated by infections and even deformity. One plastic surgeon, whose ads promised an increase of an average of two inches in length and 50% of girth, lost his medical license due to the number of complications after performing 4500 enlargements.[3]

Men are indeed spending their hard-earned money on plastic surgery: $88 million in 1992 and $130 million in 1997. While significantly shy of women's investment ($479 million in 1992 and $882 million in 1997), these numbers reflect clear trends: upward for the profiteers of Body Wars; downward for the health and well-being of both sexes. Sales for cosmetics, which exploit anxieties about masculinity just as they do about femininity, have been increasing by 11% per year, to more than $3 billion in 1996.[4]

The most telling evidence that men are seriously afflicted by body insecurity is the gradual increase in anorexia and bulimia over the past decade in men from 1 in 20 cases to possibly 1 in 12.[5] Males also comprise as many as half of people who eat compulsively[6] and 40% of binge-eaters.[7] Rogers Memorial Hospital in Wisconsin has dedicated a unit specifically for men with eating disorders, as this population has special needs, and many other programs are developing services for men.

How We Got Here

Western culture inherited a patriarchy, a male-centered social system in which both sexes are held hostage. Feminists have long criticized how such a structure silences and devalues women while simultaneously romanticizing their beauty and objectifying their sexuality. The female route to Body Wars is relatively easy to follow: diminished and disempowered, women mistakenly revert to their bodies to gain esteem, status, and self-determination. Although patriarchy may afford men power and status, this system does not value men's inner lives any more than it does women's. Encouraged to over control and deny their feelings, men strive to be hypermasculine, both physically and psychologically.[8] Their bodies then become the tools for the myth of male control; amidst a culture of Body Wars, men can also feel disembodied.

> "Most of us know by now that advertising often turns people into objects. Women's bodies, and men's bodies too these days, are dismembered, packaged, and used to sell everything from chain saws to chewing gum. But many people do not fully realize that there are terrible consequences when people become things."
> —Jean Kilbourne, author, Deadly Persuasion

Men's present overemphasis on their bodies reflects their gender socialization. Not raised to be emotionally literate, they do not have easy access to their feelings and tend to express themselves physically more than verbally. Today, they are bombarded with images of hard, muscular bodies—a new male norm for appearance. Furthermore, we have allowed a "culture of cruelty"[9] to surrounds boys, making size, strength, and prowess issues of both status and basic safety. While at one time men relied on physical strength to survive as hunters, today they must "look the part" to survive social scrutiny from both sexes.

Masculinity has become a constant performance, intensified in this body-obsessed era by cultural definitions of male attractiveness. In the workplace, men feel insecure due to an increasingly complex job market, with minimal security, economic pressures, and age discrimination. Add to that the frequency of divorce, and many men find themselves at mid-life looking for a viable job and a new relationship. Both at work and at home, they experience the impact of women's changing roles, and many feel disarmed by the upheaval of theirs. Managing traditional masculine values while adopting more liberal, modern day attitudes about emotional sensitivity and openness is a challenge for men. Increasingly, they respond to this confusion and stress, as women have, by focusing on their bodies.

Body Ideals for Men

While western women obsess about shrinking their bodies, many men strive to increase their size and proportion to take up more space. Termed "body dysmorphic disorder," this is a psychiatric condition marked by distorted body image and relentless preoccupation with particular body parts. Manifested in men who ruminate about their muscle development and size, "muscle dysmorphia," also termed "reverse anorexia," is often exhibited by excessive time at the gym and use of anabolic steroids or other enhancing potions, despite their known risk.[10] Some feel ashamed enough about their bodies to refuse to be

"Once you're in this game to manipulate your body, you want to be the best."
—16-year-old male weightlifter

seen without their shirts or to take showers after a workout or gym class. A study of male weightlifters found that 10% see themselves as small and weak despite considerable size and strength.[11]

This mentality often begins in school sports classes in which self-esteem can be damaged as easily as it is enhanced by teamwork and athletic pride. Of the approximately one-half of 9th to 12th grade boys who participate in organized athletics, 78% had taken some form of muscle-enhancing supplements such as creatine, ginseng or androstenedione, according to one study.[12] Non-athletic boys are more prone to feel inferior and ashamed, but even those who are athletic may struggle with their bodies and abilities.

"When someone offers you a shortcut and it's a shortcut you want so bad, you're willing to ignore what it might be doing to your insides. I wanted to look better. Who cares if it's going to clog up my kidneys? Who cares if it will destroy my liver? There was so much peer pressure that I didn't care."
—Alexander Bregstein, 16-year-old in *New York Times Magazine*

Just as the Barbie doll has shaped girls' body image, the equivalent male action toy affects boys. While the original G.I. Joes and other figures had basically normal proportions, now these action heroes present unattainable physical goals for boys, like Barbie does for girls. Their proportions far exceed the physique of even the largest body builders, increasing year by year as shown in the following table.

ACTION FIGURES: THE BOYS' BARBIE

Year	Figure	Description	Biceps[13]
1964	Original G.I. Joe	relatively normal proportions	12.2"
1974	G.I. Joe	bulked up with a Kung Fu grip	15.2"
1994	G.I. Joe Hall of Fame	"Ripped" bulkier	16.4"
1998	G.I. Joe Extreme	Bigger yet	26.8"
1998	Batman	Superhero	26.8"
1998	Wolverine	Superhero	32.0"

Other male action toys followed suit, with similar changes in Star Wars characters in the 20 years since their initial release. These toys are very popular, a big business in terms of both the profits ($687 million worth of male action figures were shipped in one year)[14] and the impact on boys' body image. It is little surprise that adolescent males now focus on "being cut" or "getting ripped" (meaning highly-defined musculature) or developing "six-packs" (visible divisions of their abdominal muscles).[15] Similar to the experience of a ballerina who focuses on perfection, boys strive to emulate these standards, dedicating hours to self-scrutiny and body criticism.

Adult men also struggle with body ideals in this era of rapidly changing norms for masculine models. Few today are comfortable with their natural builds. Rounded, robust bodies are no longer a sign of privilege and power; the hard, athletic, lean physique, not easily attained, is the new prototype for all ages.

While hairy chests were the earlier standard of masculinity, now a hairless look is fashionable. Hair removal techniques for men are promoted by plastic surgeons. Receding hairlines were once seen as inevitable, but now men have the "choice" to use medications, treatments, and surgeries to add hair. These options, marketed aggressively, exert tremendous pressure on men to conform. As with women, men tirelessly strive to mimic socially-esteemed body ideals.

> "What if a man...were to confide in another man with a guilty but conspiratorial smile, 'Listen, Craig, let's have a salad for lunch because I slipped and ate some chocolate last night when I was home alone.'"
> —Ellyn Kaschak, author, *Engendered Lives*

Suffering in silence, both sexes are tangled in a web of insecurity, judging others as well as themselves.

As the wise of all ages have known, in crisis there is opportunity. Because men are now vulnerable to Body Wars, they are in the unique position of being able to learn from the millions of women who have been fighting these battles for decades. Both sexes must finally join forces and create the long-awaited gender-equity we all deserve: love and acceptance of our bodies and an end to Body Wars.

STRATEGIES FOR CHANGE

The challenge to men is two-fold: building resistance against Body Wars and assisting women, as teammates, to overcome their own struggles. Starting with self-assessment, consider the pressures you feel as a man about your body. Think about these questions either alone or in a focus group with trusted friends:

QUESTIONS FOR MEN WANTING TO MAKE PEACE WITH THEIR BODIES

- What messages did your family give you about your body?

- What messages did other boys give you about your body?

- Was your body seen as acceptable or were you teased or ridiculed? Were you pushed to perform physically, either in sports or other activities?

- Were you taught to listen to or to ignore your body cues?

- Was your father (or other important male role model) satisfied with his body?

- Did he push his body to fit an arbitrary standard and was he self-critical?

- What messages do you receive about appearance, hair, skin, body size, shape, and clothing?

- What do you consider to be the male prototype or ideal?

- Do you compare yourself to males in the media, such as actors, athletes or models?

- Do you worry about your weight or physical size?

- In what ways do you want to change your body?

- Do you worry about becoming bald or developing a spare tire?

- How much do you exercise with the goal of changing your body?

- Do you compare yourself to other men?

- Are you concerned about how women feel about your physique?

Talk with other guys to realize your shared concerns. Give yourself unconditional positive regard, and then think about the other men in your life. Reach out by verbalizing messages of acceptance and validation to them. You don't have to be in competition. In fact, you could discuss how the pressure to compete has affected you and your relationships.

"How do definitions of masculinity shape the ways in which men—like me, my sons, and my male students—objectify women's bodies, sharpen their hungers, and silence their voices?"
**—Michael Levine,
Professor, Kenyon College,
Past President, EDAP**

Finally, consider how we, as a culture, can raise boys to instill positive body feelings. If boys are encouraged to attend to their own feelings, both physically and emotionally, we can help them to feel secure and to resist cultural pressures promoting body hatred.

HOW MEN CAN HELP WOMEN

- Emphasize female intellect, character, contributions, and achievements.

- Give girls the same opportunities and encouragement offered to boys.

- Be willing to share responsibilities in the home, in spite of traditional gender-based expectations about housework.

- Let your daughters know you want to be part of their lives, especially if you are separated or divorced.

- Appreciate all women's bodies even if they do not look like fashion models.

- Examine what you value in women? Is appearance more important than personality?

- Be aware of your judgments and comments about women's bodies. Are they positive or negative?

- Pay attention to the attitudes and behaviors of your friends and other men. Challenge them if they say or do things to belittle women or criticize their bodies.

- Think about the organizations in which you are involved. Do not tolerate rituals that exclude or mock women.

- Look at the images of women portrayed in your workplace. Highlight women's talents rather their appearance.

- Encourage equal pay and opportunity.

- Be aware of the power of the consumer. When you see products, companies, or advertisements that promote Body Wars for men or women, do not support them, and, let the company know why. Call or write the reasons for your boycott.

"The men of the next generation need to learn about real women. Teach (them) about love and fairness, sexuality, and the diversity of women as real human beings. Don't let them learn it at Hooters."
—Linda McBryde, M.D., author,
The Mass Market Woman

RESOURCES

DADS (Dads and Daughters)
A membership organization devoted to strengthening relationships between fathers and daughters to transform the messages that a girl's look is more important than her essence.
DADS
PO Box 3458
Duluth, MN 55803
1-888-824-3237
www.dadsanddaughters.org

The Fatherhood Institute
Part of the Families and Work Institute, is a national resource for education promoting fathers' increased involvement in families and childrearing. They have books, films, and seminars for individuals and organizations eager to transform men's role in our society.
Fatherhood Institute
307 7th Ave, Suite 1906
New York, NY 10001
www.fatherhoodproject.org

The National Men's Resources Center
Dedicated to promoting all aspects of the men's movement, including health, spirituality, and social roles informed by a profeminist and male positive perspective. They have an active website listing frequently-updated books, events, resources, and topical issues.
National Men's Resources Center
PO Box 800-W
San Anselmo, CA 94979
www.menstuff.org

National Organization of Men Against Sexism
A profeminist, gay-affirming, antiracist organization hoping to enhance men's lives by challenging old rules of masculinity. They hold an annual conference and provide resources for those committed to more positive relationships between men and women.
info@nomas.org
www.nomas.org

Rogers Memorial Hospital
Has a unit dedicated to the treatment of men with eating disorders. They also provide outreach, education, and prevention programs specifically for males.
Rogers Memorial Hospital
34700 Valley Rd
Oconomowoc, WI 53066-4599
800-767-4411
www.rogershospital.org

Books

Males with Eating Disorders
Anderson, A., New York, NY, Brunner Mazel, 1990.

Making Weight: Healing Men's Conflicts With Food, Weight and Shape
Anderson, A., Cohn, L., Holbrook, T., Carlsbad, CA, Gürze Books, 2000.

Fathering: Strengthening Connections with Your Children No Matter Where They Are
Glennon, W., Berkeley, CA, Conari Press, 1995.

The Wonder of Boys: What Parents, Mentors, and Educators Can Do To Shape Boys into Exceptional Men.
Gurian, M., New York, Jeremy Tarcher/Puman, 1996.

The Gender Knot: Unraveling Our Patriarchal Legacy
Johnson, A., Philadelphia, PA, Temple University Press, 1997.

Men Confront Pornography
Kimmel, M., New York, Meridian, 1990.

Raising Cain: Protecting The Emotional Life of Boys
Kindlon, D., Thompson M., New York, Ballantine/Fawcett, 1997.

Boys Will Be Boys: Breaking the Link Between Masculinity and Violence
Miedzian, M., New York, Anchor Books, 1991.

Father Hunger: Fathers, Daughters, and Food
Maine, M., Carlsbad, CA, Gürze Books, 1991.

Wrestling with Love: How Men Struggle with Intimacy
Osherson, S., New York, Fawcett Columbine, 1992.

Real Boys: Rescuing Our Sons from the Myths of Boyhood
Pollack, W., New York, Random House, 1998.

The Courage To Raise Good Men
Silverstein, O., Rashbaum, B., New York, Viking Penguin, 1994.

Bibliography

Chapter 1: The Challenge

[1] American Psychiatric Association (1993), "Practice Guidelines for Eating Disorders."*American Journal of Psychiatry*, 150(2), pp. 212-228.

[2] Wolf, N. (1991), *The Beauty Myth*. New York: William Morrow, p. 53.

[3] Brumberg, J.J. (1997), *The Body Project: An Intimate History of American Girls*. New York: Random House.

[4] Wolf

[5] Women's Research and Education Institute (1994), "The American Woman."1994-1995:*Where We Stand: Women and Health*. New York: Norton, p. 309.

[6] Gibbs, N. (1990), "The dreams of youth." *Time*, Special Issue: "Women: The Road Ahead," Fall, 1990, p. 12.

[7] Wolf.

[8] Wolf, p. 227.

[9] Brumberg.

[10] Steinem, G. (1994), *Moving Beyond Words*. New York: Simon and Schuster.

[11] Halloran, L. (1999), "No Holds Barred."*Hartford Courant*, September 6, 1999, pp. A1 and A5.

[12] More, T. (1992), *Care of the Soul.* New York: Harper Collins.

[13] Buchwald, E. (1993), *Raising Girls for the 21st Century.* In E. Buchwald, P. Fletcher, M. Roth. (Eds.), *Transforming A Rape Culture*. Minneapolis, MN: Milkweed Editions, pp. 179-199.

[14] Chopra, D. (1993), *Ageless Body, Timeless Mind.* New York: Harmony, p. 8.

[15] Margaret Mead. In Jackson, D. (1992), *How to Make the World a Better Place For Women in Five Minutes a Day.* New York: Hyperion, p. iv.

Chapter 2: Weightism

[1] Wooley, S.C., Wooley, W.O., Dyrenforth, S. (1979), "Theoretical, practical and social issues in behavior treatments of obesity."*Journal of Applied Behavior Analysis*, 12, pp. 3-25.

[2] Brownell, K.D. & Rodin, J. (1994), "The dieting maelstrom: Is it possible and

advisable to lose weight?"*American Psychologist*, 49(9), pp. 781-791.

3 Gaesser, G. (1996), *Big Fat Lies: The Truth About Your Weight and Your Health*. New York: Fawcett Columbine.

4 Fraser, L. (1997), *Losing It: America's Obsession With Weight and the Industry That Feeds on It*. New York: Dutton.

5 Steiner-Adair, C. (1994), "The politics of prevention."In P. Fallon, M.A. Katzman, S.C. Wooley (Eds.), *Feminist Perspectives on Eating Disorders*. New York: Guilford Press, pp. 381-394.

6 Rothblum, E.D., Brand, P.A., Miller, C.T., Oetjen, H.A. (1990), "The relationship between obesity, employment, discrimination, and employment-related victimization." *Journal of Vocational Behavior*, 37, pp. 251-266.

7 Fraser, L.

8 Rothblum, E.D. (1990), "Women and Weight: Fad and Fiction." *Journal of Psychology*, 124(1), pp. 5-24.

9 Gaesser, G.

10 Rothblum, E. (1994), "I'll die for the revolution, but don't ask me to diet." In P. Fallon, M.A. Katzman, S.C. Wooley (Eds), *Feminist Perspectives on Eating Disorders*. New York: Guilford Press, pp. 53-76.

11 "Fat Worker Wins $1 Million for Dismissal."*New York Times*, September 8, 1995.

12 Campbell, S. (1995), "Immense determination to change people's minds."*Hartford Courant*, July 4, 1995, pp. E1-E3.

13 Edell, D. (1992), "Dr. Dean Edell Medical Journal."*San Francisco Chronicle*, December 31, 1992, p. D4.

14 Berg, F. (1995), *Children and Teens in Weight Crisis*, Hettinger, ND, Healthy Weight Journal, p. 6.

15 National Association To Advance Fat Acceptance. Size Acceptance Questionaire. "Assessing Size Acceptance." From brochure, Supporting the Physical and Emotional Health of Fat People through Personal and Social Change. Reprinted with permission.

16 Rodin, J.(1992), *Body Traps*. N.Y.: William Morrow and Co.

Chapter 3: Obesity

1 Fraser, L. (1997), *Losing It: America's Obsession with Weight and the Industry That Feeds On It*. New York: Dutton.

2 Rothblum, E.D. (1990), "Women and weight: Fad and fiction."*The Journal of Psychology*, 124(1), pp. 5-24.

3 Gaesser, G. (1996), *Big Fat Lies: The Truth About Your Weight and Your Health*. New York: Fawcett Columbine.

4-5 Rothblum.

6 Garrow, J. (1974), *Energy Balance and Obesity in Man*. New York: American Elsevier.

7 Stunkard, A.J. et al. (1986), "An adoption study of human obesity."*New England*

Journal of Medicine, 314, pp. 193-198.

8 Bennett, W. and Gurin, J. (1982), *The Dieter's Dilemma*. New York: Basic Books.

9 *Women's Sports & Fitness Magazine* , Sept/Oct, 1998.

10-13 Gaesser.

14 Garner, D.M., and Wooley, S.C. (1991), "Confronting the failure of behavioral and dieting treatments for obesity." *Clinical Psychology Review*, 11, pp. 729-780.

15 Manson, J.E. etal. (1995), *Body Weight and Mortality Among Women*. New England Journal of Medicine, 333, pp. 677-682.

16 Gaesser.

17 Paffenberg, R.S., Hyde, R.T., Wing, A.L., and Hsieh, C.C. (1986), "Physical activity, all-cause mortality, and longevity of college alumni." *New England Journal of Medicine*, 314, pp. 605-613.

18 Sorlie, P., Gordon, T., and Kannell, W.B. (1980), "Body build and mortality: The Framingham Study." *Journal of American Medical Association*, 243, pp. 1828-1831.

Chapter 4: Dieting

1 Serdula, M.K., Collins, M.E., Williamson, D.F., Anda, R.F., Parnuk, E., Byers, T.E. (1993), "Weight control practices of U.S. adolescents and adults." *Annals of Internal Medicine*, 119(7), pp. 667-672.

2 Rodin, J. (1992), *Body Traps*. New York: William Morrow and Co.

3 Gaesser, G. (1996), *Big Fat Lies: The Truth About Your Weight and Your Health*. New York: Fawcett Columbine.

4 Brownell, K.D., Rodin, J. (1994), "The dieting maelstrom." *American Psychologist*, 49(9), pp. 781-791.

5 French, S.A., and Jeffrey, R.W. (1994), "Consequences of dieting to lose weight: Effects on physical and mental health." *Health Psychology*, 13(3), pp. 195-212.

6 Moses N., Banilivy, M., Lifshitz, F. (1989), "Fear of obesity among adolescent girls." *Pediatrics*, 83, pp. 393-398.

7 Garner, D.W., Wooley, S.C. (1991), "Confronting the failure of behavioral and dietary treatments for -obesity." *Clinical Psychology Review*, 11, pp. 727-780.

8 Historical Tables: "Budget of the United States Government: Fiscal Year 1992."(1991), Washington D.C.: Executive Office of the President Office of Management and Budget, p. 46.

9 Fraser, L. (1997), *Losing It: American's Obession With Weight and the Industry That Feeds On it*. New York: Dutton.

10 Gaesser.

11 Kilbourne, J. (1994), *Still killing us softly: Advertising and the obsession with thinness*. In P.Fallon, M.A. Katzman, S.C. Wooley (Eds.), *Feminist Perspectives on Eating Disorders*. New York: Guilford Press, pp. 395-418.

12 Bennett, W., and Gurin, J. (1982), *The Dieter's Dilemma*. New York: Basic Books.

13 Rothblum, E.D., (1990), "Women and Weight: Fad and Fiction." *The Journal of*

Psychology, 124(1), pp. 5-24.

[14] Fraser.

[15] Berg, F. (1995), "Children and Teens in Weight Crisis." Hettinger, N.D.: *Healthy Weight Journal.*

[16] Ernsberger, P. (1985), "The death of dieting." *American Health*, 4, pp. 29-33.

[17] Lissner, L., Odell, P.M. et al. (1991), "Variability of body weight and health outcomes in the Framingham Population." *New England Journal of Medicine*, 324, pp. 1839-1844.

[18] Gaesser.

[19] Ernsberger, P. (1997), "Adverse reactions to Dexfenfluramine." *Healthy Weight Journal*, 11(1), pp. 13-16.

[20] Levitsky, D.A. (1997), "Diet drugs gain popularity." *Healthy Weight Journal*, 11(1), pp. 8-18.

[21] Levitsky, p. 8.

[22] Curfman, G.D. (1997), Editorial: "Diet Pills Redux." *New England Journal of Medicine*, 337(9), pp. 629-630.

[23] Tye, L. (1997), "FDA requests diet drugs firms issue warnings." *Boston Globe*, August 28, 1997, pp. 1 and 29.

[24] Tye.

[25] Curfman, p. 630.

[26] Tye.

[27] Berg, F.M. (1998), "Fen-Phen Tragedy Triggers Uproar." *Healthy Weight Journal*, 12(2), pp. 17 and 32.

[28] "FDA Approves Meridia As New Diet Drug." (1998), *Healthy Weight Journal*, 12(2), p. 18.

[29] Berg, F.M. (1997) "Task Force advises against diet drugs." *Healthy Weight Journal*, 11(2), p. 27.

[30] Fraser.

[31] "FDA Warns Against "Herbal Fen-Phen." *Healthy Weight Journal*, 12(2), p. 30.

[32] Shisslak, C.M., Crago, M., and Estes, L.S.(1995), "The spectrum of eating disturbances." *International Journal of Eating Disorders*, 18(3), pp. 209-219.

[33] American Psychiatric Association. (1993), "Practice Guidelines for Eating Disorders." *American Journal of Psychiatry*, 150(2), pp. 212-228.

[34] Goldstein, L.T., Goldsmith, S.J., Anger, K., Leon, A.C. (1996), "Psychiatric symptoms in clients presenting for commercial weight reduction treatment." *International Journal of Eating Disorders*, 20(2), pp. 191-197.

[35] Gaesser, p. 153

[36] Brumberg.

[37] Gaesser.

[38] Friedman, S.S. (1994), *Girls In the 90's*. Vancouver: Salal Books.

[39] Fraser.

40 "Facts and Figures 1996." (1996), Mt. Marion, New York: Council on Size and Weight Discrimination, Inc.

Chapter 5: The Pursuit Of Beauty
1 *American Heritage Dictionary.* (1983), New York: Houghton Mifflin p. 117.
2 *Random House College Dictionary (Revised Edition)* (1979), New York: Random House; p. 119.
3 Wolf, N. (1991), *The Beauty Myth.* NewYork: William Morrow, p. 12.
4-5 Wolf.
6 Faludi, S. (1991), *Backlash: The Undeclared War Against American Women,* New York: Doubleday.
7-8 Freedman, R. (1988), *Body Love.* New York: Harper and Row.
9 Rodin, J. (1992), *Body Traps.* New York: William Morrow.
10 Wolf.
11 Freedman.
12 Rodin.
13 Brumberg, J.J. (1997), *The Body Project: An Intimate History of American Girls.* New York: Random House.
14 Cooke, K. (1996), *Real Gorgeous: The Truth About Body and Beauty.* New York: W.W. Norton, p.172.
15 Cooke.
16-17 Friday, N. *The Power of Beauty.* New York: HarperCollins, (1996), p. 369.
18-20 Wolf.
21 Wiseman, C.V., Gray, J.J., Moismann, J.E., and Ahrens, A.H. "Cultural Expectations of thinness in women: An update." *International Journal of Eating Disorders,* 11(1), (1992), pp. 85-89.
22 Wolf.

Chapter 6: Advertising
1 Twitchell, J.B. (1996), *Adcult USA: The Triumph of Advertising in American Culture.* New York: Columbia University Press.
2 Kilbourne, J. (1994), *Still killing us softly: Advertising and the obsession with thinness.* In P. Fallon, M.A. Katzman, and S.C. Wooley (Eds.), *Feminist Perspectives on Eating Disorders.* New York: Guilford Press, pp. 405-406.
3 Jackson, D. (1992), *How to Make the World a Better Place for Women in Five Minutes a Day.* New York: Hyperion.
4 Bogart, C. (1990), *Strategy in Advertising: Matching medias and messages to markets and motivators.* (2nd. ed.), Lincolnwood, IL: NTC Business Books.
5 Collins, R.K.L., and Skover, D.M. (1993), "Commerce and communication." *Texas Law Review.* 71, pp. 697-746.
6 Freedman, R. (1986), *Beauty Bound.* Lexington, MA: Lexington Books.

7 Matlin, M.W. (1993), *The Psychology of Women* (2nd ed.), Fort Worth, TX: Harcourt Brace Jovanovich.

8 Courtney, A.E., and Lockeretz, S.W. (1971), "A Woman's Place: An Analysis of the Roles Portrayal by Women in Magazine Advertisements." *Journal of Marketing Research*, 8, pp. 92-95.

9-10 Plous, S., and Neptune, D. (1997), "Racial and Gender Biases In Magazine Advertising: A Content Analytic Study." *Psychology of Women's Quarterly*, 21, pp. 627-644.

11 Freedman.

12 Kimball, M.M. (1986), "Television and Sex-Role Attitudes." In T.M. Williams (Ed.) *The Impact of Television: A Natural Experiment in Three Communities*. Orlando, FL: Academic Press.

13 Rudman, L.A. and Borgida, E. (1995), "The Afterglow of Construct Accessability: The behavioral consequences of priming men to view women as sexual objects." *Journal of Experimental Social Psychology*, 31, pp. 493 -517.

14 Gandee, C. (1994), "Nobody's perfect." *Vogue*, September, 1994, pp. 560-567.

15 Steinem, G. (1994), *Moving Beyond Words*. New York: Simon and Schuster.

16 Kilbourne, p. 413.

17 Jackson.

18 Wolf, N. (1991), *The Beauty Myth*. New York: William Morrow.

19 Jackson.

20 Kilbourne.

21 Jasper, K. (1993), "Monitoring and responding to media messages." *Eating Disorders: The Journal of Treatment and Prevention*, 1(2), pp. 109-114.

22 Levine, M.P. (1997), "Personal communication." See also, Levine, M.P., Piran, N., Stoddard, C. (1999), "Mission more probable: Media literacy, activism, and advocacy as primary prevention." In N. Piran, M.P. Levine, C. Steiner-Adair (Eds.) *Preventing Eating Disorders: A Handbook of Interventions and Special Challenges*. New York: Brunner Mazel, pp. 3-25.

Chapter 7: Magazines

1 Steinem, G. (1994), *Moving Beyond Words*. New York: Simon and Schuster, p. 153.

2 Wolf, N. (1991), *The Beauty Myth*. New York: William Morrow.

3-5 Wolf.

6 *Ladies' Home Journal* : "Women of the Year." March,1996.

7 Evans, E.D., Rutberg, J., Sather, C., and Turner, C. (1991), "Content analysis of contemporary teen magazines for adolescent females." *Youth and Society*. 23(1), pp. 99-120.

8-10 Steinem.

11 Steinhauer, J. (1995), "What do teen-age girls really, really want?" *New York Times*, May 7,1995, Styles Section, p. 59.

[12] "For The Hymenally Challenged Only: What kind of virgin are you?" *Sassy*, December, 1995, p. 79.

[13] Evans. pp 99-120

[14] Levine, M.P., Smolak, L. (1996), "Media as a context for the development of disordered eating." In Smolak, L., Levine, M.P., and Striegel-Moore, R. (Eds.) *The Developmental Pathology of Eating Disorders*. Mahwah, New Jersey: Erlbaum Associates, pp. 235-258.

[15] Wiseman et al. (1992), "Cultural expectations of thinness in women: An update." *International Journal Eating Disorders*, 11(1), pp. 85-89.

[16] Anderson, A.E., and DiDomenico, L. (1992), "Diet vs. shape content of popular male and female magazines: A dose-response relationship to the incidence of eating disorders." *International Journal of Eating Disorders*, 11, pp. 283-287.

[17] Then, D. (1992), "Women's magazines: Messages they convey about looks, men, and careers." Paper presented at annual convention of American Psychological Association, Washington, DC.

Chapter 8: Fashion

[1] Faludi, S. (1991), *Backlash: The Undeclared War Against American Women*. New York: Doubleday, p.173.

[2] Brumberg, J.J. (1989), *Fasting Girls: The History of Anorexia Nervosa*. New York: Plume. p. 251.

[3-4] Brumberg.

[5] Talcott Parsons in Freedman, R. (1986), *Beauty Bound*. Lexington, MA: Lexington Books, p.105.

[6] Freedman, p. 64.

[7] Freedman, p. 55.

[8] Wolf, N. (1991), *The Beauty Myth*. N.Y. Wm. Morrow

[9] "Facts and Figures '96." Mt. Marion, New York: 1996 Council on Size and Weight Discrimination.

[10] Wolf, p. 273.

Chapter 9: Models and Beauty Pageants

[1] Cooke, K. (1996), *Real Gorgeous: The Truth About Body and Beauty*. New York: W.W. Norton.

[2] Fraser, L. (1997), *Losing It: America's Obsession With Weight and The Industry That Feeds On It*. New York: Dutton.

[3] Gross, p. 182.

[4] Gross.

[5] Cooke.

[6] Wolf, N. (1991), *The Beauty Myth*. New York: William Morrow.

[7] Wiseman, et al. (1992), "Cultural expectations of thinness in women: An update."

International Journal of Eating Disorders, 11(1), pp. 85-89.

8 Cooke.

9 Angier, N. (1995), "Put on your best chest-it's prime time." *New York Times*, News of the Week in Review, April 2, 1995, p. 6.

10 Gross.

11 Gross, p. 2.

12 Freedman, R. (1986), *Beauty Bound.* Lexington, MA: Lexington Books, p. 123.

13 Orlean, S. (1997), "Beautiful girls." *The New Yorker*, August 4, 1997, pp. 29-36.

14 Brownell, K.D. (1991), "Dieting and the search for the perfect body: Where physiology and culture collide." *Behavior Therapy*, 22, pp. 1-12.

15 Martin, L. (1997), "Fame weighs down her crown." *Hartford Courant*. May 10, 1997, p. E5.

16 Steinhauer, J. (1995), "Miss Teen-Ager as queen of smarts." *New York Times*, March 26, 1995, pp. 45 and 47.

17 Freedman, p. viii.

18 Dee, C. (1997), *The Girl's Guide To Life: How To Take Charge of the Issues That Affect You.* Boston: Little Brown, and Co.

Chapter 10: Plastic Surgery

1 Balsamo, A. (1996), "Technologies of the Gendered Body." Durham, NC: *Duke University Press*, p. 62.

2-3 Cooke, K. (1996), *Real Gorgeous: The Truth About Body and Beauty.* New York: W.W. Norton. p. 134.

4 "Beauty and the breast." (1996), *Ms.* March/April, 1996 p. 45.

5 Faludi, S. (1991), *Backlash: The Undeclared War Against American Women.* New York: Doubleday.

6 Spindler, A.M. (1996), "It's a face-lifted, tummy-tucked jungle out there." *New York Times*, June 9, 1996, Sec. 3, p. 1.

7 Spindler.

8 Statistics provided by The American Society for Aesthetic Plastic Surgery (1999), Communications Office, 36 w 44th St. , Ste 630, New York, NY, 10036.

9 Statistics provided by ASAPS.

10 Sullivan, R. (1995), "Surgery Before 30." *Vogue,* July, 1995, pp. 156-181.

11 Freedman, R. (1986), *Beauty Bound.* Lexington, MA.: Little, Brown, and Co.

12 Statistics provided by ASAPS.

13 Faludi.

14 Selz, M. (1997), "Cosmetic surgery loans providing lift for lenders." *Hartford Courant*, January 16, 1997, p. F12.

15 Statistics provided by ASAPS.

16 Statistics provided by ASAPS.

17 Byrne, J.A. (1996), "How silicone ended up in women's breasts." *Ms.*, March/

April,1996, pp. 46-50.

18-19 Washburn, J. (1996). "Reality Check: Can 400,000 Women be Wrong?" *Ms.* March/April 1996, p. 51.

20 Byrne.

21 Faludi, p. 219.

22 Bonavoglia, A. (1996), "Alternative: Know the risks." *Ms.,* March/April, 1996, p. 43.

23 Monmaney, T. (1998), "Panel Finds No Breast Implant Disease Risk." *L.A. Times,* pp. A1 and A22.

24 Bonavoglia.

25 Brownell, K.D., Rodin, J. (1994) "The dieting maelstrom: Is it possible and advisable to lose weight?" *American Psychologist,* 49(9), pp. 781-791.

26 Levick, D. (1998), "Marketing Makeover: A New Corporate Wrinkle for Cosmetic Surgery." *Hartford Courant,* January 16, 1998, pp. D1-D2.

27 Cooke.

28 Jaret, P. (1995), "Surgical Sculpture." *Vogue,* May, 1995, pp. 287 and 344-345.

29 Cowley, G., Springer, K. (1999), "Lowdown on Liposuction." *Newsweek,* May 24, 1999, pp. 60-61.

30 "Deaths Reveal Liposuction Risks." (1997), *Healthy Weight Journal,* 11(6), p. 106.

31 Jaret.

32 Gaesser.

33 Associated Press (1995), "New Surgical technique provides alternative to fat liposuction." *Hartford Courant,* October 25, 1995, p. A2.

34 Geigis, D. (1995), "Putting on a new face." *Hartford Courant,* August 17, 1997, pp. E1-E2

35 Schmidt, W. (1995) "Skin deep." *Vogue,* Jan. 1995, p. 104.

36 Levick.

37 Turkington, C. (1995), "Beauty Answers: Baby Face." *Vogue,* September, 1995, pp. 456-460.

38 Washburn.

39 Urguhart, R. (1996), "Lunchtime lifts." *Vogue,* May, 1996, pp. 244-247.

40 Statistics provided by ASAPS.

41 Hall, M.G. (1982), *Keloid Scar Revision In,* H.E. Pierce(Ed.), "Cosmetic Plastic Surgery in Nonwhite Patients." NewYork: Grune and Stratton, pp. 203-208.

42-43 Washburn.

Chapter 11: Violence Against Women

1 Issac, N.E., and Prothow-Smith, D. (1996), "Violence." In K.M. Allen and J.M. Phillips (Eds.), *Women's Health Across the Lifespan.* New York: Lippincott, pp. 439-453.

2 Faludi, D. (1991), *Backlash: The Undeclared War Against American Women.* New York: Doubleday.

3 CCADV (1997), "Domestic Violence Fact Sheet." Hartford, CT: Connecticut Coalition Against Domestic Violence.

4-6 Wolf, N. (1991), *The Beauty Myth.* New York: William Morrow.

7 Gerbner, G. "The 1998 Screen Actors Guild Report: Casting the American Scene." Los Angeles, CA: *Screen Actors Guild,* 1998.

8 Lewin, T. (1998), "Debate Centers On Definition of Harassment." *New York Times,* March 22, 1998, pp. 1 and 28.

9 Lubanko, M. (1998), "Harassment Insurance A Hot Item." *Hartford Courant,* March 22, 1998, pp. A1 and A4.

10 Jackson, D. (1992), *How to Make The World A Better Place For Women in Five Minutes A Day.* New York: Hyperion.

11-12 Women's Action Coalition (WAC) (1993), "WAC Stat: The Facts About Women." New York: New Press, p. 53.

13 Thompson, M. (1998), "No Go: Why The Army Lost a High-Profile Sex Case." *Time.* March 23, 1998, pp. 52-53.

14 Jackson.

15 Wolf.

16 Wolf p. 38

17 Wolf.

18 Stein, N., Marshall, N.C., and Trapp, L.R. (1993), "Secrets in Public: Sexual Harassment in Our Schools." Wellesley, MA: Center for Research for Women, Wellesley College and NOW Legal Defense and Education Fund.

19 Stein, N. (1993), "No Laughing Matter." In E. Buchwald, B., P. Fletcher, M.Roth (Eds.) *Transforming A Rape Culture*, p. 313.

20-21 Friedman, S.S. (1997), *When Girls Feel Fat.* Toronto, CANADA: Harper Collins.

22 CCADV.

23 Wolf.

24 Faludi.

25-27 WAC, p. 56.

28 Issac.

29 Figures from a statement by Patricia Ireland, President NOW, on March 19, 1998.

30 ibid.

31 Issac.

32 Commonwealth Fund (1997), "Facts on Abuse and Violence: The Commonwealth Fund Survey of the Health of Adolescent Girls." New York, N.Y.: The Commonwealth Fund.

33 Warshaw, R and Books, S.L. (1988), "I Never Called It Rape: The Ms. Report on

Recognizing, Fighting, and Surviving Date and Acquaintance Rape." New York: The Ms. Foundation for Education and Communication.

34-35 Nelson, M.B. (1994), *The Stronger Women Get, The More Men Love Football.* New York: Avon Books.

36 Issac.

37 Wooley, S. (1994), "Sexual Abuse and Eating Disorders: The Concealed Debate." In P. Fallon, M.A. Katzman, and S.C. Wooley, *Feminist Perspectives On Eating Disorders.* New York: Guilford. pp. 171-211.

Chapter 12: Ageism

1-2 Friedan, B. (1993), *The Fountain of Age.* New York: Simon and Schuster.

3-6 Kuczynski, A. (1998), "Anti-Aging Potion or Poison?" *New York Times*, April 12, 1998, sec. 9, pp. 1-2.

7 Freedman, R. (1988), *Body Love.* New York: Harper and Row.

8 Bandon, A. (1999), "Longer, healthier, better." (1997), *New York Times Magazine.* March 9, 1997, pp. 44-45.

9 The American Society for Aesthetic Plastic Surgery (1999), Communications Office, 36 W. 44th St Ste. 630, New York, NY 10036.

10 Striegel-Moore, R.H., Silberstein, L.R., Rodin, J. (1986), "Toward an understanding of risk factors for bulimia." *American Psychologist*, 41(3), pp. 246-263.

11 Gross, M. (1995), *Model: The Ugly Business of Beautiful Women.* New York: William Morrow.

12-13 Friedan.

14 Kilbourne, J. (1994), "Still killing us softly: Advertising and the obsession with thinness." In P. Fallon, M.A. Katzman, and S.C. Wooley (Eds.), *Feminist Perspectives on Eating Disorders.* New York: Guilford Press, pp. 395-418.

15 Bandon.

16 "The Female in Focus: In Whose Image?" (1990), *Screen Actors Guild.*

17 Gerbner, G. "The 1998 Screen Actors Guild Report: Casting the American Scene." Los Angeles, CA: *Screen Actors Guild.* 1998.

18-19 Gerbner.

20 Rosenthal, J. (1997), "The age boom." *New York Times Magazine.* March 9, 1997, pp. 39-43.

21 Bandon.

22 Friedan.

23 Freedman, p. 186.

24 Rosen, B. and Jerdee, T. (1988), "Managing Older Worker's Careers." Research in Personal and Human Resource Management. 6, pp. 37-74.

Chapter 13: Women's Healthcare

1 Healy, B. (1995), *A New Prescription for Women's Health.* New York: Viking, p. 3.

2-3 Laurence, L. and Weinhouse, B. (1994), *Outrageous Practices: The Alarming Truth About How Medicine Mistreats Women*. New York: Fawcett Columbine, p. 14.

4-5 Healy.

6-7 Laurence and Weinhouse.

8 Miles, S. H., and August, A. (1990), "Courts, Gender, and the Right To Die." *Law, Medicine, and Health Care*, 18(1-2), pp. 85-95.

9 Clark, M. (1994), "Women: A Compelling Market." *Healthcare Forum Journal*, Jan-Feb. 1994, p. 28.

10 Clark.

11-20 Laurence and Weinhouse.

21 Commission on Women's Health (1997), "Selected Facts on United States Women's Health: A Chart Book." New York: Commonwealth Fund Commission on Women's Health, Columbia University.

22-23 Laurence and Weinhouse.

24 Quindlen, A. (1994), "What Went Wrong, What's Just About Perfect." *Healthcare Forum Journal*, Jan-Feb 1994, p. 27.

25-30 Laurence and Weinhouse.

31 Women's Action Coalition (1993), *WAC Stats: The Facts About Women*. New York: New Press, p. 26.

32 Villarosa, Linda, Ed. (1994), *Body and Soul: The Black Women's Guide to Physical Health and Emotional Well-Being*. New York: Harper Perrenial.

33 Healy.

34 Laurence and Weinhouse.

35 Healy.

Chapter 14: Kids and Dieting

1 Gustafson-Larson, A.M., and Terry, RD. (1992), "Weight-related behaviors and concerns of fourth grade children." *Journal of American Dietetic Association*, 92(7), pp. 818-822.

2 Garner, D.M., and Wooley S.C. (1991), "Confronting the failure of behavioral and dietary treatments for obesity." *Clinical Psychology Review*, 11, pp. 729-780.

3 Freedman, R. (1986), *Beauty Bound*. Lexington, MA: Lexington Books.

4-5 Kilbourne, J. (1994), *Still killing us softly: Advertising and the obsession with thinness*. In P. Fallon, M.A. Katzman, S.C. Wooley, (Eds.), *Feminist Perspectives on Eating Disorders*. New York: Guilford Press, pp. 395-418.

6 Thelen, M.H., Powell, A.L., Lawrence, C., and Kuhnent, M.E. (1992), "Eating and body image concerns among children." *Journal of Consulting and Clinical Psychology*, 21, pp. 41-46.

7 Mallick, M.J. (1983), "Health hazards of obesity and weight control in children: A review of the literature." *American Journal of Public Health*, 73(1), pp. 78-82.

8 Rodin, J. (1992), *Body Traps*. New York: William, Morrow, and Co.

BIBLIOGRAPHY

[9] Lane, C.B. (1995), "Bulking up baby." *Hartford Courant*, March 1, 1995 G1-3. (Report of Study Commissioned by Ross Products Division of Abbott Laboratories).

[10] Kilbourne, p. 397.

[11] Hirschmann, J.R., and Zaphiropoulos, L. (1993), *Preventing Childhood Eating Problems.* Carlsbad, CA: Gurze.

[12] Mellin, L.M., Irwin, C.E., and Scully, S. (1992), "Prevalence of disordered eating in girls: A survey of middle class children." *Journal of The American Dietetic Association*, 92(7), pp. 851-853.

[13] Berg, F.M. (1997), "Afraid To Eat." Hettinger, N.D: *Healthy Weight Journal.*

[14] Dietz, W.H., and Gortmaker, S.L. (1985), "Do we fatten our children at the television set? Obesity and adolescents." *Pediatrics*, 75, pp. 807-812.

[15] Berg.

[16] Mendelson, B.K., White, D.R., Schlieker, E. (1995), "Adolescents' weight, sex, and family functioning." *International Journal of Eating Disorders*, 17(1), pp. 73-79.

[17] Friedman, S. (1997), *When Girls Feel Fat.* Toronto, HarperCollins.

[18] Cooke, K. (1996), *Real Gorgeous: The Truth About Body and Beauty.* New York: W.W. Norton.

[19-20] Friedman.

[21] Rodin, J. (1992), *Body Traps.* New York: William Morrow.

[22] Mallick.

Chapter 15: Barbie Dolls and Body Image

[1] Sella, M. (1994), "Will a flying doll...fly." *New York Times Magazine*, December 25, 1995, pp. 20-25.

[2] Nussbaum, D. (1997), "The hunt is on for the toy that will make parents panic." *New York Times*, December 7, 1997, sec. 3, pp.1 and10.

[3-4] Lord, M.G. (1994) *Forever Barbie: The Unauthorized Biography of a Real Doll.* New York, William Morrow.

[5] Barbie as told to Laura Jacobs (1994), *Barbie in Fashion.* New York: Abbeville Press., p.14.

[6] Freedman, R. (1986), *Beauty Bound.* Lexington, MA: Lexington Books.

[7] *L.L. Bean: Spring 1998.*, L.L. Bean, Inc., Freeport, Maine.

[8] Lord., p. 252.

Chapter 16: Schools

[1] Piran, N. "On Prevention and Transformation." *The Renfrew Perspective*, 2(1), pp. 8-9. 1996.

[2] Collins, M.(1991), "Body figure perception and preferences among preadolescent children." *International Journal of Eating Disorders*, 10, pp. 199-208.

3 Maloney, M.J., McGuire, J., Daniels, S.R., and Specker, B. (1989), "Dieting behavior and eating attitudes in children." *Pediatrics*, 84(3), pp. 482-487.

4 Mellin, L.M., Irwin, C.E., Scully, S. (1992), "Prevalence of disordered eating in girls: A survey of middle-class children." *Journal of American Dietitc Association*, 92(7), pp. 851-853.

5 Phelps, L., et al. (1993), "Prevalence of self-induced vomiting and laxative/medication abuse among female adolescents: A longitudinal study." *International Journal of Eating Disorders*, 14(3), pp. 375-378.

6 Ferron, C. (1997), "Body Image in adolescence in cross-cultural research." *Adolescence*, 32, pp. 735-745.

7 Story, M. et al. (1991), "Demographic and risk factors associated with chronic dieting in adolescents." *American Journal of Diseases of Children*, pp. 145 and 994.

8 Facts and Figures (1996), Mt. Marion, New York: Council on Size and Weight Discrimination, Inc.

9 French, S.A. and Jeffrey R.W. (1994), "Consequences of dieting to lose weight: Effects on physical and mental health." *Health Psychology*, 13(3), pp. 195-212.

10 Sadker, M., and Sadker, D. (1994), *Failing at Fairness: How American Schools Cheat Girls*. New York: Scribner.

11 Jackson, D. (1992), *How to Make the World a Better Place for Women in Five Minutes a Day*. New York: Hyperion.

12 Sadker, p.171.

13 Debold, E., Wilson, M., and Malave, I. (1993), *Mother Daughter Revolution: From Good Girls to Great Women*. New York: Bantam.

14 American Association of University Women Educational Foundation. (1993), *Hostile Hallways: The AAUW Survey on Sexual Harassment in American Schools.* Washington, DC: AAUW.

15 Levine, M.P. and Hill, L. (1991), *A 5-Day Lesson Plan on Eating Disorders: Grades 7 through 12*. Tulsa, OK: National Eating Disorder Organization.

16 Berg, F.M. (1997), *Afraid To Eat*. Hettinger, ND: Healthy Weight Journal.

17 Steiner-Adair, C. and Purcell, A. (1997), "Approaches to mainstreaming eating disorders prevention." *Eating Disorders: The Journal of Treatment and Prevention*, (4), pp. 294-309.

18 American Association of University Women. "America Can't Compete Unless She Can." October, 1996, 10M. AAUW, 1111 Sixteenth St. N.W., Washington D.C. 20063-4873.

Chapter 17: Sports

1 *Girls Move Up*. (1999), University of California, Berkeley, Wellness Letter, 15(6) March, 1999, p. 8.

2 *Time Magazine*, August, 1998.

3-4 Ryan, J. (1995), *Little Girls in Pretty Boxes*. New York, Doubleday.

BIBLIOGRAPHY

5-6 Johnson, C., Powers, P.S., Dick, R. (1999), "Athletes and Eating Disorders: The National Collegiate Athletic Association Study." *International Journal of Eating Disorders* 26(2), pp.179-188. (1996).

7 Powers, P.S. (1999), "The Last Word: Athletes and Eating Disorders." *Eating Disorders: The Journal of Treatment and Prevention.* 7(3), pp. 249-255.

8-9 Ryan.

10 Thompson, R. H., Sherman, R.T. (1993), *Helping Athletes with Eating Disorders.* Champaign, Il: Human Kinetics Publishers.

11 Streeter, K. "Taking Their Game to the Court of Appeal." *L.A. Times,* March 9, 1999, p C1.

12 Nelson, M.B. (1994), *The Stronger Women Get, The More Men Love Football: Sexism and The American Culture of Sports.* New York: Avon Books.

13-14 "Deaths Shock College Wrestling" (1998), *Healthy Weight Journal,* 121 (3), p. 34.

15 Park, A. "Le Tour des Drugs." *Time Magazine,* August 10, 1998, p. 76.

16 Gorman, C. "Girls on Steroids." *Time Magazine,* August 10, 1998, p. 93.

17 Park.

18 Nelson.

Chapter 18: Ballet

1 Vincent, L.M. (1979), *Competing with the Sylph.* New York, Berkley Books.

2-3 Kirkland, G. (1986), *Dancing On My Grave.* New York: Jove Books, p. 57.

4 Vincent, p. 9.

5 Vincent.

6 Warren, M. (1990), *Weight Control. Seminars in Reproductive Endocrinology-8.* pp. 25-31.

7 Benson, J.E., Geiger, C.F., Eiserman, P.A., Wardlow, G.M. (1989), "Relationship between nutrient intake, body mass index, menstrual function and ballet injury." *Journal of American Dietetics Association,* 89, pp. 58-63.

8 Hamilton, L.H., Brooks-Gunn, J. and Warren M.P. (1985), "Sociocultural influences on eating disorders in professional female dancers." *International Journal of Eating Disorders,* 4, pp. 465-487.

9 Garfinkel, P.E., and Garner, D.M. (1982), *Anorexia Nervosa: A Multidimensional Perspective.* New York: Brunner/Mazel.

10 Piran, N. (1995), "What it takes for eating disorder prevention to make a difference." *National Eating Disorder Organization Newsletter,* 18, (1), pp. 1 and 10. Piran, N. (1996), "On prevention and transformation." *The Renfrew Perspective,* 2(1), pp. 8-9.

Chapter 19: Men

1 Managweth, B., Pope H.G., Hudson, J.I., Olivardia, R., Kinzl, J. and Biebl, W.

(1997), "Eating disorders in Austrian men: An intro-cultural and Cross-cultural comparison study." *Psychotherapy and Psychosomatic*, 66, pp. 214-221.

2-4 Fraser, L (1999), "The Hard Body Sell." *Mother Jones*, March-April, 1999, pp. 31-33.

5 Statistic reported by Ira Sacker, M.D. in P. J. Smith (1999), "You thought you were obsessed." *Self*, July, 1999, p. 155-157 and 169.

6 Friedman, S. (1999), *Just for girls*. Vancouver: Salal Books

7 APA (1999), *Diagnostic and Statistical Manual of Mental Disorders 4th Edition*, Washington, D.C. American Psychiatric Association.

8 Johnson, A.G. (1997), *The Gender Knot: Unraveling our Patriarchal Legacy.* Philadelphia: Temple University Press

9 Kindlon D. and Thompson, M. (1999), *Raising Cain: Protecting the Emotional Life of Boys*. N.Y: Ballantive, p. 75.

10 Pope, H.G., Olivardia, R., Gruber, A., Borowiecki, J. (1999), "Evolving Ideals of Male Body Image as Seen Through Action Toys." *International of Journal of Eating Disorders*, 26, pp. 65-72.

11 Pope, H.G., Katz, D.C. and Hudson, J.I. (1993), "Anorexia nervosa and reverse anorexia among 108 male body builders." *Comprehensive Psychiatry*, 34, pp. 406-409.

12 Hall, S.S. (1999), "The Bully in the Mirror." *New York Times Magazine*. August, 8, 1999, pp. 30-35 and pp. 58-65.

13 Pope et al. (1999).

14 Pope et al. (1999).

15 Hall.

About the Author

Margo Maine, Ph.D., author of *Father Hunger,* and Senior Editor of *Eating Disorders: The Journal of Treatment and Prevention*, is a clinical psychologist, Director of the Eating Disorder Program at the Institute of Living in Hartford, CT, and co-founder of Maine and Weinstein Specialty Group. Dr. Maine is a trustee and past-president of Eating Disorders Awareness and Prevention, Inc. and is an Assistant Clinical Professor in the Department of Psychiatry at the University of Connecticut. A lecturer, consultant, and researcher, she was also clinical consultant for the Blue Ribbon Award for Excellence winning film, *Wasting Away*, and is on the advisory boards of many organizations dedicated to women's health and eating disorders.

She has presented at numerous state, national, and international conferences including the American Psychological Association, American Association of Marriage and Family Therapy, American Women in Psychology, International Conference on Eating Disorders, National Anorexic Aid Society, International Association of Eating Disorder Professionals, The National Institute for the Advancement of Behavioral Medicine, and the Renfrew Foundation.

Order Form

Body Wars: Making Peace with Women's Bodies is available at bookstores and libraries or may be ordered directly from Gürze Books.

FREE Cataglogue

The Eating Disorders Resource Catalogue has more than 125 books on eating disorders and related topics, including body image, size-acceptance, self-esteem, and more. It is a valuable resource that includes listings of non-profit associations, and it is handed out by therapists, educators, and other health care professionals throughout the world.

___ FREE copies of the *Eating Disorders Resource Catalogue.*

___ copies of *Body Wars: Making Peace with Women's Bodies.*
$15.95 each plus $2.90 each for shipping.

___ copies of *Father Hunger: Fathers, Daughters, and Food*
$13.95 plus $2.90 each for shipping.

Quantity discounts are available.

NAME_____

ADDRESS_____

CITY, ST, ZIP _____

PHONE_____

Gürze Books (BWR)
P.O. Box 2238
Carlsbad, CA 92018
(760) 434-7533 fax (760)434-5476
www.gurze.com